Database Security

Alfred Basta, Ph.D.

Melissa Zgola, M.A., M.S.I.S.

Contributions made by Dana Bullaboy

D0165108

COURSE TECHNOLOGY
CENGAGE Learning·

Australia • Brazil • Japan • Korea • Mexico • Singapore • Spain • United Kingdom • United States

COURSE TECHNOLOGY
CENGAGE Learning·

Database Security

Alfred Basta and **Melissa Zgola**

Vice President, Editorial: Dave Garza

Director of Learning Solutions:
Matthew Kane

Executive Editor: Stephen Helba

Managing Editor: Marah Bellegarde

Product Manager: Natalie Pashoukos

Editorial Assistant: Jennifer Wheaton

Vice President, Marketing:
Jennifer Ann Baker

Marketing Director: Deborah S. Yarnell

Associate Marketing Manager:
Erica Ropitzky

Production Director: Wendy Troeger

Production Manager: Andrew Crouth

Senior Content Project Manager:
Andrea Majot

Senior Art Director: Jack Pendleton

© 2012 Course Technology, Cengage Learning

ALL RIGHTS RESERVED. No part of this work covered by the copyright herein may be reproduced, transmitted, stored or used in any form or by any means graphic, electronic, or mechanical, including but not limited to photocopying, recording, scanning, digitizing, taping, Web distribution, information networks, or information storage and retrieval systems, except as permitted under Section 107 or 108 of the 1976 United States Copyright Act, without the prior written permission of the publisher.

For product information and technology assistance, contact us at
Cengage Learning Customer & Sales Support, 1-800-354-9706

For permission to use material from this text or product,
submit all requests online at **cengage.com/permissions**
Further permissions questions can be emailed to
permissionrequest@cengage.com

Example: Microsoft® is a registered trademark of the Microsoft Corporation.

Library of Congress Control Number: 2011930892

ISBN-13: 978-1-4354-5390-6

ISBN-10: 1-4354-5390-5

Course Technology
20 Channel Center Street
Boston, MA 02210
USA

Cengage Learning is a leading provider of customized learning solutions with office locations around the globe, including Singapore, the United Kingdom, Australia, Mexico, Brazil, and Japan. Locate your local office at: **international.cengage.com/region**

Cengage Learning products are represented in Canada by Nelson Education, Ltd.

For your lifelong learning solutions, visit **www.cengage.com/coursetechnology**

Purchase any of our products at your local college store or at our preferred online store **www.cengagebrain.com**

Visit our corporate website at **cengage.com**.

Microsoft and the Office logo are either registered trademarks or trademarks of Microsoft Corporation in the United States and/or other countries. Course Technology, a part of Cengage Learning, is an independent entity from the Microsoft Corporation, and not affiliated with Microsoft in any manner.

Any fictional data related to persons or companies or URLs used throughout this book is intended for instructional purposes only. At the time this book was printed, any such data was fictional and not belonging to any real persons or companies.

The programs in this book are for instructional purposes only. They have been tested with care, but are not guaranteed for any particular intent beyond educational purposes. The author and the publisher do not offer any warranties or representations, nor do they accept any liabilities with respect to the programs.

Printed in the United States of America
2 3 4 5 6   23 22 21 20 19

Brief Contents

Table of Contents

Introduction

Over the last several decades, we have made great advancements in maintaining the confidentiality, integrity, and availability of our networked environments. These achievements are greatly due to the strides that have been made within our educational degree programs. Security research is funded at the highest rates in history, and security courses have become fundamental requirements in almost every IT-related program. Unfortunately, very little emphasis is placed on database security and as a result, IT and security professionals are left uninformed and underprepared to protect their company's most precious assets, their databases. Databases are the most valuable resources that we have. They contain our identities and hold our deepest secrets. Individuals, companies, and even countries could not exist without database security—it is our livelihood that is at stake in this technologically dependent world.

Approach and Audience

This textbook is a detailed guide to maintaining the confidentiality, integrity, and availability of a database environment. From preinstallation to postsecurity auditing, this book provides a comprehensive and in-depth explanation of database security strategies and offers general IT skills and the security know-how that professionals must have to face the growing number of threats to network security.

It has been written for information system and security administrators and analysts and emphasizes best practices in database security strategies. This book does not assume prior knowledge of databases and has been written in a casual style for both technical and nontechnical readers. It can be used in almost any basic or advanced information security or database administration course.

Organization and Chapter Descriptions

- Part I:
  - **Chapter 1** provides a full understanding of security and information technology. It defines the different types of security, intruders, attack strategies, and viruses. Security architecture is explored, along with global policy and disaster plans.
  - **Chapter 2** offers a well-rounded discussion of databases, from the definition of basic schema objects to an in-depth description of the architecture of an Oracle, MySQL, and SQL database.

- Part II:
  - **Chapters 3, 4, and 5** provide step-by-step installation guides and security practices for different vendors. Chapter 3's focus is MySQL, Chapter 4 focuses on SQL Server, and Chapter 5 focuses on Oracle 11g. With the foundation provided in the first five chapters, the student is well prepared to move on to much more advanced security concepts.

- Part III:
  - **Chapter 6** identifies authentication and authorization by covering topics such as profiles, privileges, and roles and by offering insight into how they are administered through specific vendors such as MySQL, SQL Server, and Oracle.
  - **Chapters 7 and 8** investigate the rarely explored topic of SQL injection. Based on cutting-edge research, Chapter 7 teaches learners how to identify SQL injection vulnerability and common injection strategies, while Chapter 8 explores examples of exploits and informs readers of defense techniques.

- Part IV:
  - Finally, **Chapters 9 and 10** introduce students to database security testing and auditing, covering vendor-specific processes.

Features

- *Thoughtfully organized*—The text is divided into four main parts to make finding and comparing implementation processes quick and easy.

- *Implementation focuses*—Addressing widely used database implementation, this text demonstrates how to prevent and solve problems with a practical mind-set.

- *SQL injection discussion*—SQL injection poses great challenges to database and security professionals, and *Database Security* is one of the only books on the market to address the topic.

- *Chapter Objectives*—Each chapter begins with a detailed list of the concepts to be mastered. This list gives you a quick reference to the chapter's contents and serves as a useful study aid.

- *Security In Your World*—In each chapter, real-world examples demonstrate viable solutions for various types of threats and intrusions to SQL Server, Oracle, and MySQL databases.

- *Chapter Summary*—Each chapter ends with a summary of the concepts introduced in the chapter. This is a helpful tool for reviewing the material covered in each chapter.

- *Key Terms*—All terms in the chapter introduced with bold text are gathered together in the key terms list at the end of the chapter, with full definitions for each term. This list encourages a more thorough understanding of the chapter's key concepts and is a useful reference.

- *Review Questions*—The end-of-chapter assessment begins with review questions that reinforce the main concepts and techniques covered in each chapter. Answering these questions helps ensure that you have mastered important topics.

- *Case Projects*—One of the best ways to reinforce learning about database security is to practice using the many tools security professionals use. The case projects at the end of the chapters give you practice in applying what you have learned.

- *Hands-On Projects*—Each chapter closes with one or more hands-on projects that help you evaluate and apply the material you have learned. To complete these projects, you must draw on real-world common sense as well as your knowledge of the technical topics covered to that point in the book.

Text and Graphic Conventions

Wherever appropriate, additional information and exercises have been added to this book to help you better understand what is being discussed in the chapter. Icons throughout the text alert you to additional materials. The icons used in this textbook are as follows:

The Note icon is used to present additional helpful material related to the subject being described.

Tips offer extra information on resources and how to solve problems.

Caution icons warn you about potential mistakes or problems and explain how to avoid them.

Each Hands-On Project in this book is preceded by the Activity icon and a description of the exercise that follows.

Case Project icons mark end-of-chapter case projects, which are scenario-based assignments that ask you to apply what you have learned.

Instructor Resources

The Instructor Resources CD includes the following materials (also available online at www .cengage.com):

Electronic Instructor's Manual—The Instructor's Manual that accompanies this book includes additional material to assist in class preparation, including suggestions for classroom activities, discussion topics, and additional activities.

Solutions—The instructor resources include solutions to all end-of-chapter material, including review questions and case projects.

PowerPoint presentations—This book comes with Microsoft PowerPoint slides for each chapter. They're included as a teaching aid for classroom presentation, to make available to students on the network for chapter review, or to be printed for classroom distribution. Instructors, please feel free to add your own slides for additional topics you introduce to the class.

ExamView®—ExamView®, the ultimate tool for objective-based testing needs, is a powerful test generator that enables instructors to create paper-, LAN-, or Web-based tests from test banks designed specifically for their Cengage Course Technology text. Instructors can utilize the ultraefficient QuickTest Wizard to create tests in less than five minutes by taking advantage of Cengage Course Technology's questions banks, or customize their own exams from scratch.

Figure files—All figures and tables in the book are reproduced on the Instructor Resources CD in bitmap format. Similar to the PowerPoint presentations, they're included as a teaching aid for classroom presentation, to make available to students for review, or to be printed for classroom distribution.

- Instructor Resources CD (ISBN 978-1-435-45391-3)

Software and System Requirements

Oracle 11g Release 2 (11.2.0.1.0)

    2 GB of RAM

    Virtual memory double the amount of RAM

    5.22 GB of disk space

    32-bit 550 MHz processor minimum or a 64-bit AMD64, or Intel extended memory

    256-color video

SQL Server 2008 R2

    1 GB of RAM

    3.6 GB disk space

    1.4 GHz processor or faster

    SuperVGA display

    .NET Framework 3.5 SP1

    SQL Server Native Client

    SQL Server setup support files

MySQL 5.5.13

    512 MB of RAM

    200 MB of disk space

    550 MHz processor

    256-color video

About the Authors

Alfred Basta, Ph.D., is a Professor of Mathematics, Cryptology, and Information Security. He is a member of the Editorial Board for the *Norwich University Journal of Information Assurance*, and conducts professional speaking engagements on Internet security and networking.

Melissa Zgola, M.A., M.S.I.S., is a professor of Network Technology, Information Security, and Software Architecture. She is a member of A.C.M.'s Special Interest Group for Information Technology Education and the Information System Security Association.

Acknowledgements

Thank you to all of the reviewers of this book who provided insightful comments and constructive feedback and to the Cengage Learning staff for all of the hard work put forth toward making this book possible.

To my friends and family, particularly Erin Lovas and Rae Ann Litzinger, I am enormously grateful for your unwavering compassion and moral support throughout this very long process. Thank you to Angie and Nick Madonna—"Gram and Pap"—for allowing Anthony to keep you up into the wee hours of the night, so that *"mommy can finish her chapter."*

Thank you to my mother Mary, for instilling in me the strength and perseverance to keep writing day after day, and to my late father Joe, whom I am certain was by my side smiling throughout all of the late nights of writing. *Thank you both for the sacrifices that you made in your lives, just so that I could find success in mine.*

Special love goes to my fiancé Tony, for his never-ending words of encouragement and whose constant, steadfast belief in me is what inspired the confidence that made this book a reality. *Thank you for knowing me better than I know myself, I love you!*

Finally, I would like to dedicate this book to my son, Anthony, my greatest motivation for finishing. *The stars are always within reach my sweetie, so never stop believing in the magic that life has to offer.*

—Melissa Zgola

To my wife Nadine
"It is the continuing symphony of your loving thoughts, caring actions, and continuous support that stands out as the song of my life."

To our daughter Rebecca, our son Stavros
"Fix your hearts upon God, and love Him with all your strength, for without this no one can be saved or be of any worth. Develop in yourselves an urge for a life of high and noble values. You are like little birds that will soon spread your wings and fly."

To my mother
"You are a never-ending melody of goodness and kindness. You are without equal in this world."

And to the memory of my father
"If one is weighed by the gifts one gives, your values given are beyond estimation."

—Alfred Basta

Thanks to my writing team for patiently answering my endless questions and giving me the chance to participate on this project. You are great examples of how instructors should be and now

I know that gift flows out of the classroom as well! I would like to thank the Cengage Learning staff for their support during the process. This was a great learning and growth experience for me! A huge thank-you also goes out to my friends and family who supported me during this project.

—Dana Bullaboy

Reviewers

William Figg, M.S., Ph.D., CHFI
Associate Professor
Dakota State University
Madison, SD

Roger Findley
Information Assurance Instructor
Laramie County Community College
Cheyenne, WY

Huiwei Guan, Ph.D.
Professor
North Shore Community College
Davers, MA

Robert Guess
Associate Professor
Tidewater Community College
Chesapeake, VA

Angela Herring
Instructor
Wilson Community College
Wilson, NC

David Hoehn
Assistant Professor
Brown College
Mendota Heights, MN

Britt John
New Horizons Computer Learning Center
Hiawatha, IA

B. Dawn Medlin, Ph.D.
Chair and Associate Professor
Appalachian State University
Boone, NC

Keith A. Morneau, Ed.D.
Faculty Chair
Capella University
Minneapolis, MN

David C. Pope
Instructor
Ozarks Technical Community College
Springfield, MI

Robert Sherman
Associate Professor
Sinclair Community College
Dayton, OH

Shambhu Upadhyaya, Ph.D.
Professor
University at Buffalo, The State University of New York
Buffalo, New York

Dora Zeimens
Instructor
Mid-Plains Community College
North Platte, NE

chapter 1

Security and Information Technology

After reading this chapter and completing the exercises, you will be able to:

- Define the nature of database and information systems security
- Identify the three main security objectives when protecting information systems
- Identify security threats
- Define and identify the characteristics of viruses and how they infiltrate systems
- Identify specific types of operational security and describe how to implement them
- Describe the information security life cycle
- Describe the multilayered nature of security architecture

Security In Your World

Joseph Anthony awakens on Monday morning refreshed and ready to begin his five-day workweek. On a typical weekday morning, Joe eats breakfast, watches the news, and gets dressed before walking out the door. Little did he know that this particular day would soon begin one of the worst cases of "Monday mishaps" ever experienced in the history of all Mondays.

As Joseph sits up in bed, he realizes that his alarm did not go off and he has no power at all. Remembering that there was quite a large storm in his area overnight, he assumes this is the reason for the power outage and does not give it a second thought. He glances at his watch sitting on the nightstand and notices that he is running a bit late, so he jumps out of bed, scurries to get dressed, and heads for the door.

With no power to make himself breakfast, he decides to stop at the local café to grab a doughnut and a coffee on his way to work. He orders his breakfast and swipes his debit card to pay and be on his way. To his dismay, the employee informs him that his card has been denied and that he needs to pay with cash. Insisting that the machine is incorrect, Joe asks the employee to try it again, but to no avail.

Concerned about his bank account, Joe runs back to his car and pulls out his cell phone to call his bank, yet his cell phone seems to have been deactivated. Frustrated and hoping that this was due to the storm the night before, Joseph proceeds to work and plans to call the bank from there.

Joe arrives at work, parks his car, and locates the key card that he uses to enter his employer's secure building. He swipes his card into the door's scanning device and is denied access to enter the building. Luckily, he sees a colleague heading for the door and so he asks her to let him in.

Late for work and irritated, Joe makes his way to his desk and sits down at his computer. He picks up the phone to call the bank while attempting to log into his computer. With the phone on his ear, he tries his Windows password and is denied access. He tries again and again, but eventually his repeated attempts lock the system. At this time, the bank representative answers the call and Joe explains the difficulty that he had with his debit card that morning. The bank teller asks him for his account number in hopes of identifying the cause of his problems, but when he provides her with the information, she informs him that no such account exists at their bank! They try using his Social Security number and his address, but nothing is found and so the teller recommends that Joe drive to the bank in person.

Now angry at the chain of events that have occurred thus far, Joe hangs up the phone to call his company's IT department in hopes that they can reset his password so that he can log into his computer and e-mail his boss to inform her that he must

(continued)

leave work to run to the bank. An IT representative answers the phone and asks Joe for his employee ID number. After a few minutes have passed, the IT representative explains that Joe doesn't have a user account recorded in the system. Just when Joe thought things couldn't get any worse, he was told the most frightening news he had heard this whole horrific day. According to the employee records database, Joe is not even listed as an employee of the company! Is this all a dream? Has Joe lost his mind?

We have seen this scenario in movies and on TV, and although this seems a bit extreme, it is not as far-fetched as one might imagine. In today's digital society, our identity exists as a compilation of various types of accounts, and almost every bit of personal information is stored in some type of database. Our bank accounts, medical accounts, employment records, utility accounts, phone records, car registration, income tax information, and even our Social Security numbers are all examples of important information that is stored within our current databases. The loss of our modern databases would result in the loss of our identity similar to what Joe has experienced. The obliteration of our major accounts would result in the eradication of our existence in today's digitally reliant world.

There are two types of events that are most likely to cause a scenario similar to the one described above: cyberattacks and natural disasters. This chapter will cover the measures that can be taken to detect and diminish the probability of both. Database security is defined and our enemies are identified. There is no such thing as guaranteed security, but armed with the knowledge provided in this chapter, major risks can be minimized.

Why Database Security?

Although databases can be configured within an organization to provide only local data storage and retrieval, most databases today provide access that spans several networks, and across the world. More time is spent communicating through computer networks than any other medium available and most of the transactions conducted online involve some type of database. Through e-mails, instant messages, text messages, and tweets, individuals are able to conduct business, monitor finances, maintain friendships, nurture relationships, and supervise their children. Society has progressed from one that accepts technology to a society that relies on technology to thrive.

This progression in technology has attracted an exponentially growing poll of network and database users, each outfitted with personal and business-critical information that is available through public networks. For intruders seeking destruction and monetary gain, this is a very enticing notion and has resulted in an unprecedented number of database intrusions throughout the entire globe.

Although the majority of our security efforts seem to be geared toward protecting individual and business assets, there is much more than personal identities and business finances at stake.

Advancements in technology have enabled individuals to use network databases to preserve their most critical infrastructures. Water supplies, electricity grids, and gas and oil production processes depend on a computer network to thrive. A breach to one of these data storage structures could have a disastrous impact on our livelihood. The view of a network intruder has transformed beyond the lonely hacker residing in the basement of his parent's home to a collection of hacking brigades professionally trained by the militaries of nations around the globe.

Database security has become an issue of global importance, and as networks become more sophisticated, so do intruders. Although we can never be 100% secure, we need to make every effort to minimize risks and to stay one step ahead of intruders, because the impact of a breach could be catastrophic on so many levels.

A Secure Data Environment

Deploying multiple layers of security within critical database environments is the most effective approach to minimizing the risk of a data breach. It is quite a simple concept to comprehend: if multiple layers of security are applied to a data storage environment, then intruders will have a more difficult time accessing the data. In multilayer-secured environments, an intruder who might compromise the first layer will have to find a way to bypass the second and even a third in order to obtain access, making intrusion more complex and time-consuming.

Consider a scenario in which a database administrator wants to protect his network from malicious e-mail attachments. He develops a training to teach users about the dangers of e-mail, hoping to educate them to identify the signs (such as file extensions) of dangerous attachments. If this is the only measure taken to ensure that attachments do not pose a threat to a network, then one forgetful user can cause major damage to a system.

If a second layer is added to this strategy, such as the implementation of a filter placed on the exchange server to block and quarantine certain well-known malicious e-mail attachments, the risk of a security leak is lessened. In this scenario, the attachment must fool the exchange server by changing its filenames *and* a forgetful user must download the attachment from the e-mail account.

Even a third layer can by applied, such as a firewall that is configured to deny certain types of traffic from entering the network, further lessening the risk. For a breach to occur now, the firewall, exchange servers, and user all must be fooled into allowing the attachment to intrude upon the network. Therefore, the more security layers that we can apply, the more secure our environment will be.

There are three main layers of security that need to be addressed in order to achieve a multilayered-secure data storage environment: database security, computer security, and network security. Each of these layers offers an intruder a potential way to enter the system, so to effectively secure a database, one must secure the database environment as well as the database itself.

Database Security Database security is a set of established procedures, standards, policies, and tools that is used to protect data from theft, misuse, and unwanted intrusions, activities, and attacks. Database security deals with the permission and access to the data structure and the data contained within it. Tools used to secure the database are typically included and configured within the installed database software packages, but the abilities of these packages vary by vendor (e.g., Oracle, MySQL, Microsoft SQL Server). Database security will be covered in more detail throughout the book, but the most common features made available by vendors to secure

1

the database include database-level access control, database-level authentication, and data storage encryption. Granularity varies from vendor to vendor and some vendors also offer additional software packages customized to secure their particular database management application.

Computer Security Although database security deals directly with the security assurance of the data structure and its contents, when considered independently without addressing its environment, database security is irrelevant. The security of the layers of the database environment includes the hardware and software upon which the database is installed, and is just as important as the security of the data structure itself. **Computer security** is a set of established procedures, standards, policies, and tools that are used to protect a computer from theft, misuse, and unwanted intrusions, activities, and attacks. Computer security is typically defined by the operating system used on the computer. Security features are available within the operating system and can be expanded upon using third-party applications. Common computer security features include operating system-level access control, operating system-level authentication, application security, and hardware and software monitors and logs. The features vary by vendor and operating system edition. For example, Microsoft Windows Server 2008 offers many more security features than Microsoft Windows Server 2003.

Network Security From securing the entrance doors of a building to applying firewalls to block traffic coming into the network, each and every security effort plays an important role in the overall security of a database. Network security is the outermost layer of the database and arguably the biggest security concern. Consider the potential danger for a man who secures the title to his car in a locked glove compartment, but never locks his car doors. An administrator who does not secure their network environment is essentially leaving the "car unlocked" for all to explore. **Network security** is a set of established procedures, standards, policies, and tools that are used to protect a network from theft, misuse, and unwanted intrusions, activities, and attacks. Achieving a reasonably secure network requires a combination of hardware and software devices that may include firewalls, antivirus programs, network monitors, intrusion detection systems, proxy servers, and authentication servers.

Database Security Objectives

Security measures should keep information private from an outside view, be steadfast in their efforts to maintain the consistency of data, and ensure that resources remain at a high degree of availability. The key to achieving an effective data security architecture relies in an organization's efforts to maintain the confidentiality, integrity, and availability of its environment. As illustrated in Figure 1-1, these terms are commonly known as a security model called the C.I.A. Triangle because of the three entities that connect to form one concept.

Figure 1-1 C.I.A. Triangle
© Cengage Learning 2012

Confidentiality Confidentiality refers to the efforts taken through policy, procedure, and design in order to create and maintain the privacy and discretion of information and systems. For a system to provide confidentiality, it needs to do two things:

- Ensure that information maintains its privacy by limiting authorized access to resources
- Block unauthorized access to resources

The confidentiality of resources on a database system is protected through the use of authentication and access controls. For example, an administrator can use a person's login information to restrict that person's access within a database or a database environment and therefore maintain confidentiality.

Confidentiality is not always left to the administrator's own discretion. Many of the measures that we take to ensure confidentiality are required by federal and state laws. Depending on the nature of the organization, there are state and federal laws that set the rules for privacy and confidentiality. These laws require network administrators to uphold a certain level of security to ensure the privacy of information. For example, the **Health Insurance Portability and Accountability Act (HIPAA)** defines strict laws for health institutions throughout the United States. HIPAA laws ensure the security and privacy of patient records by dictating the way files are accessed, stored, and transmitted on a network.

Confidentiality is an important goal to achieve within security efforts. A breach in confidentiality could result in a number of disastrous effects. Some of the major repercussions include identities being stolen, business's trade secrets being exposed, disaster cleanup expenses incurred, tarnished reputations, and, as mentioned earlier, even critical infrastructure failures.

Integrity Integrity refers to the efforts taken through policy, procedure, and design in order to create and maintain reliable, consistent, and complete information and systems.

Integrity within a database refers to the reliability, accuracy, and consistency of the data stored within and retrieved from the database. A database's integrity is protected by preventing both unauthorized and authorized modifications, whether accidental or deliberate, that might cause the database storage or retrieval to be unreliable and inconsistent. Integrity is the most difficult item to measure because the corrupted data are not necessarily missing, just modified.

A number of checks and balances are necessary to find changes or flaws that exist throughout a database. This process is also known as *auditing* and involves an audit professional who looks for discrepancies within the system by checking data against older backed-up versions of that data. Database auditing will be discussed in further detail later in the book, but as you can imagine, the more complex the database, the greater the auditing task. Integrity is a very important characteristic of a database, and if unsuccessfully implemented can result in system failures, unreliable data, flawed programs, and poor performance.

Availability Availability refers to the efforts taken through policy, procedures, and design to maintain the accessibility of resources on a network or within a database. These resources include, but are not limited to, data, applications, other databases, computers, servers, applications, files, drives, shares, and network access.

In order to protect our resources, we must identify those things that pose a threat to the availability of our databases, assess the level of threat that they pose, and plan an intervention accordingly. Common potential threats include technical failures (e.g., a

1

defective or broken device, a flawed program or piece of software), natural disasters (e.g., floods or fires), intrusions (e.g., viruses, Trojans, and worms), and users (e.g., accidental or intentional harm).

Unlike confidentiality and integrity, a business cannot operate without availability, because not having access to its most critical tools leaves it disabled and unable to complete the simplest of tasks.

There are many who take the availability of resources for granted. They don't realize the impact that a missing file or application can have on productivity until it is no longer available. Even with the best plans in place, one cannot assure 100% availability of all network resources all of the time. What is certain is that the longer a network or data resource is unavailable, the greater the loss that will incur. Proper identification and planning is the key to keeping a network available and a business thriving.

Who Are We Securing Ourselves Against?

Despite the expensive tools that can be purchased to aid in the protection of our data, we are defenseless against dangerous intruders without a complete understanding of those things that pose a threat.

It can be said that an uninformed security professional is similar to a sight-impaired watchdog. Both are insecure and eager to protect, having all of the tools necessary to keep the environment safe, yet they lack the ability to make the distinction between an intruder and a visitor. As a result, they blindly attack everything that enters their environment. Databases that are too restrictive are just as ineffective as those that are too accessible. Databases that are given too much access can lead to issues with security, integrity, and privacy, while those given little to no access can lead to frustrated and ineffective users. A healthy balance requires an understanding of what we need to protect ourselves against. There is a common misconception that those who pose the greatest threat to our assets are those on the outside attempting to break in. As you will learn from this section, there are a greater number of threats on the inside of a network, ready and able to destroy the resources that you work so hard to protect.

As you review the following material about the dangers that pose threats, keep in mind that the most fundamental goal for an intruder is to obtain access to the network. With access on a private network, intruders have the ability to explore and further exploit. Having access to a network provides intruders with the potential to locate and access the critical database systems. Each and every threat that is discussed in this chapter can potentially lead to the loss of the confidentiality, integrity, and availability of our database system.

Hackers

Although the term **hacker** has taken on negative connotations over the years, by true definition, it refers to those who have mastered the firmware and software of modern computer systems, and enjoy the exploration and analysis of network security with no intent to intrude or cause harm. A **cracker** refers to those individuals who break into our networks without authorization with the hope of destroying and/or stealing information. The mass media has played an enormous role in the confusion of these two terms, so they are often inaccurately used interchangeably.

Despite the general public's perception of the term *hacker*, learning to define these terms correctly is important in understanding the threats to our systems. To further clarify the difference between hackers and crackers, a new classifying system has been created and is currently in use today. This system has introduced new terminology to provide clear definitions that accommodate the changes and growth within this field, as well as naming these groups of individuals based on their motivation for exploration of networks. Table 1-1 contains information regarding the different types of online intruders.

Intruder type:	Definition:	Example:
White hat	Ethical hacker: a hacker that uses extensive experience and knowledge to test systems and provide security consultation to others; white hats pose no threat to our network systems	A security consultant hired by an organization to use different methodology to attempt to hack into their system with the intention of testing the security of that environment
Grey hat	An individual or groups of individuals that waver between the classification of a hacker and a cracker; grey hats sometimes act in goodwill and other times in malice	An individual breaks into the *Wall Street Journal*'s network and leaves notes within the system's database to alert the network team of the vulnerabilities that exist; on a different occasion, this same individual breaks into *The Boston Globe*'s human resource system to obtain sensitive employee information for personal gain
Black hat	Someone who breaks into computer networks without authorization and with malicious intent; black hats are responsible for the theft and destruction that affect our systems	An individual breaks into Walmart's point of sales system to obtain credit card information from consumers in hopes of financial gain
Hactivist	Refers to hackers and crackers who use their extensive experience and skill to use networks to share their ideologies regarding controversial social, political, and economic topics; hactivism can be malicious in nature due to the methods by which hactivists attempt to place further attention and emphasis on their cause	A group of political extremists use their computer know-how to hijack MSNBC's Web site, altering the site to display messages that disparage mainstream media
Script kiddie	Refers to an amateur cracker that uses programs and scripts written by other people to infringe upon a computer network system's integrity; script kiddies are especially inexperienced, and attacks are often experimental in nature	An individual searches for and downloads a cracking tool found online and uses it to haphazardly gain access into an organization's network and steals information

Table 1-1 **Types of online intruders**

Social Engineers

Social engineers use human interaction to manipulate people into gaining access to systems, unauthorized areas, and confidential information. They often build trust with an authorized user of a network, and through deception and trickery they convince these people to break normal security policies. One of the most common ways that intruders gain access to systems is by asking others for their passwords. By nature, human beings desire to help one another. This is one of many characteristics that facilitate the success of social engineers.

Imagine that you are working in a building that requires employees to use special key cards to enter through the main doors. Returning from lunch one day, you are walking toward the entrance and you notice a well-dressed man carrying a number of files, his briefcase, and a bag from the local fast food restaurant walking directly behind you. As you approach the door and swipe your card, you hear the man clearly struggling to locate his access key card. Do you leave him standing outside, or do you hold the door for him out of politeness and a desire to help one of your fellow human beings?

Computer Users

Well over half of the security breaches that occur on a network involve our own network users. Lack of education and a total disregard of policy are two major contributors to outside intrusions. Users are the weakest link within an organization, and the best security architecture in the world can't save us from a haphazard user. The circumstances that provide potential for user error are endless, so it is important to learn as much as you can about the users on your system and educate the users through continuing education. Here is a list of the most common errors made by users on a network:

- *Poor habits*—leaving computers unlocked and unattended while using the restroom, attending meetings, going to lunch, or visiting colleagues.

- *Password error*—choosing easy-to-guess passwords; writing passwords down on sticky notes or in notebooks and storing them in plain sight on desks, under keyboards, or on top of monitors.

- *Disregard for company policy*—visiting unauthorized Web sites and downloading unauthorized software in the process; attaching unauthorized equipment to their PCs, like USB (Universal Serial Bus) devices and external hard drives; logging into the company remotely using unapproved personal laptops and computers.

- *Opening unknown e-mails*—viewing risky attachments containing games, greeting cards, pictures, and macro files.

- *Inappropriate disclosure*—giving out information over the phone and falling prey to social engineering.

- *Procrastination*—failing to report computer or network issues in a timely manner.

Computer-literate users can be just as dangerous (if not more dangerous) as those users who are new to network and computer systems. These users generally take more risks and have less regard for security policy. They change settings and configurations, disable programs, and find shortcuts to basic security measures. These types of users tend to install more sophisticated programs, causing network-wide compatibility issues and opening doors for intruders to enter the network. Unfortunately, due to fear of exposure, these types of users are also less likely to call technical support when things go wrong. This can potentially cause major problems that are extremely difficult to detect and are detrimental to the integrity of a network.

Another type of user that we need to be aware of is the angry and disgruntled employee. Having a computer-literate disgruntled employee on your network can pose as great a threat as unknowingly hiring a security cracker. These users are more likely to intentionally cause destruction and abuse their files and access rights. These users pose a great threat because they already know the organization of the network, are aware of how to find confidential information, and have most likely already gained trust within a circle of their peers. These intelligent disgruntled workers pose a threat to the confidentiality, integrity, and availability of the database and network as a whole because they can attack from the inside, and defense is much more difficult at this level.

Network and Database Administrators

The network and database administrators and their team of specialists are not often viewed as threats to the network that they run, yet several problems can be caused at this level of administration. This department creates, maintains, manages, and monitors the entire database and/or network architecture, leaving quite a bit of room for error. As diligent and hardworking as they may be, they are only human, and they do make mistakes. Unfortunately, the mistakes made at this level are almost certain to have consequences for the integrity, availability, and reliability of the network.

Depending on the size of an organization, a great amount of change can occur over the period of a year. As employees are hired, fired, retired, promoted, and demoted, networks and databases must accommodate and adapt. When employees are hired or fired, computers and user accounts are added and removed from the network and permissions are added and removed from the database. As business is flourishing, data within the databases are changing as well, so the network and database that you have today may not be the same that you will have in a year.

This dynamic and ever-changing nature of the data environment can cause security flaws to be created in places where once no flaws existed. Therefore, it is important that virtually every component on the network is audited and reassessed on a regular basis, searching for potential, newly created security concerns and need to be frequent, comprehensive, and complete.

Overlooking security flaws within a system can cause a great deal of havoc and unfortunately it happens more often than administrators would like to admit. One prominent mistake that network administrators make much too often is forgetting to remove a user's rights and account credentials from the database environment. This is a common mistake that can have devastating results. Imagine the consequences of leaving network access available to a disgruntled exemployee who was recently fired from an organization.

So, although we rely on our network administrators to keep our environment confidential, reliable, and secure, even they can contribute to the security issues within a network.

The Internet

The environments to which we are exposed can be as threatening to our assets as the people within them. Currently, there are approximately 2 billion users and 100 million Web sites residing on the Internet. Over 75% of people within the United States have

Internet access and most of these people use the Internet to socialize, learn, and buy or sell goods.

The popularity of online education has increased tremendously over the last five years and Web sites like Twitter and Facebook are recruiting Internet users by the millions. We are locating lost family members, reuniting with old friends, finding soul mates, and developing and maintaining friendships. We have redefined the term socialization. Although many are undecided about the impact that technology is having on our culture, there is no denying that virtual has gone viral.

Sales and marketing groups have also learned that there is great potential within online markets. Billions and billions of dollars in transactions are being made online each year. Local companies are now able to reach customers on the other side of the globe, and for many products, online marketing techniques have surpassed our most lucrative traditional ones.

Yes, the use of the Internet has offered great advantages to both individuals and businesses around the world; it seems that everyone is benefiting from our virtual society. Unfortunately, with the good comes an equal amount of bad. The threats posed on the Internet are greater than ever before as intruders become more sophisticated and their numbers continue to increase. Unfortunately, the nature of the Internet makes it a main attraction for thousands of cybercriminals each year. Activities conducted online leave you susceptible to hacking and make you vulnerable to the well over 600,000 viruses that are scanning our networks today. Businesses, information, and assets are greatly threatened by the Internet and our social interactions are resulting in the greatest number of identity thefts in our recorded history.

Listed on the following pages are the most common user tools available on the Internet, along with the potential threats that they pose.

Web Pages Surfing the Web and/or Web browsing in and of itself can be a dangerous activity that poses great threat to your data. **Web pages** are documents containing a specific programming language, such as HyperText Markup Language (HTML) or JAVA, etc., that are designed to be viewable on the World Wide Web. The code contained in a Web page document usually has two purposes:

- To inform the Web browser how to display the document
- To inform the Web browser the way that it and the Web document should react to certain user responses (e.g., clicking a button, submitting a form, clicking a link etc.).

 Anything that involves programmed code can be manipulated.

Some Web sites are hacked into, also known as **hijacking**, and rewritten to react differently to users than the original Web site designer intended. These hacked sites can be rewritten to distribute malicious code upon user activity (such as downloading), or to redirect the user to a site that was built by a hacker. The intent here is to spread embedded malicious code.

Malware is an abbreviation for the term malicious software. **Malicious software** is programming code written and used by unauthorized intruders to perform a certain task on a computer.

These tasks are often intended to be harmful and destructive. Malware can be written using virtually any programming language available, so the only limitation to the impact that malware can have is an intruder's creativity.

Malware will be discussed in detail later in the chapter.

Consider a user surfing the Web who encounters a site that generates a Windows alert, or a pop-up window, which requires the user to click OK or some other labeled button in order to continue surfing. This simple window can be an invitation to disaster, programmed to initiate a response and intended to cause harm. An attacker can program the button so that when it is clicked, the Web site either begins attaching malware to the user's PC, or redirects the user to a hacker-owned Web site in hopes of obtaining the user's personal information.

Hackers build some Web sites made to look identical to other popular sites in hopes of drawing in a user. The legitimate site's address can be cloned and used to even further convince the user that the fake site is real. This is called **spoofing**. A spoofed Uniform Resource Locator (URL) is used to fool a user into believing that the site is a legitimate or well-known site, such as Yahoo! or Google.

Spoofed URLs and fake Web sites are often created to trick users into providing sensitive information like passwords or account numbers, and they are very effective tools. Spoofing a URL can be as easy as registering a domain name that is a slightly misspelled company's URL (e.g., Gogle, Yaho). After all, the user has no indication that the site is not real.

These Web sites can be accidentally stumbled upon by a user while surfing the Web, yet some Web sites are more vulnerable than others and have similar characteristics. Table 1-2 contains characteristics of Web sites that attract intruders and malicious doers.

Characteristic	Example	Reasoning
Illegal and of moral suspect	Darknets, pornography sites, and warez sites	The people who run these sites are less likely to report an incident of hacking
Social sites	MySpace, Facebook, Blogger, and Twitter	These sites are often populated with millions of inexperienced users; inexperienced users are more likely to make errors in judgment in terms of security, offering intruders a large number of potential hosts to spread or store viruses
Newsgroups and technical forums	Usenet and BinSearch	These sites are often perceived as credible knowledge bases, so users are more likely to click links provided in the forums

Table 1-2 Common characteristics for dangerous Web sites

Web Browsers All network communication is based on the same basic principles. A request to obtain a resource is sent from a source machine or application (client), to a destination machine or application (server). The request is received and processed and the client's privileges are checked to determine allowable permissions for the requested resource. Once approved, the requested resource is packaged and sent from the server to the client. Each step is handled using a set of standards or protocols that determine the who, what, when, where, and how of the communication process.

A Web browser is an application that acts as the interface for the Internet, providing a way for people to interact with and view pages on the World Wide Web. Web browsers are responsible for aiding the process of sending and receiving user requests. Web browsers pose another threat to users, because just like a Web page, they have built-in programming languages that can be manipulated. As noted earlier, anything with programming language can be attacked.

One very important job of a browser is to forward requests made by users from the source machine to the destination machine or application server. User requests occur when a user types a URL or address (e.g., *http://www.yahoo.com*) into the address field of a browser or when a button is activated on the form. When a user types an address, she is essentially requesting permission to view the Web page residing at that address. The browser reads this address, and from the information given by the user, the browser sends the request to view the page to the main Web server that holds the Web page. URLs can be manipulated and intruders can use them to obtain access to database information. Appending malicious code onto a database-directed URL is one way that intruders manipulate or trick a database into sending confidential information. This is called SQL injections, and will be discussed in much further detail in Chapters 7 and 8.

When a user fills out a form on the Web and activates a submit or send button, the browser sends the request to a separate server that contains information about what to do next. Typically, forms available on the Web are intended for communication with a database of some kind. Either a person is filling out the form to sign up for an account online (input data into a database), or to search for specific products on a Web site store (retrieve information from a database). These forms can also be using SQL injections to retrieve confidential information or perform unauthorized manipulation of the database. Again, SQL injections are discussed in further detail in Chapters 7 and 8.

The **hypertext transfer protocol (HTTP)** portion of a Web address informs the browser what protocol is used to send the request for the Web site. In our example, the Web server is told to use HTTP protocol, or port 80 (the specific port used for HTTP to send the request forward). HTTP is also used to determine how Web form information is transferred to the application server, or to the database HTTP to be configured to send all form-related data (the information that the user input into a Web form) to the database by appending the input to the URL. If this configuration is set, the user's form information can be intercepted and used by intruders to log into a database. For example, let's say that you have the capability to log into your school to check your grades online. Once you enter the address for your school (e.g., the URL), the browser sends the request to your school's Web server and returns to you a form that instructs you to insert your username and password. If you were to log in, you essentially send a request to your school's database server, asking it to retrieve the grade information for the username and password that you input into the form. If HTTP is configured to append the information that you input (username and password) onto the URL, this information can be intercepted by an intruder before it reaches the application server. In this case, you might provide the intruder with a username and password to the school's database and enable him to send unauthorized requests using your credentials.

Besides the SQL injections, there are other ways the URLs can be manipulated for the purpose of obtaining access to a network. The Web address, *www.yahoo.com*, tells the browser where to find the main server to send this request. Before the request can be sent, the URL needs to be changed into an Internet Protocol (IP) address to make it routable across the network. The browser needs to first send the address to the Domain Name Server (DNS), which holds a database of domain names and their respective IP addresses. The DNS looks up the IP address for *yahoo.com* and sends this IP address to the Web server. The Web server can now send the request to the main server holding Yahoo's main Web page.

It is possible for the DNS server to be attacked, an intrusion called **DNS poisoning**. When DNS poisoning occurs, a cracker gains control over the DNS server and changes the domain name's respective IP address, redirecting requests to sites that the cracker has built and maintains. These fake sites will look and feel identical to the Web sites the user has attempted to access. Therefore, the user is fooled into providing their **personal identifiable information (PII)**, which is personal information that identifies a person or entity, and may include information such as names, passwords, Social Security numbers, etc. These fake sites may also hold malware, which the user unknowingly downloads just as described in the preceding spoofing example. The whole process takes place without the user suspecting a thing.

A Web browser also contains menus which allow organizations or individuals to customize and configure security and personal settings. These settings can be compromised using malware and cracking techniques, as well. An example of a browser setting that can be changed by a user is a home page setting. A browser's home page setting allows a user to customize the main **startup page** (the Web site that is displayed when the browser is started). In a home environment, a user can set his browser startup page to be directed to his favorite news Web site or search engine. Within organizations, this setting is often configured to be directed to the company's Web site.

Common Web Browsers Some common Web browsers include Internet Explorer, Firefox, Netscape Navigator, and Opera. The most common of these Web browsers is Microsoft Internet Explorer (IE). IE comes installed on Windows machines by default.

A good rule of thumb to consider with security and the Internet is that the more popular a system is, the more likely it is that it will be violated. Most crackers want to do as much damage as possible, so they attempt to crack into systems and sites that attract the most people. The more people there are who use a system, the more available hosts there are to carry the virus. Therefore, unless Microsoft changes their default Web browser, IE will be more vulnerable to attacks than any other Web browser. IE has been the victim of many attacks throughout the history of the Internet. These attacks have been accomplished by crackers finding security weaknesses and vulnerabilities within the application. Each time a browser is attacked, Microsoft locates the weakness and creates an update to the browser to patch that vulnerability.

Patches will be discussed later in the chapter.

1

These patches are normally included as part of a Windows Update, yet in large and enterprise organizations where patches are centrally managed, it is the administrator's responsibility to install or apply the most recent patch. If an old version of the Web browser exists, or updates to the Web browser are not completed on a regular basis, the Web browser can be left vulnerable to attacks. Web browsers are also vulnerable to hijacking as well. This is also the case for database systems. If a database administrator does not update the database software as new updates are made available, the system can be vulnerable to security breaches.

Misleading Applications

The fear of the many viruses and threats floating through cyberspace makes users vulnerable to fearmongering and phishing techniques, designed to trick users into downloading malicious code. **Misleading applications** are applications that deceive users into believing that their computer's security has been breached, therefore tricking the user into downloading and purchasing rogue antivirus tools to remove the bogus breach. The application often is very believable, and may look like common spyware and antivirus removal tools.

For example, the user performs some activity, such as clicking the link or installing the software, and once downloaded, the misleading application will hijack the PC and obtain personal information, destroy files, and collect data. Misleading applications are found throughout the Internet and are most often found in earlier shareware sites, social sites, and newsgroups. These applications can also hide in banners and advertisements, as well as in programming code of legitimate sites.

The victim essentially pays to have malware installed onto their PC, which robs them of their PII, retrieving the malware that was installed, thus compromising the reliability of their system. All of this is done without the user's knowledge, and they are left with a false sense of security that potentially leads to future threats.

E-Mails

Electronic mail has become one of the most common forms of communication in today's society. E-mail is used to send critical, sensitive, personal, and business information daily. E-mail has become vital to the success of businesses, and yet it poses the biggest threat to a network and the database environment. E-mail provides crackers with a simple channel of attack, and is the most common way that malicious code gains access into a business. Along with the basic vulnerabilities that come with sending and receiving e-mail, Web e-mail accounts carry the vulnerabilities that come with browsers. The most common threats to e-mail are attachments, phishing, and HTML code attacks.

Attachments Attachments are the largest threats to an e-mail system. Although we can train ourselves and our users to carefully consider attachments, crackers make it very difficult to identify a fake attachment. Crackers can send an endless array of malicious programs through attachments provided in an e-mail, yet in order for these intrusive programs to be effective, the user must download and initiate them. Crackers often use attachment names and/or file extensions in an attempt to gain trust.

Intruders understand that attachments coming from strange e-mail accounts are not likely to be opened, and file extensions of common virus types are likely to be blocked, so they use techniques like e-mail spoofing and strategic filenaming, such as pjb.jpg.exe, to help their cause. Spoofing e-mail addresses, like spoofed URLs discussed earlier, fools a user into believing that the sender is a friend or a colleague.

Spoofing an e-mail address can be as easy as using a stolen e-mail address from the "from" and "reply" fields of an e-mail account. Like URLs, spoofed addresses are very effective. Imagine that a user receives an e-mail that she thinks is from a colleague, and this e-mail contains an attachment with a filename related to the nature of her business; the user is very likely to open the attachment.

The cracker only needs to fool one user into opening an unknown attachment for an entire system to erupt in chaos. Imagine this scenario: A cracker sends an e-mail containing a malicious attachment to 1,000 people. One of the 1,000 people opens this attachment, initiating code that sends a copy of their contact list back to the cracker and begins to attack the user's machine. Most important, the virus has gained access to the network, allowing it to propagate, affecting the network and the database environment, and affecting each and every machine (including the servers) along the way. With each machine affected, the intruder receives a contact list of e-mail addresses. Now the intruder has broken the integrity of the network and potentially the database environment, obtaining potentially thousands of e-mail addresses to spoof, to gain trust of other users, improving the possibility that the next attack will result in many more opened attachments. This is a dangerous, never-ending cycle.

Phishing   Phishing is the attempt to obtain PII from people through the use of spoofed e-mail addresses and URLs. Phishing relies on spoofing to gain trust. While spoofing is the act of cloning accounts, URLs, and IP addresses, phishing is the act of trying to fish information out of people.

Imagine receiving an e-mail from your company's IT group informing you that your account password was about to expire unless you changed it immediately by using the link provided in the e-mail. Without making a call to the IT group, you might fall prey to giving a stranger your system username and password. This can be disastrous for your organization as well as your professional career.

Phishing can also include the act of convincing a user to click a link, therefore redirecting the user to a cracker-owned site where attacks can then ensue. A very effective phishing technique used to redirect a user is through the use of fake holiday and birthday card e-mails. Sending cards through e-mail has become a grand gesture around the office. When an individual sends another individual an electronic greeting card, an e-mail is normally sent to the recipient that provides them a link to click to view the greeting card. These electronic card e-mails can be spoofed, and phishing can convince users to click a link provided in the e-mail. Instead of receiving a birthday wish, the recipient of the bogus card would be led to a cracker-built Web site where exploitation is initiated.

1

Web-embedded HTML Today, it is not necessary to use Webmail to send and receive HTML-based messages. E-mail clients, even local, have advanced from simple text files to colorful formatted documents that hackers use to exploit the programming code. HTML allows e-mail to be formatted using font, colors and styles, as well as many other formatting features available in a word-processing application. It can also include scripting languages such as JavaScript and active content such as ActiveX controls.

As said previously, anything that contains programming code can be manipulated. These e-mails have been and continue to be exploited by viruses, because malicious software can be created using scripting language and active content. In cases like these, in which malicious programs can be embedded directly into the e-mail's programming code, users do not have to initiate the virus, so they cannot be blocked as easily as attachments. Intruders do not have to rely on users to download risky attachments or click unfamiliar links. Users only have to read their e-mail for the malware to attack. As they open and read their mail, the malicious code is obtaining information, corrupting files, and forwarding e-mail addresses to the individual who created the virus.

Instant Messages

Instant messaging has become more than just a way to connect and socialize with a network of friends and family members. It is used much more frequently throughout the culture of organizations to help employees meet business goals, and it provides a quick and convenient way for employees to communicate, share files, and even hold brief chat sessions. It is a great tool to increase a team's productivity and solidarity as a whole.

Instant messaging is also being implemented to improve customer service and build client relationships. It provides a way for customers to immediately chat with product representatives, to ask product questions, receive technical support, or finalize business transactions.

The evolution of instant messaging has made this technology much more attractive to crackers who are looking to obtain sensitive information and break into confidential database environments, and it provides a viable option due to its insecure and vulnerable nature. Instant messaging does not encrypt data on either file transfer or peer dialog. In fact, it circumvents the security architecture put into place to protect such resources. Instant messaging provides an ideal environment for phishing that involves spoofed buddy names and redirection techniques to lead users into the traps of the cracker's custom-built malicious code distribution sites.

Tweets

Twitter.com is a Web site that provides members with a miniature blog-like service where a person can post small messages (140 characters maximum) onto the Twitter site for friends and family members to see. These messages are most often updates of a person's activities or status throughout the day. A person can post a tweet using a cell phone, a computer, or any device that provides access to the Internet.

Tweeting has become quite popular over the last few years, and as with any other popular social site, Twitter is a haven for intruders looking to invade. Like instant messages, images and links can be included within a tweeted message, posing great threat to any unsuspecting Twitter member. Twitter accounts are quickly falling prey to phishing, spoofing, and redirection techniques. As was expected by security professionals throughout the world, Twitter is now the cracker's new playground.

Malware

As mentioned earlier in the chapter, malware is capable of performing harmful and destructive tasks on the computers of those who fall victim to it. Because it can be written using so many different programming languages, an active imagination is all a cracker needs to wreak havoc on scores of users. Falling under the umbrella of malware are:

- Computer viruses
- Worms
- Trojans
- Spyware
- Adware
- Bots

Computer Viruses

Computer viruses are a form of malware intended to spread from one computer to another without detection. Viruses vary in degrees of danger; while some viruses only cause annoying disturbances to a computer system, others can copy sensitive information, corrupt files, delete data, or destroy entire systems. There are currently about 600,000 viruses floating around on our computer networks. The most common channel for virus transmission is e-mail.

Before we explore the different types of viruses, it is necessary to first identify the characteristics often found within malicious code. These characteristics are often built into the code of viruses, worms, and Trojans, and act as defense strategies to avoid detection and removal. Common characteristics and defense strategies include:

- *Self-encryption*—**Encryption** is the transformation of data by using sophisticated algorithms in an attempt to make the data unrecognizable. Viruses are often recognized by their **signature**, which is a pattern of characters that is identified for a specific family of viruses. Most antivirus programs use character string recognition scanning techniques to identify virus signatures on a network, so encryption can be a very effective method for viruses to avoid exposure. If a virus is able to disguise the way it appears to a network (pattern of numbers or characters), then antivirus programs searching for common characteristics of this virus will have a very difficult time recognizing the virus.

- *Stealth*—Every program that is installed onto a system makes changes to that system in some way or another. Whether these changes involve the use of memory or an increase in file size, once a program enters a system, a change is inevitable. Antivirus programs regularly monitor these changes by requesting information from the operating system (OS) looking for unauthorized altered system files, suspect registry entries, etc. If changes are found, antivirus programs look to attack. In order for a virus to remain successfully hidden within a system, it needs to cover its tracks by concealing any changes that it makes. This is what stealth code does to avoid detection. Stealth involves the interception of the requests from the antivirus programs and answers them instead of the OS. The malicious program provides information to the antivirus program, making it appear as though there haven't been any changes made to the system. This misleads the antivirus program into believing that the system is clear of viruses. When users are unaware of their presence, viruses with stealth defenses can remain on a system corrupting files or collecting sensitive information for quite some time.

- *Polymorphism*—As mentioned before, antivirus programs look for signatures and patterns found within data. **Polymorphism** refers to the incidence of changing forms, or self-modification. Viruses that use polymorphism as a defense take encryption to another level by changing forms subsequent to each infection. This means that code that is polymorphic changes its signature each time it infects a file, and that each file infected is infected by a different copy of the original code. The dynamic and ever-changing nature of this code makes it the most serious and difficult threat to detect.

- *Residence*—The general term for a virus that requires users to initiate it by downloading a program or opening up an e-mail attachment is **nonresident virus.** Nonresident viruses cannot affect a system unless users make them active. Once active, these viruses attack software that resides on the hard drive. A virus that installs itself or takes residence directly in the main system memory of a computer is known as a **resident virus.** Unlike nonresident viruses, resident viruses are viruses that do not need users to make them active. Because these viruses reside within random access memory (RAM), they attack any and all programs that become active on the computer system. Resident viruses take advantage of the multitasking feature of a computer system, and therefore can infect programs at a much faster rate. These types of viruses usually result in the need to reinstall virtually every piece of software on the computer. Resident viruses are much more common because they are much more effective.

Classes of Viruses
Just as with defense strategies, there are certain categories of viruses that can apply to some or many other types of viruses. This section explores these categories by defining the components of both a logic and time bomb virus, and describes the characteristics of spyware and adware.

- *Logic bombs and time bombs*—**Time and logic bombs** are general terms for viruses that do not become active until predetermined specific conditions are met. These viruses can lie dormant and undetected for many months before the effects of the virus begin to appear. A time bomb or time-delayed virus involves conditions in which the variables are times, days, or specific dates. For example, a time-delayed virus may be written to corrupt certain systems at regular intervals (e.g., every other Tuesday), or once on a specified date. The variables and conditions are predetermined and written within the code of the virus. A logic bomb has an endless amount of possible variables. These conditions normally depend on the environment in which the logic bomb resides. For example, a logic bomb might be set to corrupt data or systems only when a specific user logs into a network, or only if a specific name appears within a database query. These viruses are often thorough and purposeful in intent. Historically, these viruses have been written by disgruntled employees or people seeking revenge on a specific organization or individual.

- *Spyware*—**Spyware** is a general term for any software that intentionally monitors and records a user's computer and/or Internet activities. Spyware gathers sensitive information about users or businesses, compiles this information into some type of document, or **transmission packet,** and then forwards this information back to the originator or creator for use as the creator sees fit. Spyware is most often downloaded and/or installed accidently from users surfing the Internet, yet it can be manually installed on an individual's computer as well.

- *Adware*—**Adware** is a general term for software that uses typical malware intrusion techniques to obtain marketing data or advertise a product or service. There are a few different types of advertisement software that fit the definition of adware. One form of adware is a software program that collects information for advertising and market research purposes through using attractive pieces of software that are offered to computer users at free or a reduced cost. Some adware, once installed, automatically generates advertisements in the form of pop-ups and Web site redirects. For example, a Web site might offer a free calendar and meeting-organizing software that, once downloaded, gathers information about the user's Internet activities for purposes of market research or personalized advertising. This type of adware can also be considered spyware because the software gathers information about your activities without your explicit knowledge. Another more invasive form of adware automatically generates advertisements on a person's PC once the free software is installed and used. The advertisements can be displayed using pop-ups and Web site redirects. This form of adware can take up a great amount of resources on the network or a computer system, causing the computer and/or Internet to become slow, and in some cases unusable. The effect on the computer and the network is dependent on the amount, frequency, and origin of the advertisement displays. Although some adware can cause slow networks and computers, adware by definition is not designed with the intent to harm a person's PC, a network, or a database environment.

Virus Types Viruses come in many forms and are often written to attack specific vulnerabilities, objects, and locations. The following section will review the different types of viruses that exist, as well as explore the vulnerabilities and objects of which they take advantage.

- *Boot Sector Viruses*—A boot sector virus loads itself into the boot sector of a computer's hard disk drive. The **boot sector** of a hard disk drive is an area of the drive that contains records necessary to the boot process of a computer. If the boot sector is compromised, then so is the entire boot process. Boot sector viruses normally infiltrate a system via an infected floppy disk left in a floppy disk drive. Due to advancements in technology, most new computer systems do not include floppy disk drives as a default firmware device, so boot sector viruses are not as common as they were in the past.

- *Macro Viruses*—A **macro** is a small program that enables users to automate a large number of repeated processes within a document. Macros are found within many Office-related applications, such as word-processing and spreadsheet-rendering programs. Macro viruses can either be attached to a macro or can replace a macro within a document. Macro viruses run automatically when the document containing the infected macro is opened or closed, and because people are often more comfortable opening and sharing documents of this type, macro viruses spread pretty quickly and easily, most often through e-mail attachments. Once the virus is initiated, it affects all documents of the same type on that computer or network drive. The affected documents include those that have already been saved, and any documents that are saved in the future. These viruses are easy to write and can be quite dangerous. They corrupt data, install external software, and in some cases, like the infamous Melissa virus of 1999, they can take down entire networks of computer systems.

- *File-infected viruses*—Most file-infected viruses come from users on the Internet (e.g., downloaded e-mail attachments, instant messaging file transfers, and downloaded programs). Unlike macro viruses, which attack the data within a file, a file-infected virus will attach itself to an executable file that requires a user to run it before it can propagate and corrupt the system. File-infected viruses can begin as nonresident viruses that are downloaded from the Internet and require a user's action to become active. Once file infectors become active, they become resident viruses by copying themselves to the system memory. As with resident viruses, the effects are devastating to a computer system because the virus stays in memory.

- *Multipartite viruses*—A multipartite virus combines the characteristics of a boot sector virus with those of a file-infected virus. A multipartite virus can be obtained and activated in the same way a file-infected virus can be obtained. The difference is that the multipartite virus also infects the boot record of the boot sector on the hard disk drive, so that at the next boot, the virus will be distributed throughout the entire system.

Worms

Worms can be defined as self-replicating malware that are able to harness the power of networks and use this power in their attacks against the networks. Worms and viruses share a number of the same characteristics, yet, unlike viruses, worms do not need users to travel from one computer to another. In addition, worms propagate across networks, while viruses primarily propagate across computer systems.

A worm takes control of one computer, using weaknesses and vulnerabilities that were learned while maintaining control over its previous target computer. A worm uses information from the computer it is currently victimizing to look for vulnerabilities in nearby systems. Once these vulnerabilities are identified, a worm attacks these vulnerabilities and takes control of the next target computer. A worm repeats this pattern as it travels across networks, destroying systems along the way.

Elements of a Worm's Travel All worms, regardless of the type, share common elements that make up the self-replication process. As illustrated in Figure 1-2, the common process of a worm's travel across a network is as follows.

USER

Figure 1-2 Elements of a worm's travel
© Cengage Learning 2012

This example refers to a worm traveling across the Internet, yet the same concepts apply to all other modes of travel.

1. *Find a weak target*—The enormity of the Internet leaves room for much vulnerability. The first element of a worm's travel across a network is to identify and take advantage of these vulnerabilities in order to find an open door onto the network and get closer to a potential database target. A worm looks for vulnerabilities such as those discussed earlier in the chapter (e.g., e-mail, file sharing sites, and insecure passwords) and then uses its knowledgeable code to obtain its first victim.

2. *Take control of the machine*—Once a worm gains access to its identified target through the use of e-mail, cracking passwords, or utilizing insecure file-sharing technologies, the worm installs itself onto the system. At this point, infection of the system begins. The level of harm that a worm can cause depends on the directives that the creator has included as part of its payload. The worm's **payload** is the component of the worm that contains a list of action commands, which the worm will follow for each machine that it encounters. These instructions can include steps for deleting files from a machine, opening back doors into a system, or forcing **denial of service (DoS) attacks** across a network. DoS attacks are concerted efforts made by malware to keep system resources busy, halting normal functionality. A **back door** is a path created to enable unauthorized access that evades all system and environmental security measures. Opening a back door into a system allows an intruder unauthorized and undetected access to a system or its environment.

3. *Interrogate the machine*—After the damage to the first target is complete, the worm hidden within the system begins searching for a new target. The worm looks for a new target by interrogating the system in which it currently resides. E-mail addresses and network configurations are pulled in search of a nearby computer to exploit. DNS queries are made to the nearest DNS servers, looking to obtain the IP addresses of nearby machines. Much information is discovered during this process.

4. *Testing a new target*—Once IP addresses, e-mail addresses, and network neighbor information is collected, the worm sends a series of packets to nearby machines to test their vulnerability and the effectiveness of the techniques that the worm used to obtain control of the current PC. Based on these tests, a new target is identified and the process starts all over again.

Types of Worms   There are several types of worms that are categorized by the modes of travel by which these worms spread. Table 1-3 identifies and gives a brief description.

Trojan Viruses

A **Trojan**, or Trojan horse, is a form of malware that disguises itself and its harmful code. Trojans often hide within enticing programs such as software updates, games, and movies. Unlike viruses and worms, Trojans cannot replicate. Their primary purpose is to gain access into your system in order to obtain sensitive information, destroy important files, or to create opportunities for downloading and installing bigger and better threats, such as bots, onto your systems.

Types of Trojans   Just as with viruses and worms, there are several varieties of Trojans. Trojans are categorized by their purposes. In this section, we will examine the different types of Trojans that exist and explore the damage that they have the potential to cause.

Worm types	Description
E-mail worm	Propagate from e-mail to e-mail using messages that contain worm-infected attachments or links that redirect users to worm-infected Web sites
Instant Messaging worm	Travel from messenger to messenger by sending links that redirect users to worm-infected Web sites; these links are often sent using a target's entire buddy list
Internet worm	Travel across the Internet using Internet scans and information found within a target (see example in the section titled "Elements of a Worm's Travel")
IRC (Internet relay chat) worm	Travel from chat to chat by sending worm-infected files and redirect links to worm-infected Web sites
File-sharing network worm	Travel from file-sharing network to file-sharing network by making copies of itself and placing them in a shared folder with an appropriate name

Table 1-3   Types of worms

- *Remote access and administration Trojan (RAT)*—Provides remote access capability to the cracker from whom the virus originated. Remote access provides a user's complete control and access to your computer from a remote location. Remote access also gives a cracker the ability to record content (such as video from your Webcam and voice from a microphone), which is a cracker's own personal reality show—your life at his fingertips. Remote access is potentially the most dangerous capability a cracker can have.

- *Data-sending Trojan*—Obtains sensitive data from your computer and transmits it back to a cracker. Key loggers are the most often used data-sending Trojans. A key logger is an application that logs your keystrokes in an attempt to retrieve sensitive data. Key loggers can remain on your system unnoticed for months, silently recording every key that you punch into your keyboard. These records are then sent via e-mail to the cracker for review at previously specified intervals. As with other malware, the most common way that Trojans spread is through e-mail.

- *Destructive Trojan*—As its name suggests, a destructive Trojan is installed on your computer with the intent to destroy your system as a whole. Destructive Trojans are more like viruses than any other Trojans. They randomly delete files and folders and corrupt the registry. If left undetected for too long, this type of Trojan will leave you with a corrupt OS and an inoperable PC.

- *Proxy Trojan*—Enables a cracker to use someone else's computer to access the Internet in order to keep her identity hidden. Using your computer to access the Internet means that the attacker will be using your IP address to commit cybercrimes. Your IP address is registered to your home address through your ISP (Internet service provider) and is used to identify you on the Internet. Therefore, any crime committed with your IP address could potentially result in you being investigated for identity theft or other cybercrimes.

- *File transfer protocol (FTP) Trojan*—Allows the attacker to use someone else's computer as an FTP server. Installing this Trojan onto your computer would enable the intruder to download files from his PC to yours, which could provide another avenue for more installation of malware. It also can enable the intruder to download files from your PC to his. Establishing your PC as an FTP server could also lead to the attacker storing illegal or pirated material (e.g., software, music, movies) on your computer, from which other Internet users could download. Again, this situation could potentially result in you being investigated for the illegal server.

Bots

Bots, also called software robots, are so named due to their ability to perform a large array of automated tasks for an intruder at a remote location. These tasks range in severity from spamming a system to initiating DoS attacks on systems. A DoS attack can slow down or completely shut down a database system or network of systems by flooding and overwhelming them with requests. For example, think about what would happen if there were one hundred applications running on your PC simultaneously. The PC would slow down tremendously due to the RAM overload. This is one strategy that a bot uses to compromise a system.

Bots can be hidden in games and other enticing programs downloaded by unsuspecting users, e-mailed from one infected machine to another, downloaded from infected Web sites, and/or can break into a person's computer through vulnerabilities found in the security architecture.

Bots allow intruders to gain access and full control of a number of computer systems from a distance, without an administrator or antivirus program ever becoming wise to the attack. Removal and detection of a bot often requires the use of a special antivirus program created specifically to look for bots. Because of the complexity of a bot, the detection of one bot normally requires the reinstallation of the whole system. You can never be completely sure that all bots have been removed from a system. Even with these specialized programs, bots are often not detected because:

- Not all bots are alike.
- Bots know how to update themselves, so new versions are created daily.
- Like Trojans, bots have the ability to hide and disguise themselves, and are aware of all the necessary steps to avoid being detected.
- Bots run in the background, virtually in silence.

Bots are only one component in a larger scheme to destroy networks. Once a computer is under the control of a bot, it becomes a part of a network of bots, called a **botnet**. This botnet is controlled by an individual often referred to as a **botmaster**. A botmaster accumulates a number of bots and then rents these botnets to other intruders and cybercriminals for the purpose of spamming, phishing, and other more serious types of cybercrime.

Security Architecture: A Never-ending Cycle

There is a great amount of uncertainty in the security field. Creating a security architecture that effectively ensures the confidentiality, integrity, and availability of database environments is no easy task. In considering the steps to achieving security goals, one message should remain in the forefront of our minds: security is never 100%, and we can never be 100% secure.

The techniques that are used to attack databases and other systems are developed using the same technology that is used to protect these systems. This means that as security systems become more sophisticated, viruses, Trojans, and worms become more sophisticated as well, and as technology becomes more advanced, so do intruders. With a virus population of approximately 600,000 and growing, there is no time to rest. By the time you reach a level of security where you feel comfortable, several new intrusions will have been developed and the process starts all over again. In this section, we will review the process of creating and maintaining security architecture.

Phase 1: Assessment and Analysis

Assessing and analyzing an organization's data security needs involves the identification of vulnerabilities, threats, and assets that exist within an environment's devices, resources, and vendor relationships. A security audit must be thorough and exhaustive, searching for every type of potential threat that may exist within the database environment. These threats can range from social engineering gaps to external firewall faults. They can be present within any of the computer, network, and database layers, so all types of security should be addressed.

An audit can be a difficult task for a group of security professionals. The process can take quite a bit of time and resources to complete, so audits can be conducted either internally or by paying a third-party company, such as a group of white hats.

By identifying risks, defining the likelihood of a threat to an asset, and determining the cost of a breached or lost asset, you can prioritize and plan reasonable measures to counteract these threats. Security measures that are created to counteract risks found on a network or database system should never exceed the value of the assets that they are protecting. Questions that are often asked during the assessment and analysis phase are:

- What are the devices and resources within the database environment?
- What type of threats exist within the database environment?
- What are the assets that need protection?
- What value do the assets have?
- What cost would the threats incur?
- What is the likelihood that each threat will occur?
- What level of security is needed for each threat?

Steps that are often taken to complete a risk assessment include:

1. Create a list of all devices and resources within a database environment.
2. Identify the vulnerabilities and the assets involved with each resource and device.
3. Define the value of these assets as well as the cost of any damage from the threats.
4. Using the information from Step two, as well as an understanding of the likelihood of each threat, create security measures to counteract these threats.
5. Prioritize your security measures.

Phase 2: Design and Modeling

The design and modeling phase involves the creation of policies and prototype security architecture that fit the needs of a business. A model for security will rely strictly on the results of the assessment and analysis phase. The prioritized lists of threats that are created dictate how the model is developed and what policies are put into place. In the design and modeling phase, security policies and procedures are created, necessary firmware and software changes are defined, and security tools or applications that are used to minimize risk are identified.

The entire organization must be included in this process. From senior management to human resources to network users, all should be made aware of the security efforts taking place. Involving the entire organization in this process will ensure that policies are correctly focused and realistic for both user and business needs. Questions that are often asked during the design and modeling phase are:

- What policies need to be put into place to meet the security goals?
- What firmware changes need to take place to minimize vulnerabilities and support policies and procedures?
- What software is put into place to minimize vulnerabilities and support security policies and procedures?
- What are the steps for the implementation of the plan?
- What additional staff training will be necessary?
- How will success and failure be determined?
- What is the communication plan?
- How will the communication and training be delivered?
- How will firmware and software be tested?

Steps that are often taken to complete a risk assessment include:

1. Define the policies and procedures that need to be put into place.
2. Define the firmware and software changes that support the policies defined in Step one.
3. Identify the implementation plan.
4. Create baselines to determine success and failure.
5. Define a plan for user training and awareness.

Phase 3: Deployment

During the deployment phase, the security policies, firmware, and tools defined in previous phases are put into place. These security measures are deployed using the steps that were defined in the design and modeling phase. Deployment usually occurs in a test form first. A test environment is often created to simulate the environment in which deployment will take place. Firmware and software is purchased and also tested to ensure that unforeseen variables do not affect the overall deployment and security goals. Changes to user training and awareness are put into place in this phase as well. Questions that are often asked during the deployment phase are:

- Have user training adjustments been well accepted?
- Are all firmware and software tests successful?
- Are the security measures ready for full deployment into the active environment?

Steps that are often taken to complete a risk assessment include:

1. Adjust user training and awareness based on user acceptance.
2. Test firmware and software changes in a controlled simulation environment.
3. Deploy changes as defined by the deployment plan.

Phase 4: Management and Support

The management and support phase involves the ongoing support, maintenance, and assessment of the security architecture that was deployed in the previous phase. During this phase, performance of the security system is monitored, and any failures or breaches would result in the reevaluation of the security architecture. Security policies can go through minor changes, yet too many minor changes or a failure in a system should initiate the need to repeat the entire process from the beginning. Questions that are often asked during the management and support phase are:

- Is the security plan protecting the intended assets?
- Are enough time and resources invested in high-priority threats and assets?
- What impact do the security measures have on the users' ability to complete their tasks?
- What impact do the security measures have on the network's ability to complete a function normally?
- Are minor revisions needed?
- Are the security measures out of date?
- Have breaches increased?
- Is it time to reassess the environment?

Steps that are often taken to complete a risk assessment include:

1. Monitor performance of security architecture as well as user security awareness and training.
2. Make minor policy revisions as necessary.
3. Identify the need for a reassessment and initiate the start of the security life cycle.

Global Policies for the Database Environment

Operational information security ensures the secure operation of an organization through the development and reliability of an environment's policies and procedures. It focuses on security policies, change management, update management, and disaster recovery plans and is a necessary component for maintaining the database environment.

Security Policies

Security policies define the overall goal of security, identify the scope of what to secure, and define the roles and responsibilities of people within the organization. In addition, they identify specific communication processes and discus the enforcement of the policies. These policies are vital to the success of a security architecture. Without a security policy in place, employees are forced to make up their own rules for security-related decisions, resulting in disastrous effects within a database environment. A security policy's effectiveness can affect how quickly a company will recover from a threat to a system.

The amount of loss incurred from a security breach can also be dependent on the effectiveness of the security policy. Security plans should be written by a committee of individuals, all whom have a stake in the success of the business. Security policies should not be created by IT professionals alone. The more invested the stakeholders are in this process, the more effective the policy will be. A security policy must include the following information:

- *Define the overall goals of the policy*—The goals of a security policy should show a direct relationship to the overall business goals.

- *Provide the scale of the security policy*—The policy should define which data, people, departments, facilities, and technology are included and protected by the policy. Assets should also be clearly identified and included in the scope of the security policy.

- *Define the roles and responsibilities of all employees*—The policy should identify the roles of those involved in maintaining the security of the environment. These roles should include the identification of a security team, decision makers and policy enforcers, and user responsibility in keeping the network secure.

- *Identify processes*—This component of the policy should include processes for prevention, detection, and reaction of security threats that include, but are not limited to, securing, updating, maintaining, managing, and monitoring a network. This section should include instructions for both accidental and purposeful attacks.

- *Handle noncompliance*—The policy should include the consequences for not complying with the security policy. What disciplinary actions will take place? Disciplinary actions should be based on the severity of the situation, yet need to be flexible enough to be applied consistently to everyone in the organization. Consequences should not be based on the role an employee plays within an organization (e.g., senior managers should face the same consequences as administrative assistants).

Once these components are defined and the security policy is complete, a plan for communication of the policy should be created. Security policies can be communicated using a regular training regimen, or delivered to employees individually. Either way, security plan awareness should be conducted regularly. The plan for dissemination should include a plan as to how new employees will receive the information and how updates to the plan will be communicated. Another process that should be considered after the security plan is complete is the process of assessment and revision. The security plan should be regularly assessed and revised based on changes made to business goals.

Update and Upgrade Management

Defining procedures for updating a database environment's software and firmware is as important to a security system's architecture as the security plan itself. **Update management policies** should include procedures for patch updates, software upgrades, OS upgrades, and firmware changes. An update or change to a system should never be done without careful planning and thoughtful consideration.

1

The first question that must be answered prior to a system update is: Is the update necessary? To help answer this question, we must first distinguish between an update and an upgrade.

An **update** is a change to a system that is added to software or firmware that is already installed on a network. This can include the database application, database server, client applications, and client machines. Updates are often minor changes made to software or firmware to slightly improve upon the functionality of a system or to help ensure that your current software or firmware maintains compatibility within a database environment. They are often small changes that are easy to apply and easy to reverse. They are normally distributed from a vendor free of charge. An update is represented as going from version 1.0 to version 1.1. Updates may be necessary if they provide fixes to the current version of the software or firmware residing on your database, if there are known security vulnerabilities within the software or firmware on your system, or are necessary to maintain compatibility throughout an environment.

On the other hand, upgrades are usually larger, more intrusive changes. **Upgrades** are normally replacements for older versions of software or firmware. They are more difficult to apply and even more difficult to reverse. Upgrades normally need to be purchased. An upgrade is represented as going from version 1.0 to version 2.0. One could be necessary when older versions are no longer being supported by the vendor, if they provide a significant amount of improvements to a system, or if the older version no longer fits an organization's needs. Unless absolutely necessary, an upgrade should not be applied to a database or its environment immediately after release. Upgrades are often complete overhauls of previous versions of software and firmware. They often do not become stable for months, and, in some occasions as with operating systems, years after the upgrade's release.

Vendors of software and firmware cannot fully test their systems against all components that might be found within a database environment; therefore, upgrades are often released to the public with bugs or glitches that are not found and fixed until after some time. Bugs and vulnerabilities of new programs are often discovered through reports made by companies and individuals who purchased the software early. It is good practice to wait until a software upgrade becomes stable before applying one to a database or its environment.

The next question in determining whether to apply an update or an upgrade to your system is: What are the possible repercussions of the install? Understanding the possible compatibility issues or negative consequences that can result from a change made to your environment can be vital to maintaining the integrity and availability of the resources. Unfortunately, software vendors are not eager to share the possible issues that might arise from updating or upgrading their product, so this information can be difficult to find. Here are a few suggestions to find out what known complications and compatibility issues exist with a software or firmware upgrade or update:

- Check the vendor's help and troubleshooting pages.
- Search technical support forums, newsgroups, and blogs.
- Ask your peers and colleagues who may have recently installed the product.
- Check within your own database manual for software and firmware specifications to ensure compatibility.

You must be relentless in your search to ensure that you are not putting your database environment and resources in jeopardy. If possible, create a test database environment in which to install your upgrade. Test database environments, although not foolproof, can often give you clues as to what issues you may encounter. The time and effort that you put forth early in this process will pay off greatly in the long run by possibly saving you time, money, and many late hours at the office.

Prior to making any changes within the database environment, a recovery and restore plan should be put into place including failsafe options, such as reversal and backup. Instructions are often included with updates to allow an administrator to reverse an update in the event that the installation fails or the database rejects the new software. So before applying an update, check to be sure that an update has a reversal technique, and locate and read the reversal instructions so you are prepared for problems that may occur.

To add extra redundancies, back up your files. In case the reversal does not work, a backup can save your database settings. In addition, if at all possible, schedule the update during off-hours so as not to interfere with your users' work hours. Finally, after an update has been applied, it is important to document the changes that were made. Sometimes negative effects do not appear right away. Without a document showing recent changes, it can be quite difficult to pinpoint the problem and restore your system.

Types of Updates and Upgrades There are different types of updates and upgrades that can be performed within an environment. Understanding the different types of updates and upgrades is vital to the success of an update and upgrade management policy. This section focuses on patches, software upgrades, and operating system upgrades to determine the level of commitment that is required to complete each one.

A **patch** is a small program that is used to fix or update software programs or firmware devices. A patch is often created as a response to a newly discovered vulnerability found within a program. Because it is impossible for software vendors to test their software in every single environment, they are forced to release programs to the public that contain certain vulnerabilities, glitches, and compatibility issues that can result in a security breach.

Vendors learn about these vulnerabilities as well as other software issues from organizations who install and report them early on. Once a vulnerability or compatibility issue is found, a vendor will develop a patch to fix the problem and fill in security holes. If a user does not update or patch their system, the system will remain vulnerable. A system that has not been updated allows malware to take advantage of these vulnerabilities to intrude upon a database environment.

Therefore, it is a best practice to develop a strategy for receiving notification, managing installation, and documenting or tracking patches that are applied on your system's software and firmware. Some vendors' software programs include a tool that automatically searches for and installs updates and patches online (e.g., Windows Automatic Updates). Some vendors send e-mail alerts and text messages to inform their clients of critical or recommended software patches available, while other vendors require administrators (or the people that they have designated within the security plan) to search a company's Web site looking for patches on their own.

Often, software or firmware vendors will combine a number of patches to create a new version of the software, called a **software upgrade**. As mentioned earlier, upgrades are more intrusive than updates because they involve changes to the system, so careful, thoughtful planning is necessary to avoid availability and reliability issues.

1

An **OS upgrade** is accomplished by installing a new version into a host or a server. They are the most significant and risky upgrades that can be installed onto a network. These upgrades often involve radical changes to both clients and servers. Database server upgrades affect every single client within the environment and if the clients are Web applications or Web forms online, they can impact the external user's ability to access the database. Therefore, without proper planning, scheduling, research, and testing, an OS upgrade can result in a great amount of wasted time and money for a business. A failed OS upgrade can potentially leave networks and resources completely unavailable for days at a time. Imagine the loss for a company like Walmart if their point of sales servers (register software) stopped working for an entire day!

Just as with most projects, proper planning is critical to the success of the upgrade and requires a strong understanding of the current environment, future objectives, and the beginning and end points. Servers maintain all of the structure and the resources available within the database environment. They determine the logical structure of the data within the database, the user rights and access with the database, and the general resource availability of the database to internal and external clients. Therefore, a plan should carefully consider the impact that the new database system will have on the environment. The research required to do this is quite a task within itself.

The sheer scale of a server OS upgrade makes choosing the right time to schedule it extremely important. As with any smaller software upgrades, scheduling the deployment after business hours is ideal, yet with a server OS upgrade, the time of year is also critical. Because our servers essentially maintain every detail of our database as a resource, a great deal of budget resources and time are needed. Therefore, even a successful upgrade can negatively impact a business if it is scheduled during busy seasons.

Just as with smaller software upgrades, a test environment in which the main elements of the database environment can be tested and configured will help you identify potential threats that the upgrade will pose. Although test environments do not provide a foolproof way to maintain a secure network, they do provide a good deal of help and can be the step that separates success from failure when upgrading a system.

Backup Management Plan

A **backup** is an intentional copy of your data, program files, and system configurations, and is used to archive and store information. A backup can be used to replace or restore your files and systems after a network failure or malware attacks. A **backup management plan** is a process developed to ensure the safety of the data on a network. Without a backup management plan in place, the risk of losing valuable data and network resources is immense.

Backup Solutions There are many backup management solutions available today, and choosing the solution that best fits your data and business goals is important. In customizing a backup management plan that works best for your organization, several questions must be answered:

- *What type of media should I use?*—One of the first decisions that needs to be made once a backup management plan is created is what type of media will be used to store your backup data. There are different types of media available for saving your data, and choosing the right one for your business will depend on the cost, compatibility with the environment, labor, and potential for growth. Table 1-4 illustrates the types of backup media available today.

Type	Storage size and technology	Effort
CDs (compact discs), CD-RW (compact disc-rewritable) DVD (digital versatile discs) and DVDs	Use optical digitized data; lasers burn image onto the disc CDs and DVDs can be written onto one or both sides The size of the disc depends on the type of CD or DVD, but ranges from 700 MB to 17 GBs of storage	Require a computer with a suitable CD or DVD drive; process can be automated only to a certain extent; CDs and DVDs must be changed often and require a fair amount of supervision
Tape backup cassettes	Small cassette tapes Use magnetic tape to store information onto a cassette Can store up to 366 PB (petabytes) of information	Process is fully automated; removing and changing tapes require supervision Require special backup server and software
External drives, hard drives, jump drives	Thumb drives, external hard drives, USB, PCMCIA; FireWire uses flash memory technology Can range from 1 GB (gigabyte) of information to 1 TB (terabyte) of information	Process has very little automation Requires very little supervision

Table 1-4 Media storage types

- *Where is the backup to be placed?*—Backups should be saved in areas of the network other than the original data location to avoid both the original and copy being destroyed at the same time. Backups should never rely on the same system as the original data. It is not uncommon to move daily backup media off-site in order to save it. For example, once a tape or CD backup has completed for the day, the administrator drives the media to a local bank's safety deposit box to ensure the safety and security of the data. Many third-party data storage companies offer online storage and backup of your organization's data as well. Third-party systems require the creation of a secure connection, but it is available.

- *What should be backed up?*—Involves assessing and mapping data throughout the environment, as well as the identification of critical information, and should ensure that critical data receives backup priority.

- *How often should information be saved?*—The frequency with which data should be saved should correlate with the importance of the data being saved. In other words, the more valuable and critical the data, the more frequent should be the backup of that data.

- *What time of day or night should backup occur?*—Backup should occur during downtimes and/or the end of the work day. Backup should not be completed while information is being saved and updated.

- *What type of backup should be completed?*—There are different types of backups. A **full backup** will back up all of your information, regardless of its critical nature, age, and prior backup activity. An **incremental backup** conducts a backup on only the data that has changed since the last full or incremental backup. As the incremental backup completes, it flags data that is being updated so that it is not included in the next incremental backup. A **differential backup** will save only the data that has changed since the last backup was complete (full, incremental, or differential). As the differential backup completes, it does not flag any data, so that the data is stored again when the next incremental or full backup occurs.

1

The Disaster Plan

A **disaster plan** is a plan developed to ensure the quick reinstatement of a network that has fallen victim to a human or naturally caused disaster (e.g., earthquakes, fires, floods, snow, ice, hurricanes, tornadoes, explosions, chemical fires, hazardous spills, smoke, water, solar flares, and human error).

The goal of a disaster plan is to ensure the speedy reinstatement of the most critical aspects of the business. Disaster plans should not focus on minor outages, but on major disturbances that could potentially cause devastating results for an organization.

A disaster plan should include the contact names and phone numbers for emergency coordinators that will execute the disaster recovery response, as well as roles and responsibilities of emergency response staff.

Details of the network backups should be included to ensure that the most recent accurate data can be restored and these details should include information about the data and servers that are being backed up, how frequent these backups occur, where backups are stored, and information on how these backups can be recovered.

Any and all agreements made with national services carriers should also be outlined at both the local and regional level for cases when the regional service carriers are hit by the disaster as well.

Communication strategies should be defined for communication to employees and customers before, during, and after the disaster. Communication strategies should include means for communicating in scenarios where regular modes of communication are not available.

Information related to any contracts that are currently in place with organizations that specialize in disaster recovery services and provide off-site help should also be included.

Third-party disaster recovery organizations offer cold sites, warm sites, and hot sites that offer solutions to concerns about disaster recovery.

A **cold site** is a facility that provides the basic necessities for rebuilding your network. A contract that involves a cold site would promise the use of a facility that provides water, power, air conditioning, or heat. A cold site only offers the environment necessary to rebuild the network, and does not include the computer's software or firmware. This is the least expensive agreement that can be made. Rebuilding at a cold site would involve restructuring a network from the ground up.

A **warm site** is an agreement that promises the existence of a facility that contains the basic environmental concerns, as well as computers, connection firmware, and software devices necessary to rebuild a network system. Applications are not included. Rebuilding at a warm site would involve restorating all applications from backups available. A warm site provides the technical infrastructure, and the customer rebuilds the logical infrastructure.

A **hot site** is an exact replica of an organization's network, in other words, a mirror site. A hot site promises that the vendor will assume all responsibility for ensuring that the network is readily available in the event of a disaster. Hot sites are very expensive, but for critical environments they are well worth the financial cost.

Shared site agreements are arrangements between companies with similar, if not identical, data centers; there is compatibility in hardware and software that enables companies who agree to a shared site to back up each other's data. If a disaster occurs and a shared site agreement is in place, the affected organization would move to the unaffected organization's building and continue business there. This is a great alternative to a hot site, yet it is very difficult to find a company with a close enough match to enter into this agreement. Shared sites are usually different locations of the same company.

Chapter Summary

- Database security refers to the efforts taken through policy, procedure, and design to achieve the absence of threat or harm within our database systems.

- The key to achieving effective database security involves achieving confidentiality, integrity, and availability. It is important for security professionals to have experience and remain up to date in order to identify threats and vulnerabilities to the system they are protecting.

- Some potential threats to database systems include crackers, social engineers, computer users, network administrators, malware, Web browsers, and e-mail.

- Malware is an umbrella term for malicious software and can come in many forms, such as computer viruses, worms, Trojans, spyware, adware, crimeware, and bots.

- A virus is a program that spreads from one computer to another without detection, either through network connections or storage devices. There are over 600,000 viruses currently residing on our networks, and that number grows daily. They use different defense strategies to remain undetectable, and have common traits that make them extremely resilient. These strategies include self-encryption, stealth, polymorphism, and residence.

- There are different classes of viruses. For example, logic and time-dependent viruses initiate when certain variables are met. Other viruses, like spyware, only focus on gathering sensitive information. An adware virus's main purpose is marketing by obtaining potential customer information and/or excessively promoting products.

- Unlike viruses, worms do not need users. They self-replicate by harnessing the power of the networks and using this power to attack those networks.

- All worms share common elements in replicating themselves across the network. First, they find a weak target, using vulnerabilities found on a network. Next, they take control of the target and pull all viable sensitive information from it. Finally, they test the network looking for new vulnerabilities, and, therefore, targets.

- A Trojan horse is a form of malware that disguises itself in its harmful code. Trojans may come in the form of music, software, or movies, using this disguise to infiltrate a system in order to corrupt, transfer files, and log user activities.

- Bots, or software robots, have the ability to perform a large array of automated tasks for a botmaster at a remote location. Bots are difficult to detect because they self-update, morph exceptionally, and run virtually in silence. Often it requires a special program to remove a bot from a system.

- Security is never 100% and we are never 100% secure. Security is a never-ending cycle of assessing a network, designing security policies, deploying security architecture, and testing security performance.

- Operational information security ensures secure operation within an organization through the development of policies and procedures. It focuses on policies that record and define changes, updates, and failsafe measures that are made within a database environment and it provides comprehensive disaster recovery plans.

- A disaster plan ensures the quick reinstatement of a network that has fallen to a disaster. Such plans define the dynamics of hardware, software, and user correlation throughout the organization's environment and make provisions for restoring the network in jeopardy.

- Security must never be one-dimensional. Building a secure architecture requires a multifaceted, strategic approach. Careful attention to structural layers must be considered in order to build an exceptional and reliable infrastructure.

Key Terms

adware A general term for software that uses typical malware intrusion techniques to obtain marketing data or advertise a product or service.

availability The efforts taken through policy, procedures, and design in order to create and maintain the accessibility of resources within a database environment.

back door A method created during the programming of a worm in which access is gained into a system by avoiding normal security, which gives the creator of the worm undetected access into the system.

backup An intentional copy of data, program files, and system configurations that is used to archive and store information in the event of network failure or malware attacks.

backup management plan A process developed to ensure the safety of the data on a network.

black hat Someone who breaks into computer networks without authorization and with malicious intent.

boot sector An area of the hard disk that contains records necessary to the boot process of a computer.

boot sector virus Malware that infiltrates a system by loading itself onto the boot sector of a hard disk via an infected floppy disk left in a floppy disk drive.

bot (software robot) A form of malware that has the ability to perform a large array of automated tasks for an intruder at a remote location, ranging in severity from spamming a system to initiating DoS attacks on systems.

botmaster An individual who controls a network of bots and who accumulates a number of bots and then rents these botnets to other intruders and cybercriminals for the purpose of spamming, phishing, and other more serious types of cybercrime.

botnet A network of bots.

cold site A facility that provides the basic necessities for rebuilding a network. A contract that involves a cold site would promise the use of a facility that provides water, power, air conditioning, or heat.

computer security A set of established procedures, standards, policies, and tools that are used to protect a computer from theft, misuse, and unwanted intrusions, activities, and attacks.

computer virus A form of malware intended to spread from one computer to another without detection.

confidentiality The efforts taken through policy, procedure, and design in order to create and maintain the privacy and discretion of information and systems.

cracker An individual who breaks into our networks without authorization with hopes to destroy and/or steal information.

database security A set of established procedures, standards, policies, and tools that are used to protect data from theft, misuse, and unwanted intrusions, activities, and attacks.

data sending Trojan Malware that obtains sensitive data from your computer and transmits it back to a cracker.

denial of service (DoS) attack A concerted effort made by malware to keep system resources, such as Internet sites, from functioning correctly.

destructive Trojan Malware that is installed on a computer with the intent to destroy a system as a whole by randomly deleting files and folders and corrupting the registry.

differential backup An intentional copy of data, program files, and system configurations that only saves the data that has changed since the last backup was complete.

disaster plan A plan developed to ensure the quick reinstatement of a network that has fallen victim to a human or naturally caused disaster.

DNS poisoning An intrusion where a cracker gains control over the DNS server and changes the domain name's respective IP address, redirecting requests to sites that the cracker has built and maintains.

encryption The transformation of data by using sophisticated algorithms in an attempt to make the data unrecognizable.

file-infected virus A form of malware that will attach itself to an executable file that requires a user to run before it can propagate and corrupt the system.

file transfer protocol (FTP) Trojan Malware that allows the attacker to use someone else's computer as an FTP server.

full backup An intentional copy of data, program files, and system configurations that stores all information, regardless of its critical nature, age, and prior backup activity.

grey hat An individual or groups of individuals who waver between the classification of a hacker and a cracker, and who either act in goodwill or in malice.

hacker Someone who has mastered the hardware and software of modern computer systems and enjoys the exploration and analysis of network security with no intent to intrude or cause harm.

hactivist Hackers and crackers who use their extensive experience and skill to use networks to share their ideologies regarding controversial social, political, and economic topics.

Health Insurance Portability and Accountability Act (HIPAA) Strict laws for health institutions throughout the United States that ensure the security and privacy of patient records by dictating the way in which files are accessed, stored, and transmitted on a network.

hijacking A process in which Web sites are hacked into and rewritten to react differently to users than how the original Web site designer intended.

hot site An exact replica of an organization's network, or a mirror site, that promises the vendor will assume all responsibility for ensuring that the network is readily available in the event of a disaster.

hypertext transfer protocol (HTTP) The portion of an Internet address that informs the browser what protocol is used to send the request for a particular Web site.

incremental backup An intentional copy of data, program files, and system configurations that is conducted on only the data that has changed since the last full or incremental backup.

integrity Efforts taken through policy, procedure, and design in order to create and maintain reliable, consistent, and complete information and systems.

logic bomb Malware that can lie dormant until a specific predetermined variable is met, whose variables typically depend on the environment in which it resides.

macro A small program that enables users to automate a large number of repeated processes within a document.

macro virus Malware that can either be attached to a macro, or can replace a macro within a document, and that runs automatically when the document containing the infected macro is opened or closed.

malicious software A programming code written and used by unauthorized intruders to perform a certain task on a computer.

malware An abbreviation for the term malicious software.

misleading applications Applications that deceive users into believing that their computer's security has been breached, therefore tricking the user into downloading and purchasing rogue antivirus tools to remove the bogus breach.

multipartite virus A form of malware that combines the characteristics of a boot sector virus with those of a file-infected virus.

network security A set of established procedures, standards, policies, and tools that are used to protect data from theft, misuse, and unwanted intrusions, activities, and attacks.

nonresident virus The general term for malware that requires users to initiate it by downloading a program or opening up an e-mail attachment.

operational information security Ensures the secure operation of an organization through the development and reliability of an environment's policies and procedures that focus on security policies, change management, update management, and disaster recovery plans.

OS upgrade Installing a new version of an operating system onto a host or a server.

patch A small program that is used to fix or update software programs or hardware devices.

payload The component of a worm that holds all of the instructions on how to affect each computer that it encounters.

personal identifiable information (PII) Personal information that identifies a person.

phishing The attempt to obtain PII from people through the use of spoofed e-mail addresses and URLs.

polymorphism The incidence of changing forms, or self-modification.

proxy Trojan Malware that enables a cracker to use someone else's computer to access the Internet in order to keep their identity hidden.

remote access and administration Trojan (RAT) Malware that provides remote access capability to the cracker from whom the virus originated, who in turn is provided complete control of and access to someone else's computer from a remote location.

resident virus Malware that installs itself or takes residence directly in the main system memory of a computer.

script kiddie Amateur crackers that use programs and scripts written by other people to infringe upon a computer network system's integrity.

security policy A document that defines the overall goal of security and identifies the scope of what to secure, as well as the roles and responsibilities of the people within the organization.

shared site agreement An arrangement between companies with similar, if not identical, data centers.

signature A pattern of characters that is identifed for a specific family of viruses.

social engineer An individual who uses human interaction to manipulate people into gaining access to systems, unauthorized areas, and confidential information.

software upgrade A combination of a number of software or hardware packages that creates a new version of software.

spoofing A process that involves hackers building Web sites to look identical to other popular sites in hopes of drawing in a user.

spyware A general term for any software that intentionally monitors and records a user's computer and/or Internet activities.

startup page The Web site that is displayed when the Web browser is started.

time bomb (time-delayed virus) Malware that can lie dormant until a specific variable is met, such as times, days, or specific days that are predetermined and written within its code.

transmission packet Sensitive information about users or businesses compiled by spyware that is sent back to its original creators for use as they see fit.

Trojan (Trojan horse) Malware that disguises itself and its harmful code and often hides within enticing programs such as software updates, games, and movies.

update A change to a system that is added to software or firmware that is already installed on a network.

update management policy A document that includes procedures for patch updates, software upgrades, OS upgrades, and firmware changes.

upgrade Replacements for older versions of software or firmware.

warm site A facility that contains the basic environmental concerns, as well as computers, connection firmware, and software devices necessary to rebuild a network system.

Web browser An application that acts as a user interface of the Internet, allowing users to interact and view Web pages on the World Wide Web.

Web page A document containing a specific programming language (e.g., HTML or JAVA) that is designed to be viewable on the World Wide Web.

white hat An ethical hacker; hackers who use their extensive experience and knowledge to test systems and provide security consultation to others.

worm Self-replicating malware that is able to harness the power of networks and use this power in its attacks against them.

Review Questions

1. Identify the three main items that are utilized in achieving security objectives in order to protect our database systems.

2. Identify and define three objectives that are key to achieving effective security architecture.

3. List and define the different classifications created to clarify the difference between hackers and crackers.

4. List six common errors that users make on a network. Give examples of each.

5. Identify three ways that the Internet can be used as a tool to compromise information security.

6. List the destructive tactics that uneducated computer users can run into when using e-mail.

7. Define the following: computer viruses, worms, Trojans, spyware, adware, and bots.

8. List and define each phase in the process of creating and maintaining a security architecture.

9. List and describe the information that should be included in a security policy.

10. Explain the difference between an update and an upgrade.

11. List six questions you should ask when creating a backup management plan.

12. Which backup media would be most appropriate for a large enterprise or network?

13. Identify and explain the four options available for restoring your network in the event of disaster.

14. Explain the multilayered nature of security.

15. Identify the five layers of security and give examples of each.

Case Projects

Case Project 1-1: Locating Recent Vulnerabilities

Use one or more of the links provided below and write a paper that includes the top ten most current exploits and vulnerabilities identified. Include a description of these vulnerabilities as well as any known fixes or counterattacks.

- *http://www.microsoft.com/technet/security/advisory/default.mspx*
- *http://www.us-cert.gov/*
- *http://www.exploit-db.com/*

Case Project 1-2: Legal Privacy Compliancy

HIPAA is one example of a well-known act passed by Congress that has identified compliancy and privacy laws for certain types of organizations. Choose at least two other acts from the list provided and discuss the rules for privacy and confidentiality that are set forth in these acts. Include at least one policy, procedure, and design strategy that an organization can take to comply with each act discussed.

- Payment Card Industry (PCI) Data Security Standard (DSS)
- The Health Information Technology for Economic and Clinical Health (HITECH)
- The Sarbanes-Oxley Act (SOX)
- Among other changes to financial laws, the Gramm-Leach-Bliley Act
- The Basel II
- ISO 17799 Compliance
- FFIEC Compliance
- CA SB 1386 Compliance
- DCID 6/3 Compliance
- DoD 8100.2 Compliance
- FISMA Compliance
- NISPOM Compliance

Case Project 1-3: Understanding the Risks That Users Pose

Organizations take great measures to ensure the secure design of their organization architecture. Write a paper that discusses the ways users can harm this architecture if they are not properly trained. Include in your paper the policies and procedures that you will recommend to ensure that users will support the security of your network.

Hands-On Projects

Hands-On Project 1-1: Assessing and Prioritizing Risks

You have been hired as the security professional in your current work or school environment. Your department has experienced a recent breach within its database architecture. Your manager feels it is time to reassess the network as a first step in a phased approach to hardening the network security. You have been delegated to lead this assessment. Research your organization or school to determine its database architecture. Write a paper describing your assessment process. Include the following information in your paper:

- Define who would be included in the assessment of the database environment.
- Identify the assets that you are protecting.
- Define the threats you are protecting yourself against.
- Using the following table, assign a risk value to each threat, based on its likelihood and cost to the company.
- Prioritize your threats based on their risk value (5 being the highest risk and 1 being the lowest).

Risk values 5 = high, 1 = low

	High cost	Medium cost	Low cost
High probability	5	4	3
Medium probability	4	3	2
Low probability	3	2	1

Hands-On Project 1-2: Designing Your Security Defense

You have been hired as the security professional in your current work or school environment. Your department has experienced a recent breach within its database architecture. Your manager has delegated you to lead an effort to eliminate threats within your database environment.

Based on the results that you found in your assessment, five priority threats have been identified. Define each threat identified in Hands-On Project 1-1 and indicate the policy, procedure, and design changes that need to be taken to ensure the security of your network. Ensure that your measures follow the multilayered approach to security by using the following table:

Layer	Computer layer measures	Network layer measures	Database layer measures
Threat 1			
Threat 2			
Threat 3			
Threat 4			
Threat 5			

Hands-On Project 1-3: Implementing a Strategy

You have been hired as the security professional in your current work or school environment. Your department has experienced a recent breach within its database architecture. Your manager has delegated you to lead an effort to eliminate threats from the database environment. Based on the results from your assessment, five priority threats have been identified. Changes in policy, procedure, and design need to take effect in order to ensure protection from these threats. Using the five priority threats you identified in Hands-On Project 1-1, create a plan for implementation. Your plan for implementation should include the following:

- The phases in which you intend to implement the project
- The cost of the implementation, including a list of all new firmware and software to be purchased as well as training costs

- The plan for communicating these changes to network users
- The plan for training network users on changes, if necessary
- The time frame for implementations
- The time of day that the implementations will occur
- The testing strategy

chapter 2

Database Review

After reading this chapter and completing the exercises, you will be able to:

- Review the basic components of a database
- Define a database and identify the basic components of a database management system
- Identify the different database management system models and applications
- Identify and describe the architecture of Oracle, MySQL, and Microsoft SQL Server

Security In Your World

Lady's Inc. is a music management company based out of Miami, Florida. The company, well known for its representation of some of the hottest talent in the state, has recently fallen victim to a major security breach. A list of phone numbers, addresses, and birth names of high-profile clients was stolen from the company's database and leaked to the press. Worried about the potential impact that this might have on the organization's reputation, and concerned for future prospects, the board of directors of Lady's Inc. decided to hire Amber E., one of the most sought-after and highly-respected security consultants in the state of Florida. With more than 15 years' experience securing network and database environments, Amber is well known for her exhaustive network environment audits and iron-clad security strategies.

After a few hours of extensive testing and exploration, Amber had identified the main source of the breach. Although great measures were put into place to secure the network and the computers where the database resided, there were significant deficiencies in the security measures that were applied to the logical data structure components. Many of the fundamental strategies that are necessary for securing a database system were missing, and critical database architectural components were left completely exposed.

Based on what she found, Amber was able to make accurate inferences about the previously hired consultant. In her report to the board, she stated that although it seemed that the previous security consultant appeared to be talented, based on the obvious neglect of the fundamental database components, it was clear that he did not have much knowledge or experience working with database systems. Had the prior consultant taken the time to research the basic architecture and conduct a general review of the components of a database, this breach could have been avoided.

As discussed in the previous chapter, there are three layers of security that must be addressed in order to maintain the integrity of a database system: network security, computer security, and database security. Prior knowledge of all three of these types of architectures is a necessity in order to provide security assurance within a database environment. This chapter provides an overview of database components and explores the architecture of an Oracle, MySQL, and SQL Server database system.

Database Defined

A **database** is a collection of data stored on a computer using an application called a database management system. A **database management system (DBMS)** is an application that allows others to search stored data in order to locate specific information. The goal of a DBMS is to provide users the means to manipulate, analyze, store, and retrieve information.

2

A simple example of a database is your school library. Whether you take classes online or at a traditional school, your school library stores literature and materials that you can search through to find specific information that you need. In this example, the librarian (in an on-campus library) or the Web site (for an online campus library) acts as the database management system. The DBMS provides you with the means to conduct a search and access the information that is stored within the library.

Database Structure Components

The way information is stored within the database depends on the database type. For example, addresses in an address book are normally stored alphabetically, while books in a library are stored using a sophisticated numbering system like the Dewey Decimal system. Digital database management applications have common components and use common strategies for storing and organizing information. The common components that are found within these systems are introduced below.

Tables

A **table** is one of the most basic units of storage within a database, typically representing unique and specific data objects. For example, in Lady's Inc.'s database, a table can be created to hold information about an artist or an album. Tables are composed of vertical columns and horizontal rows. A **column**, also known as a **field**, is the component of a table that maintains a general category of information with similar datatypes. A **row**, often referred to as a **record**, or a **tuple**, holds distinct units of data, and each record or row within a table is identified using unique strings of numbers or characters.

For example, referring to Figure 2-1, you can see that the column *Name* is a general category of information that holds similar data, while the second row holds a distinct unit of data that is identified by the unique number two. When referring to columns of a group, the table name is included to indicate the table in which that particular column belongs. For example, Figure 2-1 displays a typical table within a database along with its naming convention. Tables are often used in conjunction with other tables to access information, so referencing rows and columns in a table correctly is critical to the effectiveness of a database.

NOTE

We refer to a column similarly to the way we indicate the paths of a file in a Windows file system. For example, if a folder named *Budget* is saved on the main drive of a Windows PC (the C: drive), and a file called *Dec.docx* is added to this folder, the full reference to the **Dec.docx** file would be C:/Budget/Dec.docx. In Figure 2-1, the ID column is referred to as the Artists.ID and the Name column is referred to as the Artists.Name.

Keys

Keys are another concept within the structure of a database, and there are several different types. A **key** is a single field or group of fields used to identify an entry in a table. In a relational database, a key is used to access or manipulate records or rows within a table of a database.

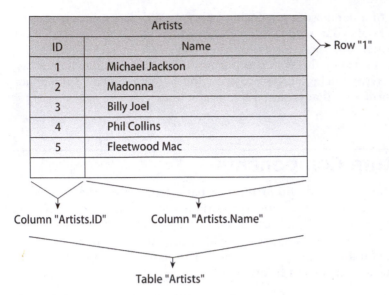

Figure 2-1 Common table found in a database
© Cengage Learning 2012

Keys are contained within the unique ID columns of a table and allow databases to be more resilient and flexible to changes. As you will discover later in this chapter, referring to a key rather than the specific table entry has a few advantages:

- Lowers the possibility of data entry errors and redundancy within a database
- Allows for less-taxing data entry changes
- Creates a more object-oriented relational environment in certain database models

Primary Key A **primary key** is a field that contains a unique label by which we can identify a record or row in a table. Each table should have at least one primary key that must be unique to all other record keys within the same table, and that cannot change over time. To ensure the uniqueness of the primary key, often the key is a sequence or pattern of numbers that guarantees the absence of duplication. It is a best practice, but not necessary, to use keys that are meaningful to the data being stored. Examples of primary keys are employee ID numbers, student IDs, ISBNs, and Social Security numbers.

The use of Social Security numbers as a unique identifier is controversial. In some instances, it can be considered illegal due to inherent privacy concerns.

Foreign Key A **foreign key** is a field within a table that contains a label that is used to build a relationship between two tables. Often, a foreign key refers to a unique entry or primary key in a table different from the table where the foreign key resides. Figure 2-2 displays the use of a foreign key, where the numbers found within the Songs.Artist column represent a foreign key that refers to our primary key, Artists.ID from the Artists table. In

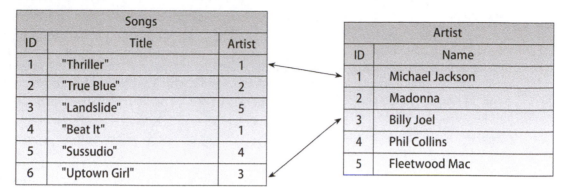

Figure 2-2 Use of foreign keys
© Cengage Learning 2012

most DBMSs, data can be added into a foreign key column only after the entries to where foreign keys point exist within another table. For example, we could not add a new song into Figure 2-2 and use the number six before we have identified an entry for six in our original Artists table.

Not all DBMSs allow foreign keys to be used. MySQL does not support the use of foreign keys. Although foreign keys can be included with the specifications for creating a table, it won't actually do anything. MySQL will not support foreign keys in this sense. This is a limitation in the way that MySQL implements the relational database management system (RDMS) model, yet the trade-off is that you get a significant performance boost.

Other Keys So far, two main types of keys have been discussed. Several other types of keys can be implemented, yet they do not exist as frequently. These keys are worth noting, and so it is important to understand this terminology. The usage of these keys varies, and depends on the administrator, the DBMS, and the database model within an environment:

- *Secondary or alternative key*—A field with values that contains nonunique data and that can refer to several records at one time. For instance, Michael Jackson sings two songs from another table.

- *Candidate key*—A field with values that meet the requirements for a primary key. This key meets the characteristics of a primary key.

- *Composite key*—A group of two or more fields where their values can be combined to be used as a primary key.

- *Sort or control key*—A field with values that are used to sequence data.

- *Alternate key*—A field with values that are not chosen as a primary key, but can be used in cases where the primary key is not available. For instance, if a Social Security number is used as the primary key and an employee is hired from outside the United States, then an alternate key is used.

Queries

A **query** is a search initiated by users in an attempt to retrieve certain information from the database. A query consists of sets of variables or keywords that are formatted in a way that is defined by the programming language being used to query the DBMS in hopes of retrieving specific information. The query language to which we will refer throughout this book is known as Structured Query Language (SQL). A query written using SQL looks similar to this:

```
SELECT title FROM songs, artists, WHERE songs.artists = groups.ID
AND groups. Name= 'Madonna'
```

This query asks the database to pull all of the song titles for the songs written by Madonna. A query displays information within a **report**, which is a document that contains a formatted result of a user's query.

Database Models

As mentioned earlier, a database is a collection of data stored on a computer using a database management system. A **database model** is a representation of the way data is stored. The model for which a database is constructed also determines the way the data can be retrieved and manipulated. In this section, we will discuss four main database models: flat, relational, hierarchical, and network.

Flat Model

A **flat model** is a two-dimensional list of data entries, where all data within a field are understood to be similar, and all data within a record are understood to be related to one another. Essentially, a flat model system is similar to a sign-in sheet at a doctor's office. When a person arrives at the doctor's office, he normally writes his name in the first column, the time of arrival in the second, and the doctor he came to see in the third. All information provided in the first column is assumed to be similar (names), as well as with the second and third. All of the rows on this sheet are assumed to be related to individuals who sign in (name, time in, doctor, etc.), and each time a patient visits the doctor, he must add another row to the sheet, filling the information out again. This is certainly not a very sophisticated model, yet it is important to understand the advantages and disadvantages of this to be able to move toward the more complex relationship based on database storage models.

Consider this scenario: You work at a radio station and are asked to keep track of all of the songs that are played within an hour. You are given an Excel spreadsheet that looks like the one in Figure 2-3.

Here we have another example of a flat model database. The first column stores the same type of data (artist) and each row represents information that relates to each other row (artist's songs). The DJ plays the Billy Joel song "Uptown Girl" first, so you input this into the table. If Billy Joel is played again that hour, his name needs to be written in the table again.

Disadvantages to this system include multiple efforts and redundant data, as well as wasting time and storage space. This may not seem like much added effort, considering that only

Artist	Song

Figure 2-3 Flat database model
© Cengage Learning 2012

around 15–20 songs are played on the radio in an hour. Imagine the wasted space of a much higher frequency and greater amount of records, for example, 20,000 entries an hour. At this level, it becomes much more of an issue.

Even though multiple efforts and redundant data are major problems, they are not the main issues with a flat database storage model. The main issues is the large margin for error that this system allows. For example, if one of Billy Joel's songs is played again later in the day and a new person is tracking the music, that person could create many mistakes. It could be something simple, such as not knowing the name of the individual who is singing the song, which could result in typing the incorrect name. Other instances include inconsistencies such as not using capital letters, placing an incorrect space in the title (e.g., "Up Town Girl," rather than "Uptown Girl"), or spelling Billy Joel incorrectly (e.g., Billie Joel). The possiblity for error is endless.

If inconsistency does exist and a query is run to find out how many Billy Joel songs were played that day, the results will not be accurate. Computers are literal when searching for identical character strings, so a query asking for B.I.L.L.Y. followed by J.O.E.L. would not return items that aren't an exact match, causing unreliable results. There are many issues with this system, and in some definitions of a DBMS, the flat model does not fit. It is important that we learn the disadvantages of this system to fully understand the advantages of the others.

Hierarchical Model

Popular in the late 1960s and well through the 1970s, hierarchical database structures are found mostly in legacy servers. The **hierarchical database structure** is a treelike storage schema that represents records and relationships through the use of tiers and parent-to-child relationships.

Similar to a family tree, relationships within a record in this schema are represented by layers. This one-to-many approach greatly minimizes redundancy (unlike the flat model) in the database and creates a more simplified view of the environment's data. The hierarchical structure restricts designers to one-to-many relationships between parent-and-child entities, whereas parents can have several children, yet children only have one parent. This model builds direct relationships only within one stem, creating one upward link to data. No direct relationships are made vertically *across* the tree, which would make searches through this storage model cumbersome and resource intensive. These restrictions have caused designers to conform their data to fit the structure, which means that data is less logically and conceptually stored than in relational database structures. Figure 2-4 illustrates the hierarchical database structure.

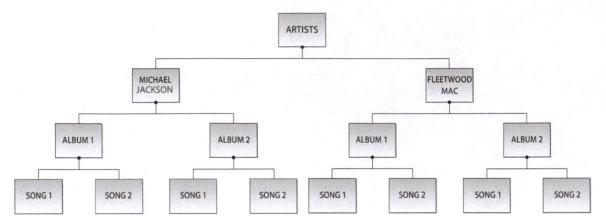

Figure 2-4 Hierarchical database model
© Cengage Learning 2012

Network Model

The network database model was developed as a solution to the one-to-many restrictive nature of the hierarchical database model. Popular during the same period as the hierarchical model, it provided an alternative for those environments that required many-to-many relationships. Much like the hierarchical data model, the **network database model** is a treelike structure that stores information in the form of a hierarchy, using tiers and parent-child-like entities to represent relationships.

Unlike the hierarchical model, the parent is referred to as a set of which the child entities are members. It is possible for child entities to be a member of more than one set (to hold more than one parent). This many-to-many relationship provided a more conceptual and logical design than the hierarchical model, and it was less resource intensive and easier to navigate. Figure 2-5 illustrates a network database model structure.

Relational Database

Developed in the 1970s, relational database storage became the flexible and conceptual solution of its predecessors. A **relational database** is a storage model in which common entities are stored within separate tables that use unique key identifiers to build relationships among these entities. There are three main concepts to understand when referring to a relational database: entities, keys, and relationships.

An **entity** is defined as a person, place, or thing stored within a table of a database for which attributes and relationships exist. An entity can be thought of as a noun. An **attribute** is a characteristic or variable that describes or further identifies an entity. An attribute can be thought of as an adjective. A **relationship** defines the association between two entities and binds them. A relationship can be thought of as a verb. Entities, attributes, and relationships together are the quintessential concepts on which relational databases are built.

Unlike a flat database model, which stores all information in one large table, a relational database is a logical and conceptual representation of information stored in several smaller

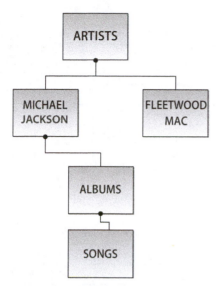

Figure 2-5 Network database model
© Cengage Learning 2012

tables. Each table is given a unique name and the database management system uses this name to retrieve and manipulate the data within the database. These unique identifiers (keys), are used to reference and build relationships with other tables or entities. A query in this model uses table names to retrieve information from the database. Figure 2-6 illustrates an example of information stored within a relational database model.

As you can see in this figure, the table Songs now includes the Album ID and the Artist ID, creating a relationship among these three tables. These relationships, as well as the object-oriented nature of relational databases, provide for a robust, flexible storage system. The issues inherent to the flat database model (e.g., redundancy, multiple efforts, and typographical errors) are greatly lowered because if designed well, data needs to be stored only once.

Object-Oriented Databases

With the advancement of Web technologies and programming languages, complex data-types such as multimedia files have become more prominent and in demand, and so has the need to store them. Relational database management systems (RDBMSs) allow only simple datatypes such as strings and numbers to be stored within a table. Therefore, storing and retrieving a media file such as a 3-D graphic within a relational database is quite cumbersome. For this to happen, essentially all graphical information must be broken down into numbers and strings to be placed into storage, and retrieving the information requires the reconstruction of the graphic using a combination of SQL and programming code. For example, consider the process of storing a 3-D graphic of a house in an RDBMS. Each component (e.g., window, door, roof) would need to be stored separately in its own individual table and then broken down into integers that represent the position of that particular portion of the graphic as one part of the whole. To reconstruct the house, these tables must be retrieved and joined using SQL and then repositioned and drawn using different object-oriented programming code.

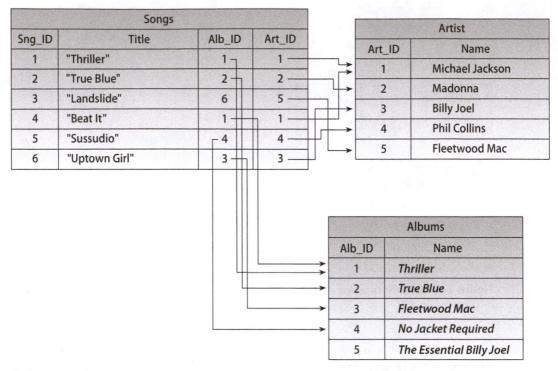

Figure 2-6 Relational database model
© Cengage Learning 2012

Object-oriented database management systems, or OODBMSs, were introduced as the means by which programmers can store objects and complex datatypes within a database. OODBMSs store objects rather than data in tables and all objects are stored as a whole, so there is no need for reconstruction. Objects are stored within the database as subclasses of a class from which subclasses inherit attributes. Object-oriented programming languages such as Java, C++, and .NET parallel those concepts and techniques of an OODBMS, as they both use the same type of objects and references to objects. Therefore, retrieval of objects from within the OODBMS is ideal for object-oriented programmers, as there is much less time wasted trying to reference application objects to their corresponding database objects.

Unfortunately, OODBMSs were introduced in 1985, well before the popularity of multimedia and object-oriented programming, so they did not catch the interest of database administrators right away. Also, OODBMS technology is quite a big leap from the relational database management systems that most administrators were used to, so the learning curve also affected the adoption of the system.

Still, OODBMSs are used in a number of specialized areas and offer great advantages for organizations that require the frequent storage and retrieval of CAD files, artificial intelligence objects, XML-compatible objects, and general multimedia (e.g., audio, video).

A special query language has been developed and standardized for OODBMSs, named object query language, or OQL. OQL is an alternative to object-oriented languages for retrieving and storing objects in the object-oriented database management system.

Object-Relational Database

Object-relational database management systems, or ORDBMSs introduced in the 1990s as a middle ground between relational and object-oriented database management systems. An ORDBMS is essentially a relational database management system with an expanded group of datatypes to accommodate object classes and inheritance. General programming languages and SQL can be used to retrieve information, and custom datatypes can be developed. This might seem like the best of both worlds for programmers and database administrators alike, yet at the time of this writing, relational database management systems are still the prominent choice in the market. Only the future can tell the potential for an ORDBMS.

NOTE Most database administrators and programmers use a relational database management system in combination with an object-relational application as a way to obtain the advantages of an ORDBMS without having to obtain one.

Relationships

Relationships define the association between entities and bind them together. The two entities in a relationship are often called parent and child entities. The types of relationships implemented between two entities are one-to-one, one-to-many, or many-to-many. Figure 2-7 displays these relationship types.

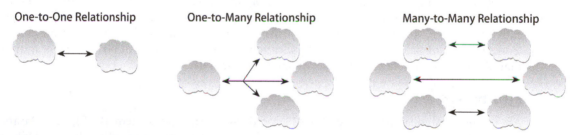

Figure 2-7 Entity relationship types
© Cengage Learning 2012

- *One-to-one relationship*—Often expressed as 1:1. This is the most simplistic relationship that two entities can have. This relationship has only one entity in both directions. These relationships rarely occur within a relational database. They are found only in unique situations. Too many one-to-one relationships found within a relational database schema usually indicate poor design choices. An example of a 1:1 relationship is an instructor who teaches a specific section of a course. Anthony Joseph teaches section two of the database security course, and the database security course contains only one instructor. Although these are rare, there are some security policies created in order to ensure that 1:1 relationships keep private information separate.

- *One-to-many relationship*—Often expressed as 1:N (N represents an indefinite number). This is the ideal type of relationship within a relational database schema. This relationship involves one entity who has a sole relationship with an entity that has a relationship with several other entities as well. For instance, an instructor may belong to only one department within the university (e.g., Information Security), yet that department has many instructors that are members.

- *Many-to-many relationship*—Often expressed as M:N. This is a type of relationship that refers to an entity that has one or many partnerships with another entity that also has one or many other partnerships. For example, an instructor may be a member of several school committees, and school committees may have several members. This is used effectively within databases as long as the entities do not have many-to-many relationships with one another. A situation in which a many-to-many relationship causes issues is one where there are duplicate tables within a database to represent a many-to-many relationship. This type of redundancy is unnecessary and an inefficient way to store data. It can make querying the database difficult and confusing for both users and administrators.

Database Types

Databases can be used for many purposes and are capable of storing many types of data. The type of database that is used is determined by the data that will be housed in it.

OLTP

An **online transaction processing (OLTP) database** is a database that is created for real-time storage and manipulation of data within an organization. An OLTP was created to be used in an active environment and is optimized to serve thousands of users simultaneously. Typically, an OLTP stores data that results from large volumes of short transactions, usually from a point of sale or data entry application. A **point of sales (POS) system** is a system that is meant to handle cash register or sales transactions.

OLAP/DSS

An **online analytical processing (OLAP)**, or **decision support system (DSS)**, is a database that stores large volumes of historical data for report generating and analyzing. DSS and OLAP systems typically retrieve their data from an OLTP. The data stored is analyzed within a business environment as a way to improve productivity or meet a specific need. These systems are also referred to as data warehouses, or repositories, for an organization's digitally stored data. Designed to store large amounts of data and draw reports for analytical intentions, these types of systems do not cater to real-time, frequent, large-volume, or short transactions.

Database Management Systems

As defined earlier in this chapter, a database management system is an application that provides users with the means to manipulate, analyze, and query data. Almost all DBMSs in existence today are developed to be used with relational databases. These applications are known as Relational Database Management Systems (RDBMSs).

There are several relational database management systems in existence today. For this book, we will be focusing on the three most prominent and fastest-growing RDBMSs: Oracle, Microsoft SQL, and MySQL. The following section will explore the major components of their architectures.

Oracle

Oracle is an RDBMS developed by Oracle Corporation in the late 1970s. Holding 52% of the DBMS market in 2009, it remains one of the most popular database servers. Oracle is well known for being portable, its ability to run on almost any operating system, and its dominant role in providing solutions on which businesses rely to achieve their core competencies. Oracle databases offer a number of storage solutions, and can be found maintaining business-critical data such as human resources, billing, and financial records throughout the globe. The most current version and the version on which this book will focus is Oracle 11g.

MySQL

MySQL is an RDBMS developed by Sun Microsystems. Showing tremendous growth each year and well known for its speed, MySQL is the most popular open-source database server today. The term **open source** refers to software that has been written to be distributed for use and download free of charge. Besides cost, open-source applications provide the advantage of customization.

Anyone is able to view and study the code and can contribute to it by providing additional customization or features that fit several environments. A large contribution has already been made to MySQL, so several variations of tools have already been created that support almost any network configuration. MySQL is platform independent, and like Oracle, it is implemented to solve business needs, both large and small.

Microsoft SQL

Microsoft SQL is often referred to simply as SQL Server. SQL Server is an RDBMS developed by Microsoft to provide a fast, secure, and scalable data access platform. SQL Server's primary query languages are T-SQL and ANSI SQL. The scalability of the SQL server architecture is its most attractive feature, as it was developed to run equally in a wide variety of environments. From a database running on a personal computer servicing only one user, to a database stored on a cluster of servers servicing several thousands of users, SQL Server can meet the needs of any Windows environment.

Database Similarities

Two main areas of focus that exist in all database management systems are read consistency and query management. Obtaining an understanding of read consistency and query management is imperative in order to identify the different ways these applications address these items.

Read Consistency

Read consistency refers to the accuracy and reliability of data within a database and is dependent on a database's ability to process and commit transactions in a timely manner, as well as control concurrency effectively by applying the following locking mechanisms:

- *Transactions*—Initiated by a user via a request to change or obtain information from a database. A user initiates a request by querying the database using an API or a programming language such as SQL. A **transaction** is the group of statements or queries processed by the database to execute a user's request to update or change the database. In order to meet the standards of the database industry, transactions must operate as a single unit, maintain consistency of the database, work in isolation, and be durable enough to persist even after system failures.

- *Concurrency*—One of the greatest concerns within a multiuser environment is how to handle simultaneous access to data and resources in such a way that integrity and reliability of that data is maintained. For example, if two users are accessing data within the same table of a database at the same time and both are making changes to this table, problems will occur. One user's change will override the other's, making the database inaccurate for at least one of the two users. Concurrency is the term used to describe this concern. **Concurrency** is the simultaneous access of resources and data. Oracle, MySQL, and SQL Server handle concurrency in different ways, yet each application uses locks to maintain system integrity.

- *Locks*—A **lock** is a mechanism within a DBMS that controls concurrency by allowing users to take hold of the data until changes being made are completed or committed. If two users attempt to commit changes on the same data at the same time, a deadlock will occur. A **deadlock** is a situation when two transactions cannot proceed because each user has data that the other needs.

- *Commit*—A transaction is committed after it is processed by the database. To **commit** a change means to make it permanent and visible to other users.

- *Undo*—Transaction commits can be undone. To undo a transaction commit is to roll back changes made through users' API or SQL transactions. The undone transactions are reverted to the state they were in before the user committed the most recent transaction.

Query Management

Query management refers to the steps taken by a database management application to process a user query. Query management often involves retrieving, parsing, and optimizing user SQL requests. Query processing can be conducted on queries within a local table, within a partitioned table, or on a distributed server.

Each database application has a different process for parsing queries, yet in general terms, **parsing** involves the act of analyzing the construction of a query for correct syntax and semantics. During the parsing process, the database applications also identify the tables and data the user is requesting, checking that these items exist as well.

Optimization is the process of locating the quickest and most efficient way to retrieve the data requested by the user. Modern database applications often optimize using the variables of cost and speed to determine the best plan for executing a SQL statement. Cost is the amount of resources needed to retrieve data in a certain way.

Queries can be processed individually, where one process parses and optimizes one query at a time, in batches, where one process parses and optimizes several queries at one time; or in parallel (known as **parallel processing**), when more than one server process processes one query at the same time.

Oracle Architecture

Before you can install, use, or secure Oracle, you should have a basic understanding of the architecture of Oracle and how it conceptually works. This section will begin by identifying the two main components of the Oracle server—the instance and the database—and then will review the physical structure, memory structure, logical structure, and processes of the Oracle architecture. Oracle architecture is illustrated in Figure 2-8.

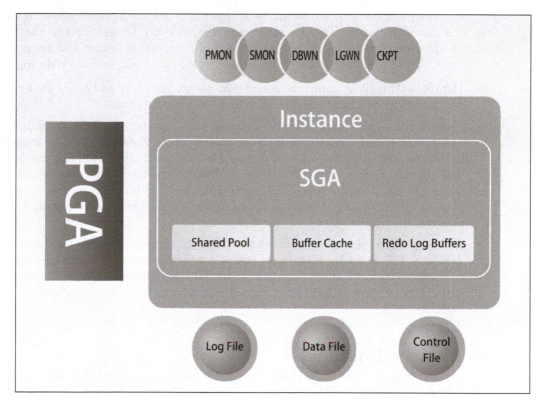

Figure 2-8 Oracle architecture
© Cengage Learning 2012

The Instance and the Database

An **instance** is a broad term that refers to the background processes and structured memory used during interaction with the database. To create an instance, a user must connect to the database and establish a session. A session begins when a user connects to the database and it ends when the user logs out of a database. The set of background processes in the instance include the performance monitor (PMON), the system monitor (SMON), the recovered (RECO), the log writer (LGWR), and the checkpoint (CKPT), and will be discussed in more detail later in this section. It is important to note that these resources play a vital role in Oracle's dependability and performance. Two critical memory structures included within an Oracle instance are the System Global Area (SGA) and the Program Global Area (PGA). These will be discussed in greater detail later in this section.

The database portion of an Oracle server holds the database files that an environment needs to run the Oracle database. This set of files helps to configure the instance, make it possible for SQL executions to be processed, and ensure alert and recovery from hardware and software failure. Example files found in this area are the control, the redo log, and the data files. These files will be discussed in detail in the next section.

The Physical Structure

For the most part, the physical structure is dependent on the operating system on which Oracle is installed, yet, a few files are required with every Oracle install. The files contained within the physical structure interact with the operating system and are transparent to the user. These common files are the datafile, the control file, and the redo log.

- *Datafile*—This file contains the actual data for the database and holds the information for all logical structures (tables, records, etc.) in the database.

- *Control file*—This file contains the location and important credentialing information of other files, and is critical to the functionality of the database. Because it contains location information for other important files, if your control file fails, the database will not run. Examples of information held within the control file are: read/write status of files, database unique ID, point of failure if failure occurs, and the name and location of the datafile. Duplicate copies of the control file should be made for fail-safe reasons.

- *Redo log*—This file contains information about all changes made to the data within the database. This is similar to an undo button for the database. The redo log can be used to restore data in the event that data is lost. All installations of Oracle include at least two copies of the redo log, and it is good practice to make a duplicate copy for fail-safe reasons.

The Memory Structure

The memory structure of Oracle holds the secret to why this RDBMS works so efficiently in a multiuser environment. As it is known in the information technology field, the main memory and cache is the quickest accessible storage area in any system. Therefore, running processes directly from memory will ensure that your systems are efficient and reliable.

In Oracle, practically everything happens from within the main memory. Even the users connect to the memory through the server process (defined later in this section). This is one reason that Oracle RDBMSs are capable of reliably servicing hundreds upon thousands of users concurrently.

One example of the way Oracle utilizes memory to speed up processes is in its query caching. **Caching** is the process of saving a duplicate of requested data to another area of a system in hopes of saving resources and speeding up the future requests for that same data. In an Oracle database, queries are cached into the buffer area to further utilize memory, and therefore increase the speed of future query returns. The memory structure of Oracle is divided into two main parts: the System Global Area (SGA) and the Process Global Area (PGA).

System Global Area The System Global Area (SGA) is the central area in which all shared data and processes are stored. The information contained in the SGA includes information shared by users and database processes. The SGA also holds the control data for one single instance in Oracle. Oracle 11g uses dynamic SGA, which means the data can be changed and an SGA is created for each new instance of Oracle. The SGA contains a number of required and optional memory structures. Tables 2-1 and 2-2 illustrate the required and optional memory structures found within the SGA.

Process Global Area The Process Global Area (PGA) is the central area where information is stored for background and server processes. Similar to the ways that the SGA allocates space for each new instance, the PGA allocates space for each individual background process. The Process Global Area content varies depending on the configuration of Oracle.

Structure	Description	Information and examples
Database buffer cache	Used to cache information read from the data files as well as recently used SQL and PL/SQL queries	A user executes a query on a client machine, and when the client connects to the dedicated server process. The server process first checks the cache to see if the file already exists. If it does, it passes the result to the users; if it is not in the cache, the server process takes data from the datafile and loads it into the buffer cache for future use
Shared pool	Stores the most recently executed SQL statements and data definitions Contains the library cache and data dictionary cache	When you execute a SELECT query, once executed, the statement is saved in the shared pool; it checks the rights of the user to ensure the user can view the requested information and then removes the requested information from the datafile, loading it into the buffer cache for the user to view
Library cache	Used to cache metadata information	An SQL statement is stored here parsed while the syntax is checked by the database; once validity is confirmed, it searches in the shared pool for a cached version of the statement
Data dictionary cache	Caches recently used data dictionary information	User account information, datafile names, etc.
Database buffer cache	Stores blocks of table and database data that has been retrieved in the past	A query is sent to the server process; the server process first looks in the database buffer to find the information needed to access the hard disk, thus speeding up performance
Redo log buffer	Stores all changes that have been made to the database	When the redo buffer gets filled, the excess moves to the redo file

Table 2-1   Required memory structures within the SGA

Structure	Description	Information/example
Large pool	Stores large jobs to avoid filling the shared pool	RMAN backups
Java pool	Stores and caches Java commands	Necessary only when Java is installed
Streams pool	For advanced queuing	Only used in Oracle 10g and 11g

Table 2-2 Optional memory structures within the SGA

The Processes

A **process** is a set of instructions that is executed by the operation system and intended to complete a task. To complete an instance in Oracle, two tasks must take place. First, a user must run an application tool, such as SQL, to request a connection to the Oracle Server. This is referred to as a user process. Next, the server must handle the user's request and run a process to create the Oracle instance and complete the connection, referred to as a server process. Once the Oracle instance is created, background processes run to maintain relationships and resources among the Oracle structures.

Server processes can be shared or dedicated. In a dedicated server environment, each session owns a dedicated server process for executing SQL statements and handling user requests. Within a shared server environment, users must share server processes for handling requests and SQL statements. The configuration is dependent on an organization's size and needs. Larger organizations may opt for a shared server environment because it minimizes the number of processes running on the server, while smaller organizations may be less concerned with the server overhead.

There are several background processes that begin with every Oracle instance. Some are required, while others are options. Table 2-3 illustrates the different background processes found within an Oracle instance

Process name	Example process task
PMON (process monitor)	Cleans up after processes complete or processes fail
SMON (system monitor)	Recovers the database in case of failure by using the redo logs as well as database files
DBWN (database writer)	Writes changes from the database buffers to the database files
LGWR (log writer)	Writes modifications from the redo log buffer to the redo log files
CKPT (checkpoint)	Writes to the control file's established commit points where recovery begins, if necessary

Table 2-3 Background processes

MySQL Architecture

The MySQL architecture has been developed for multiplatform use. MySQL can be found on Solaris, Linux, or Windows. The architecture components defined in this section are the components that remain consistent on all three of these operation systems. This section will explore the main structures of the MySQL server architecture: the database connection manager, query engine, transaction manager, and storage engine. The MySQL architecture is illustrated in Figure 2-9.

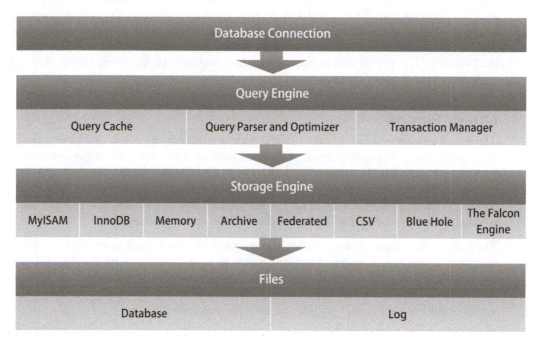

Figure 2-9 MySQL architecture
© Cengage Learning 2012

Database Connection Manager

The **database connection manager** does just what its name implies. It manages connections to the MySQL server. The connection management layer is very versatile, enabling virtually any client to connect to a MySQL server. An open-source application built to run on virtually any platform, MySQL has provided several ways for clients to connect via the connection management layer. Developers can create clients and application programming interfaces (APIs) in virtually any of today's modern programming languages (e.g., C, C++, Perl, and PHP), and clients using Open Database Connectivity (ODBC), Java, and .net are provided support through MySQL's interface.

Although there are several options for connecting to MySQL through the connection management layer, TCP/IP is the most common type of connection utilized. Not only is TCP/IP secure, but it can be used in virtually any OS environment (Windows, UNIX, OS/2 Linux and Solaris), making it a very attractive choice for users. It is safe to assume that most applications connecting to MySQL servers are running using TCP/IP.

Each server connection creates its own thread, to which MySQL dynamically assigns buffer space during query execution. A **thread** is an execution that runs independently from other processes and utilizes a portion of the CPU. These threads handle all requests from the client during a connection, including authentication and query processing. There are as many threads as connected users at any given time. Although this dedicated thread approach provides advantages to the user, it can cause great overhead to the server, so systems are in place to ensure that threads are utilized efficiently.

Besides managing the actual connections to the database, the database connection manager allows clients to connect to local and remote databases using predefined connection profiles. These profiles allow users to define a specific role based on their intended use of the database, and then save that role along with its configuration parameters for later use when connecting to the network. The profile dialog box offers great convenience for users, eliminating the need to reconfigure the connection each time.

Query Engine

The **query engine** is the component of the architecture that optimizes and manages queries and SQL statements. The query engine has been built to use resources at the greatest efficiency, therefore, it can equally support data from both OLTPs and DSSs. This is partly because the queries in MySQL are written using a variation of the standard version of SQL that provides for much more powerful searching. In this section, we will review the process for receiving, parsing, and optimizing queries within the MySQL query engine.

Typically, when users connect to MySQL using their client application and the configuration manager, a query is initiated. Once the query request is received by the MySQL server, it is the responsibility of the data manipulation language (DML) to find relevant SQL statements and retrieve them from the client-side application. The data definition language (DDL) then provides access for the SQL to interact with the database.

Before the access takes place, the query parser creates a treelike structure based on the SQL statements extracted. The parsed SQL is then checked for validity within the syntax and the semantics of the tree. If the statement is not valid, an error message is sent back to the user. If the statement is indeed valid, then the integration manager determines whether the users have access to obtain the information that they are requesting.

The query optimizer runs testing speed variables. While most RDBMSs optimize for cost of resources, MySQL optimizes for speed, which is the reason for its success in this area. Once the fastest path to retrieving the information is found, the query is then executed by the query execution engine.

A memory component that plays a role in ensuring that query processing is successful is the **query cache**. The query cache maintains a set of recently requested queries within its storage space to save time and resources in the event that a similar query is requested again. If a similar query is requested, that would produce exact results of those in the query cache, resulting in shortened query processing, because there would be no need to parse the query. The query cache returns the previous results instead.

Transaction Manager

A MySQL transaction is a group of MySQL queries that are treated like one single process. As described earlier the transaction manager's task is to maintain concurrency throughout the database. This means that the transaction manager must ensure that simultaneous data handling will not cause the data to become corrupt or unreliable. The **transaction manager** is responsible for avoiding and resolving deadlocks and corrupted data by initiating the

COMMIT and ROLLBACK commands on the server. InnoDB and BDB are the storage engines that have been added to MySQL to manage transactions.

There are database environments that are transactional and some that are nontransactional; it depends on the needs of the organization. MySQL is a transaction-safe, ACID-compliant environment. In order to pass the ACID test, a transaction must maintain atomicity, consistency, isolation, and durability. As you will see in the next section, a MySQL administrator can choose whether or not to have a transactional database within the environment. MySQL's pluggable storage engines add this customization and are a feature that only MySQL provides. Table 2-4 illustrates MySQL's ACID compliance standards.

ACID characteristic	Description	MySQL sample compliance
Atomicity	SQL statements operate together as one entity group or alone as one entity; a group passes and/or fails as one process	MySQL statements begin and end, as well as pass and fail, together using the BEGIN and COMMIT, UNDO, and ROLLBACK statements
Consistency	Transactions do not affect the state of the database; consistency remains despite the success or failure of a transaction	MySQL uses logs (binary logs) to record all changes to the database as well as to help recover from a failure; the ROLLBACK statement is used if needed
Isolation	Transactions run separated from other transactions and are not viewable until committed	MyISAM permits locking, which avoids data corruption and visibility
Durability	Transactions persist despite system failures	Binary logs can be reverted

Table 2-4 ACID compliance and MySQL

Storage Management

As with Oracle, MySQL stores its data in files in secondary storage (/var/lib/mysql). Dynamically traversing these files is just not fast enough for our database needs. **Storage management** refers to the process of storing and retrieving data throughout the database. As with Oracle, most of the work takes place within the main memory (the fastest memory), and buffers take on the greatest load. Storage management in MySQL is a three-tiered process involving the resource manager, buffer manager, and storage manager. Figure 2-10 displays the efforts of storage management within MySQL.

The Storage Engine

Storage engines are components of a MySQL database architecture that read and write data to and from the database and offer services to enable customization of an environment. MySQL's pluggable storage engines differentiate MySQL from the rest of the RDBMS, because in MySQL, administrators can *pick and choose* which storage engines they want to use for certain tables and/or applications.

Having this option gives an administrator more control over the reliability and security of the data of an environment, yet the decision should be made early on in the design process to

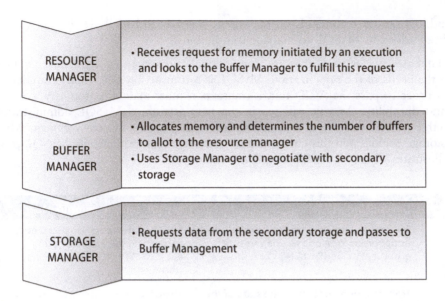

Figure 2-10 MySQL storage management
© Cengage Learning 2012

avoid issues later in the developmental cycle. This section will review each of the storage engines available in MySQL, as well as discuss the considerations that should be made before choosing one storage engine over another.

- *MyISAM*—As MySQL's default storage engine, providing variable row lengths and 256 TB of data, MyISAM is one of the most-used storage engines supported in all MySQL configurations. Fitting for both OLTP and DSS type servers, MyISAM offers fast searches and merge engine features. This engine can provide nontransactional environments as well as enable table locks.

- *InnoDB*—Another highly popular storage option, yet specifically designed for OLTP. InnoDB is a transaction-compliant engine that provides great performance for short-lived frequent transactions. InnoDB includes COMMIT, ROLLBACK, and row-level LOCK.

- *Memory*—Formally known as HEAP, this engine stores everything in RAM, so it is perfect for situations where you need fast access with data that never changes. This engine is great for DSS environments and aggregated data.

- *Archive*—This engine is great for storing and retrieving archive data. The archive engine only supports INSERT and SELECT queries where a full table scan is necessary for each SELECT statement.

- *Federated*—Enables separate MYSQL servers to be linked, referring to remote servers for all operations. This engine stores everything on the remote servers, so it is good for distributed environments where data does not need to be stored locally.

- *Comma-separated values (CSV)*—Stores data by comma delimitating within text files. Useful for certain kinds of logging, this engine provides easy exchange of data between applications.

- *Black Hole Engine*—Accepts data, but has no storage utility, therefore it discards every INSERT and does not retrieve data. These are useful in distributed environments or in replication configurations.

- *The Falcon Engine*—Designed for 64-bit processors and larger memory banks, but flexible enough to work in smaller environments as well. Falcon is a transactional-safe engine capable of handling short and frequent transactions.

Microsoft SQL Server Architecture

Microsoft SQL is often referred to simply as *SQL Server*. SQL Server is an RDBMS developed by Microsoft to provide a fast, secure, and scalable data access platform. SQL Server's primary query languages are T-SQL and ANSI SQL. The scalability of the SQL server architecture is its most attractive feature, because it was developed to run equally in a wide variety of environments. From a database running on a personal computer servicing only one user, to a database stored on a cluster of servers servicing several thousand users, SQL Servers can meet the needs of any Windows environment. Figure 2-11 displays the architecture of a Microsoft SQL Server.

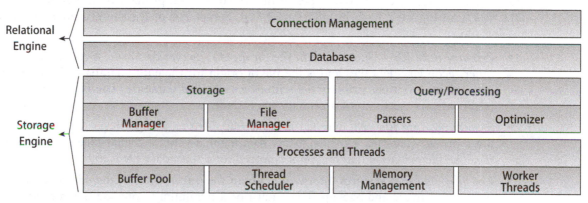

Figure 2-11 Microsoft SQL Server architecture
© Cengage Learning 2012

Architecture and Engines

The Microsoft SQL Server architecture has been developed for Windows platform use. This section will explore the main structures of MySQL. The topics covered in this section include connectivity, the relational engine, query processing, the storage engine, transaction processing, and the physical files.

Clients that connect to the server do so using the Tabular Data Stream, a Microsoft proprietary format. **Tabular Data Stream (TDS)** is a Microsoft-defined protocol that describes the specifications as to how the SQL Server and a client can communicate. TDS describes the specifications for which type of data, as well as the means by which data can travel. TDS is often encapsulated within another transport protocol such as TCP/IP, so clients that want to transmit data to and from a SQL server can do so using TCP/IP, as well as other transport protocols in which TDS is encased. The SQL Server relational database management system architecture can be broken down into two main components: the relational engine and the storage engine.

- *The relational engine*—The relational engine's primary responsibilities lie in query processing and data retrieval. The tasks that the relational engine completes are initiated by user queries and include parsing the SQL, optimizing the execution plan, and retrieving the results for the user.

- *The storage engine*—The storage engine's primary responsibilities are to ensure the effective management of files, memory, recovery, logging, and transactions. The storage engine assures that memory is available and being allocated appropriately, files are being effectively utilized and stored, backup is being completed as often as necessary, and data or structures can be restored reliably if needed.

The Physical Structure

Every database management system needs a place to store data. Microsoft SQL Server is a database installed within an operating system, so its system is stored in a set of operating system files which are then broken down into pages (pages are described later in the chapter). SQL uses three different types of files to store data: primary data files, secondary data files, and log files. Each installation of SQL Server has at least one primary file and one log file.

- *Primary data file*—The main data file for an SQL Server database, it references all other secondary data files and is the file of origin for the entire database. There must be a minimum of one primary file with every installed database. The file extension (although not enforced) of a primary file is .mdf.

- *Secondary data file*—An optional data file found within a SQL Server database that is not a primary data file. Essentially, any data file that is not a primary file is a secondary file. The file extension (although not enforced) of a secondary file is .ndf.

- *Log file*—A file that stores information about the transactions in the database to be used for recovery and backup. There must be a minimum of one log file in every database. The file extension (although not enforced) of a log file is .ldf.

In an SQL Server, data files can be collectively combined and placed into one group called a filegroup. Building filegroups enables administrators to create secondary files in the same group to better organize and place data. A **filegroup** is a collection of one or more physical data files within a SQL Server database. Only data files can reside in the same filegroup; log files must remain separate. There are two main types of filegroups:

- *Primary filegroup*—The collection of files that contain all of the SQL Server system files, including the primary data files

- *User-defined filegroup*—A collection of files created by a user

These filegroups can be used to organize a database into logical units of resources. The way filegroups are used will be dependent on the environment and the data that is stored within, yet ineffective organization of filegroups can have a negative impact on the backup and recovery of a database. A database has only one filegroup.

Memory Management

One of the most noteworthy characteristics of SQL Server's memory architecture is that it can dynamically allocate its own memory without a need for an administrator's intervention. By default, each instance of SQL Server dynamically acquires memory as needed without creating a shortage in the system. The goal of the database, as with MySQL and Oracle, is to limit the number of times that the secondary storage is accessed. The hard disks are the slowest and most resource-costly storage. By minimizing the reads and writes to them, the server performance will be increased.

As was explained earlier in the chapter, the goal is to maintain speed by maximizing the use of main memory and the system cache. Accomplishing this goal requires a great deal of monitoring and balancing. The main memory is used for many database processes within the server, so although increasing the size of the storage allotted to these processes will help maximize its use, using too much of it to store and retrieve data would starve the rest of the system of memory. Therefore, proper memory management is one of the keys to the success of SQL Server's dynamically allocated memory.

The virtual memory plays a large role in proper memory management. **Virtual memory** is a technique for extending the availability of memory where by units of storage located on different memory devices are used to store data from one entity in such a way that it appears the data has been stored in one continuous block of the same memory. The fixed units of storage that are transferred or *swapped* from one storage device to another are known as **pages**. The page is the primary unit of data storage in SQL Server. Pages are often swapped from the main memory (RAM) to a secondary form of memory (a hard disk drive) to handle overflow and/or ensure ideal utilization of storage. The dedicated swap space for the page is known as a **pagefile**. The **virtual address space** is the complete virtual memory area allotted to a program.

The goal is to maximize the use of the main memory for the database without exceeding the available memory on the server. In order to achieve this goal, SQL maintains a buffer cache in memory to hold pages that were previously read from the database. As stated earlier, the larger the size of the buffer pool, the fewer reads and writes to the hard disk are necessary. If the buffer cache uses up too much of the main memory, the result is that the operating system begins implementing virtual memory by swapping memory to and from the dedicated pagefile. This process ultimately uses fewer resources and increases performance.

There are two major components of the SQL server virtual memory architecture: the memory pool and the executable code. Figure 2-12 displays the memory architecture of an SQL Server machine.

The Executable Code The executable code is essentially the server engine within SQL Server. It includes the executable (exe) and dynamic link library (dll) files for the server itself. The executable code includes the following components:

- SQL Server code
- Server Net-Library DLLs
- Open services code
- Extended stored procedures

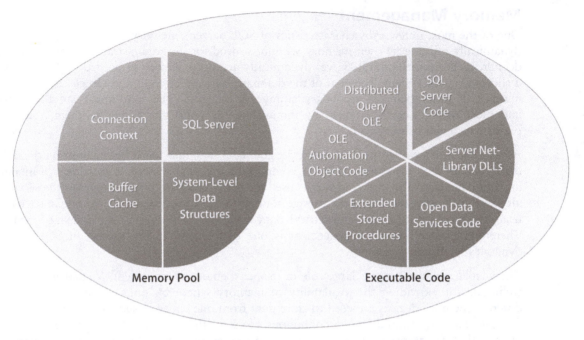

Figure 2-12 Microsoft SQL Server memory management
© Cengage Learning 2012

- OLE Automation
- Object code
- Distributed Query OLE DB provider DLLs

The Memory Pool The memory pool is the total amount of memory available for an instance of SQL Server. Virtually everything that uses memory in an instance of SQL Server uses the memory pool. The size of the memory pool depends on how many instances and applications are running. It is the most dynamically changing portion of a SQL Server instance.

The memory pool can fluctuate between an established minimum and maximum value as it attempts to fulfill the needs of the applications and instances and maintain a level of virtual memory allocation just below the true amount of physical memory (4–10 MB). The min server memory and the max server memory configuration settings are the established minimum and maximum amount of memory that can be used by the memory pool.

A server instance begins with the amount of memory that it needs (not the min server memory value) and then adds and frees memory as determined by the number of applications, instances, and user requests. The memory pool never exceeds the amount specified within the max server memory value, and if at any time the memory value reaches that established within the min server memory size variable, more memory is acquired. Five main objects within the memory pool are allocated memory:

- *System-level data structures*—Stores all data that is global to the instance.
- *Buffer cache*—Stores data pages from the database to avoid reads and writes to the hard drive

- *Procedure cache*—Stores execution plans for all currently and recently run SQL statements
- *Log cache*—Stores pages that are read from and written to logs
- *Connection context*—Stores a record of the current state of the connection

Buffer Management

Buffer management is vital to the performance of the SQL Server machine. As is apparent in the earlier section, buffers provide the location within physical memory where data is stored, minimizing the reads and writes to secondary storage devices. There are two important components within buffer management. The **buffer manager** is a portion of the SQL Server responsible for accessing data pages and updating the database. The **buffer pool**, or **buffer cache**, as described earlier, is the area where data pages from the database are stored to minimize the need to read and write from the database file located on the hard disk.

Once the SQL Server starts, it determines and reserves the buffer cache size by calculating the amount of remaining physical memory. The reserved space for the buffer cache is called the **memory target**. The buffer cache acquires from this only what is needed for a current instance.

When a request is made for data (and after query processing), the buffer manager accesses the database files stored on the hard disk and retrieves the requested data. The data is placed in the buffer cache pages, and from there the data is read. If changes are made to the data while in the buffer cache, it is considered dirty. A dirty page is one that has been modified within the buffer cache, but not yet written back to the database. A dirty page can go through several modifications before it is written back into the database.

With each modification, a transaction row is added to the log cache to maintain recovery integrity. Once the transaction has been logged, and the dirty page has stopped being referenced (by users or SQL statements), then the buffer cache frees the data to be written back into the database.

Threads and Processes

Microsoft SQL server uses thread and sometimes fibers to perform several simultaneous tasks within the operating system. As described in an earlier section, a thread is a process that contains tasks or executions that run independently from one another, yet utilize the same resources (portions of the CPU). The use of threads enables several different tasks to be performed simultaneously with minimal resource consumption.

When an instance occurs within the SQL Server database, an operating system process is created to handle that instance, which could potentially contain thousands of simultaneous user requests. To help manage these requests, the process is broken into different, independently working executions or threads that can run concurrently using very few resources.

A **fiber** is a subcomponent of a thread, and is handled by the server to accomplish a task. Fibers are not used in SQL by default; they must be configured. Where a thread is handled by the operating system and allocated one per CPU, a fiber is handled by the server and allocated one per user command. Therefore, there can be many fibers within one thread. Fibers are typically found in large enterprise environments where the processes generated are quite heavy and several CPUs exist on the server.

SQL server keeps a pool of either threads or fibers for all user connections; these pools are called **worker processes**. The amount of threads or fibers available within one worker process depends on the size of the network. A value can be set to limit the number of threads within a worker process to lower resource consumption, yet this should be carefully considered. If the value of requests exceeds the value available, threads will be pooled, causing users to wait for a thread to be available to connect. If the value is set too high, too many resources will be consumed. Within Microsoft SQL Server, threads are prioritized on a scale from 1 to 31. If a thread is waiting to be executed, the operating system checks the priority and sends out the one with the highest priority. SQL Server threads have a priority of 7, giving them a normal priority level, which is enough to access resources without interfering with any other processes or applications. This value can be changed as well, yet again at a cost if not carefully considered.

Chapter Summary

- A database is a collection of data stored within a database management system that allows others to search, analyze, and manipulate stored data.

- Data is stored within a database using a table structure, whereas general categories can be found within columns; distinct units of data are contained in rows.

- Keys are used to identify distinct entries within a database and are used to access or manipulate rows of data. Using keys to reference data creates an object-oriented storage system that lowers the probability of redundancy and makes data entry and manipulation simpler.

- There are several types of keys used to reference data within a database: primary, foreign, secondary, candidate, composite, sort, and alternate.

- One primary key is required for each row of a table, as it provides a unique identifier for referencing that row.

- Foreign keys can be used to build relationships between tables and are not supported by all database management systems.

- Query languages act as the intermediary for users and DBMSs, providing users a way to retrieve and manipulate data from a database. There are a variety of query languages, but SQL is the most common query language in modern database systems.

- Different database models describe the way data is stored within a database: flat, hierarchical, network, and relational, to name a few models. Building relationships between tables, such as within a relational database model, is the most common and efficient way to store data in today's databases.

- The most common relationships formed between tables in a relational database are one-to-many relationships. These types of relationships are defined by which one entity relates with several other entities of that same database. Other examples of relationship types created within databases include one-to-one and many-to-many.

- Databases can be built to handle very active, high-volume query environments such as online transaction processing and POS environments, or stagnant, low-volume query environments such as a historical data warehouse or data support systems.

- There are several different DBMSs available today, each having unique advantages and disadvantages. The most commonly used database management systems are Oracle, MySQL, and Microsoft SQL Server. It is important to understand a DBMS's architecture before choosing one for a specific environment.

- Two very important aspects of a DBMS are read consistency and query management. The method by which a DBMS accomplishes read consistency and query management can indicate the system's efficiency and reliability.

- Read consistency is dependent on a database's ability to manage multiple processes and refers to the accuracy and reliability of data. Read consistency is achieved through the use of efficient transaction processing, concurrency handling, and data-locking mechanisms.

- The general query processing steps of a database are parsing, optimization, and execution of a SQL statement.

- Oracle's architecture has two main components, the instance and the database. The instance begins with a user's connection and includes the background processes and memory managment of the application, while the database component involves the physical file structure.

- MySQL's main architectural components include the connection manager, query engine, and storage management engine. The connection manager handles connections to the database, the query manager processes SQL statements, and the storage engine manages memory and storage for the application.

- The main components of SQL Server include the relational engine and the storage engine. The relational engine involves query management, threads and processes, and the physical file structure, while the storage engine includes buffer and memory management.

Key Terms

alternate key A field with values that are not chosen as a primary key, but can be used in cases where the primary key is not available.

attribute A characteristic or variable that describes or further identifies an entity.

buffer manager A portion of the SQL Server responsible for accessing data pages and updating the database.

buffer pool (buffer cache) The area where data pages from a database are stored to minimize the need to read and write from the database file located on the hard disk.

caching The process of saving a duplicate of the requested data to another area of a system in hopes of saving resources and speeding up the future requests for that same data.

candidate key A field with values that meet the requirements for a primary key.

column (field) The component of a table that maintains a general category of information with similar datatypes.

commit To make a change within a DBMS that is permanent and visible to other users.

composite key A group of two or more fields where their values can be combined to be used as a primary key.

concurrency The simultaneous access of resources and data.

control file A file within a database that contains the location and important credentialing information of other files.

database A collection of data stored on a computer using an application called a database management system.

database connection manager Manages connections to the MySQL server.

database management system (DBMS) An application that allows users to search stored data in order to locate specific information.

database model A representation of the way data is stored.

datafile A file that contains the actual data for the database and holds the information for all logical structures (tables, records, etc.) within the database.

deadlock A situation when two transactions cannot proceed because each user has data that the other needs.

entity A person, place, or thing stored within the table of a database and for which attributes and relationships exist.

fiber A subcomponent of a thread, which is handled by the server to accomplish a task.

filegroup A collection of one or more physical data files within a SQL Server database.

flat model A two-dimensional list of data entries, where all data within a field are understood to be similar, and all data within a record are understood to be related to one another.

foreign key A field within a table that contains a label used to build a relationship between two tables.

hierarchical database structure A treelike storage schema that represents records and relationships through the use of tiers and parent-child relationships.

instance A broad term that refers to the background processes and structured memory used during interaction with the database.

key A single field or group of fields used to identify an entry in a table.

lock A mechanism within a DBMS that controls concurrency by preventing users from taking hold of data until changes being made are completed or committed.

log file A file that stores information about the transactions in the database to be used for recovery and backup.

memory target The reserved space for the buffer cache.

network database model A treelike structure that stores information in the form of a hierarchy, using tiers and parent-child-like entities to represent relationships.

online analytical processing (OLAP), (decision support systems [DSS]) Databases that store large volumes of historical data for report generating and analyzing.

online transaction processing (OLTP) database A database that is created for real-time storage and manipulation of data within an organization.

open source A term that refers to software that has been written to be distributed for use and downloaded free of charge.

optimization The process of locating the quickest and most efficient way to retrieve the data being requested by a user.

page A fixed unit of storage that is transferred or swapped from one storage device to another.

pagefile The dedicated swap space for a page.

parallel processing When more than one server processes one query at the same time.

parsing The act of analyzing a construction of a query for correct syntax and semantics.

point of sales (POS) system A system that is meant to handle cash register or sales transactions.

primary data file The main data file for an SQL Server database which is the file of origin for the entire database and references all other secondary data files.

primary filegroup The collection of files that contains all of the SQL Server system files, including the primary data files.

primary key A field that contains a unique label by which we can identify a record or row in a table.

process A set of instructions that is executed by the operating system intended to complete a task.

Process Global Area (PGA) The central area where information is stored for background and server processes. It allocates space for each individual background process.

query A search initiated by a user in an attempt to retrieve certain information from a database.

query cache A memory component that plays a role in ensuring that query processing is successful.

query engine A component of the architecture that optimizes and manages queries and SQL statements.

query management The steps taken by a database management application to process a user query.

read consistency A term that refers to the accuracy and reliability of data within a database.

redo log A file within a database that contains information regarding all changes made to the data within the database.

relational database A storage model in which common entities are stored within separate tables that use unique key identifiers to build relationships between these entities.

relationship Defines the association between two entities and binds them.

report A document that contains a formatted result of a user's query.

row (record, tuple) The component of a table that holds distinct units of data identified using unique strings of numbers or characters.

secondary (alternative) key A field with values that contains nonunique data and that can refer to several records at one time.

secondary data file An optional data file found within an SQL Server database that is not a primary data file.

sort (control) key A field in which values are used to sequence data.

storage engine A component of the MySQL database architecture that reads and writes data to and from the database and offers services to enable customization of an environment.

storage management Refers to the process of storing and retrieving data throughout the database.

System Global Area (SGA) The central area where all shared data and processes are stored, including information shared by users and database processes.

table One of the most basic units of storage within a database, typically representing unique and specific data objects.

Tabular Data Stream (TDS) A Microsoft-defined protocol that describes the specifications as to how the SQL Server and a client can communicate.

thread A process that runs independently from other process. It utilizes a portion of the CPU and contains tasks or executions that share the same resources, yet run independently from one another.

transaction The group of statements or operations processed by a database to execute a user's request to update or change the database.

transaction manager A component of the MySQL database architecture that is responsible for avoiding and resolving deadlocks and corrupted data.

user-defined filegroup A collection of files created by a user.

virtual address space The complete virtual memory area allotted to a program.

virtual memory A technique for extending the availability of memory by which units of storage located on different memory devices are used to store data from one entity in such a way that it appears as though the data has been stored in one continuous block of the same memory.

worker process A pool of either threads or fibers that SQL Server keeps for all user connections.

Review Questions

1. What is a database?

2. What is the main goal of a DBMS?

3. What are the common components found within DBMSs?

4. List the common components of a table.

5. What are the advantages to using keys rather than specific table entries?

6. Identify and define the four main database models.

7. Explain the concept of relationships within a database.

8. Identify the three relationship types and give a brief explanation of each.

9. List the two types of databases, as well as their purposes.

10. What are the three most prominent and fastest-growing RDBMSs?

11. Identify two main areas of focus that exist in all DBMSs.

12. List the five locking mechanisms used in maintaining read consistency.

13. What are the main components of the Oracle architecture?

14. What are the main componenets of the MySQL architecture?

15. What are the most noteworthy characteristics of the SQL Server's memory architecture?

Case Projects

Case Project 2-1: Real-World Examples

Use the Internet or your current work environment and provide a practical, real-world use of an OLAP and a practical, real-world use of an OLTP. Include in your answer the name of the organization, the nature of the business, and the way in which the database is being manipulated.

Case Project 2-2: Database Management System Vendors

Oracle, MySQL, and Microsoft SQL Server are only three of the many database management systems. Use the Internet and find three more database management systems available in today's market. Provide a brief description of the systems that you found, include the year that they were developed, and the operating systems that can be installed, as well as the main features of the applications.

Case Project 2-3: Understanding ACID-Compliant Transactions

Choose one database management system from Case Project 2-2 and determine whether it is ACID-compliant. Create a table similar to Table 2-4, providing examples as to how the database does or does not meet ACID standards.

Case Project 2-4: Understanding Query Management

Choose one database management system from Case Project 2-2 and discuss its query management process.

Hands-On Projects

Hands-On Project 2-1: Improving Upon a System

A convenience store located within an apartment complex uses a log similar to the following one to keep track of customer purchases. The goal of the database is to keep track of the inventory sold in hopes of using the data to better meet customers' convenience store needs. From the information gathered, the store owner is able to obtain statistics that help her plan future inventory. Data such as the number of products sold, the highest and fewest products sold, the frequency and amount of customer purchases, and the total purchases made by a specific apartment aid the owner in determining how best to suit her customers' needs. Write a paper that discusses how you might achieve the owner's goal in a more efficient manner using a database. Answer the following questions in your paper:

- What database model would you implement?
- What type of database fits this scenario best?
- What DBMS is best suited for this scenario, and why?
- What would be the cost of implementing your proposed system?
- How would training and maintenence of the system be handled?

Customer name	Apt #	Product name	Product price	# Purchased
Joseph Anthony	1125	Orange juice	4.59	1
Joseph Anthony	1125	Bread loaf	2.29	1
Yolanda Burns	3221	Milk	3.67	1
Yolanda Burns	3221	Candy bar	1.19	3
Frances Jordan	1138	Gum	.99	2
Steve Miller	2221	Gum	.99	1
Cho Lin	2239	Bread loaf	2.29	1

Hands-On Project 2-2: Building a Relational Database

You have been hired to design a relational database for a convenience store which is located within an apartment complex. The goal of the database is to keep track of the inventory sold in hopes of using the data to better meet the customers' convenience store needs. Up until your arrival, the store kept track of each customer's purchases using a flat database log, as shown in the following table. Using the information provided, build a relational database that will allow for querying things such as products sold, customer purchases, total apartment purchases, and total spent per apartment. Include any created tables and identify the keys and key types that are used. Identify all relationships, labeling them 1:1, 1:N, or M:N.

Customer name	Apt #	Product name	Product price	# Purchased
Joseph Anthony	1125	Orange juice	4.59	1
Joseph Anthony	1125	Bread loaf	2.29	1
Yolanda Burns	3221	Milk	3.67	1
Yolanda Burns	3221	Candy bar	1.19	3
Frances Jordan	1138	Gum	.99	2
Steve Miller	2221	Gum	.99	1
Cho Lin	2239	Bread loaf	2.29	1

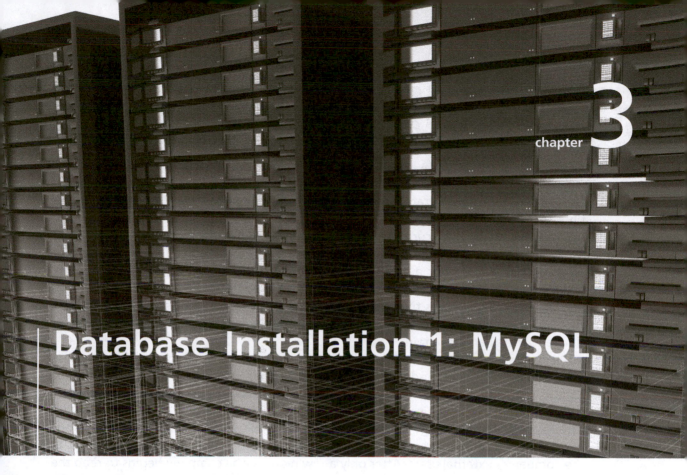

Database Installation 1: MySQL

chapter 3

After reading this chapter and completing the exercises, you will be able to:

- Identify the considerations that an administrator must take into account prior to installation
- Download and install the binary distribution of MySQL for the most common operating systems
- Configure a MySQL database for both Windows- and UNIX-based platforms
- Secure the installation and configuration of MySQL server

Tony, the system administrator for Haphazard, Inc. is about to install MySQL for the first time. The company has experienced a bit of success, so a larger database storage plan became necessary. Their current implementation of Microsoft Access no longer meets the needs of their growing clientele and so Tony has been asked to find an inexpensive solution that would offer a way for their external customers to access their inventory through the Web. Tony researches the current available database management systems and decides that MySQL is the best fit for the organization. He presents his proposal to the senior managers, explaining that MySQL offers a free, scalable DBMS that seems simple to install and maintain.

Pleased with his proposal, Haphazard managers promote Tony to the database administrator role and send him to training to prepare him for the administration of MySQL. Unfortunately for Tony, and as often is the case, the training focused primarily on planning and building a database schematic with little emphasis on security.

Equipped with his new knowledge and focused on data administration, Tony migrates the company's Access database with MySQL and begins providing access to the company's external users. After only a few months, the company begins to reap the benefits of the new system and the project seems successful. The clients are pleased with their new real-time access, and the managers are pleased with the speed with which orders are being delivered.

Three months after the implementation, Tony is sitting proudly at his desk when his phones all begin ringing simultaneously. It seemed that several customers were experiencing issues connecting to the database. Unable to access the data himself, Tony called MySQL support for help. To his dismay, the database appeared to be infected by a virus, which had corrupted several major tables within the database.

After many hours and several unsuccessful attempts at recovering the data using antivirus programs, MySQL embedded recovery tools, and the most recent backups, Tony had no other choice but to call a third party to help recover the database. In the end, the company lost money due to the database outage, the technical support fees, and the third-party application. The customers lost trust in the company and its ability to maintain secure and private data and the managers lost faith in Tony as a database administrator. All of this could have been avoided if only Tony had taken a few small security precautions during the software installation process.

It is not uncommon for database administrators to focus on the design of the database and its administration, leaving few resources for database security. This chapter will cover the information needed to download, install, and configure MySQL, as well as learn the basic security precautions for the initial setup.

Preinstallation Preparation

MySQL is a reliable and robust open-source application licensed under the General Public License (GPL). It is the most popular open-source database application used today. MySQL offers many features to its users, and can be customized to fit almost any business or personal environment. MySQL can be found servicing major Internet Web sites as well as popular enterprise corporations.

Flexibility brings choices, and there are a few considerations that an administrator must take into account prior to installation. This section contains the necessary preinstallation considerations needed to ensure the best fit for an environment. Topics covered in this area include distribution formats, MySQL versions, supporting platforms, and technical support lines.

Choosing a Distribution Format

Due to MySQL's open-source nature, there are different ways MySQL can be installed. These options vary from simple prepackaged executions to individualized custom downloads. The two main installation formats in which you can choose to install MySQL are source code installation and binary code installation.

Source code is a group of statements or functions that are written using a specific programming language and then combined to create a specific type of application or utility. Source code usually refers to the main code that makes up an application. A **programming language** is a type of synthetic language developed with specific syntax and semantic rules that allow individuals to create statements or functions to interface and control the behavior or functionality of a machine. **Source code installations** of MySQL allow users to download the actual MySQL source code, change it, customize it, and compile it into a binary file for installation execution.

A **binary file** is a file that contains code that can be read by machines and run as an executable file. **Binary code installations** of MySQL are already packaged as binary files and are ready to be installed without the need for compiling the code to enable it to be run as an executable file on a particular machine. **Compiling** refers to the act of converting source code that is written in one language into a different programming language or machine language.

MySQL is written using C and C++ programming languages. There are several different types of programming languages, and each is developed to interface with a particular type of system or device. Compiling source code results in a binary file. Compiling MySQL can be time consuming, taking up to 60 minutes to compile.

There are advantages and disadvantages to both source code and binary distribution formats. Although most environments choose to install the binary distribution formats, it is important to know what each distribution offers prior to installation. Source code distribution formats require more steps to complete than binary file installations. Although they allow for customization within an environment, expertise is necessary to achieve this goal. In this case, software programmers would be used to create a slightly different, more compatible version of MySQL for installation within their own environment. For example, an environment that requires a small lightweight database application may choose to install the source code distribution format and remove all of the features that exist within the default packaging of a specific version of MySQL. This would be done prior to compiling and can greatly increase a database network's efficiency.

Another reason for using the source distribution format would be for strict environments where specific compilers must be used; however, this is a unique scenario. Despite its customization, installing a source code distribution format can be quite cumbersome because it requires additional steps and longer compiling times. Source distribution installations also require detailed documentation that describes any customization that has taken place. This is to ensure that any updates to the software are handled appropriately, given the original changes that were made.

Binary distribution formats are easy to install and require less time and expertise. Since they are already executable files, customization cannot take place and compilers cannot be changed. As you will see in this chapter, binary distribution installations are as simple as downloading and installing a small software application found on the Internet.

Prior to making a decision about using source code distribution installations, all alternative choices should be thoroughly considered. MySQL offers a number of different versions from which to choose, and there are also third-party vendors that distribute their own versions of MySQL with customized features to meet the needs of specific environments and operating systems. Only around 5% of the MySQL installations are of source code distribution formats, which should offer a clue as to how many different versions and flavors are available.

 Although third-party distributions of MySQL can appear to be a great fit for a specific environment, the templates are often out of date and do not include the updates, fixes, and features that are available with the most current Sun distribution.

Choosing a Version of MySQL

As mentioned in the preceding section, MySQL comes in many different version releases and includes third-party vendor developed binary files to offer custom templates of MySQL installations. These releases are systematic and predictable. Identifying the most stable MySQL available is important to the success of an implementation of the database application.

Sun Microsystems releases new versions of MySQL subsequent to one another while they are at different levels or stages of maturity. New versions of the database are released in their testing and debugging phase, while older, more stable versions are still available. This allows organizations to test upcoming versions in a controlled environment prior to their true production release. It is important to review the phased releases of the database application prior to exploring the available versions of MySQL to ensure that the most stable versions are explored and installed. Originally, there were four main phases of maturity for a release of MySQL: General Availability (GA), Release Candidate (RC), beta, and alpha.

- *General Availability*—General Availability-labeled software is ready for production. In this stage of maturity, it is a stable application and there are very few known bugs.

- *Release Candidate*—Research Candidate-phase software is considered somewhat stable, though it might have serious bugs that still exist, but do not affect everyone. Normally these bugs only affect unique and rare environments.

- *Beta* —In the beta phase of the application, there are known issues that exist with the software. This software should be used for texting and experimental purposes only. These versions should not be downloaded for use in a working environment.

- *Alpha*— The alpha phase is where new features are added. This is the very early stage of testing. Like the beta stage, software in this phase should not be downloaded for use in a working environment.

Around the time that the MySQL 5.1 production phase was released in 2008, a new approach to the phase and release cycle was introduced, called the milestone model. This model was implemented to improve the efficiency of the version phase and iteration process as well as allow for smaller, more frequent, and controllable releases of the MySQL database software. Unlike the previous phased approach, the new milestone approach focuses on smaller iterations of updates and changes. In the prior phased approach, where applications are released in a beta form with many changes to the application being released, the milestone model does not release MySQL in any stage lower than the beta stage. The version numbers use a more specific naming scheme, and a suffix has been added to the version number to indicate the phase of a particular release. Let's examine the release version MySQL 5.5.0-m2:

- The first number of a version indicates the main file format for a particular application. In this case, we have a five. All MySQL applications with the major version number 5 maintain the same file format.

- The second number is the release level and indicates the number of major changes or updates that have been applied to a particular application. For the preceding example, there have been five major changes or added features to this release.

- The third number indicates the number of smaller changes that have been tested and released for that particular application. In our example, there have been no minor changes.

As you can see from the example, the suffix that has been added to the version number is *m2*. This suffix indicates how stable the application is, similar to the old GA, RC, beta, and alpha system. There are three main categories for which the suffixes apply. Table 3-1 defines these suffix types.

Suffix	Meaning	Example
m1, m2, m3, etc.	A suffix of m1, m2, m3, etc., indicates the number of milestones that have been achieved thus far This stage is similar to the beta stage described earlier.	MySQL 5.5.0-m2 For this example, two milestones have been achieved; a milestone is a small focused change or feature added to an application that has been tested rigorously
rc	A suffix of rc indicates that an application is a release candidate	MySQL 5.5.0-RC For this example, the application is considered to be somewhat stable, although it may have serious bugs that still exist but do not affect everyone; normally these bugs only affect unique and rare environments
None	If no suffix is provided at the end of a version of a MySQL application, then the application is considered to be of General Availability	MySQL 5.5.0 For this example, the application is ready for production; in this stage of maturity, there are very few known bugs and it is a stable application

Table 3-1 Suffix types

Another goal of the milestone model was to provide releases that are more predictable than in the past. With the milestone model, RC releases occur every 3–6 months, while GA releases occur every 12–18 months. Refer to Table 3-2 for a complete history of MySQL releases and added features. More details on the MySQL lifecycle policy can be found at *http://www.mysql.com/about/legal/lifecycle*.

Year	Version	Notes
1994	Original development	
1996	Public release for Solaris	
1998	Windows version released for Windows 95 and NT	
2000	Version 3.23 beta release	BDB and InnoDB engines
2001	GA production release of version 3.23	
2002	Beta version 4.0 release	
2003	GA production release version 4.0 three months after Beta release version 4.01	Version
2004	Beta and production versions of 4.1 are released	Subqueries R-trees, B-trees, prepared statements
2005	Beta and production versions of 5.0 are released	Cursors, stored procedures, triggers, views, XA transaction Federated Storage Engine included as a default engine
2006	Beta release version 5.1	Partitioning, row-based replications, plug-in storage engine API, server log tables, and event scheduler
2007	6.0 Alpha version released	Falcon and Maria storage engines and online backup
2008	Sun Microsystems acquired MySQLAB version 5.1 production, version production release 5.4-m1	Version 6.0 withdrawn Version 5.4 upgraded features: improve scalability on multicore CPUs, I/O subsystem changes, enhanced Solaris support, diagnostic, and monitoring capabilities
2009	Version 6.0 cancelled Version 5.5.0-m2	Semisynchronous replication, key caching for index, two new users defined, enhanced XML functionality

Table 3-2   Timeline of MySQL releases

New versions of MySQL are released every 3–6 months, and third-party vendors supply their own editions or templates of the database application. In 2007, MySQL 6.0 was released in the alpha phase, yet only a year later the milestone model was introduced. To maintain consistency with the (then new) milestone model, MySQL 6.0 was withdrawn due to its advanced maturity. When choosing a version of MySQL to install for the first time, it is recommended that you use the most stable version, which is the current Generally Available version. This version can be identified with no suffix added to the milestone model versions.

Supported Platforms

Users are encouraged to download, modify, and use MySQL free of charge. It is for this reason that MySQL has obtained widespread popularity. MySQL works on several different operating system platforms. These platforms include AIX, BSDi, eComStation, FreeBSD, HP-UX, i5/OS, Linux, Mac OS X, Microsoft Windows, NetBSD, Novell NetWare, OpenBSD, OpenSolaris, OS/2 Warp, QNX, IRIX, Solaris, Symbian, SunOS, SCO OpenServer, SCO UNIXWare, Sanos, and Tru64. You can find more details, as well as a complete list of the platforms supported, on MySQL's site.

Platform information for the Community Edition of MySQL can be found at *http://dev.mysql .com/doc/refman/5.5/en/which-os.html*. You can also find platform information for the Enterprise Edition of MySQL at *http://www.mysql.com/support/supportedplatforms.html*.

As with operating systems, MySQL is available as a 32-bit and 64-bit system. The suggested install is 64-bit. Ideally, MySQL would be installed as a 64-bit software application residing on a 64-bit operating system.

Locating Help

There are a great number of places to locate support for MySQL. One option for obtaining help is through a Sun Microsystems paid service called MySQLAB. This service will connect users and administrators directly to MySQL developers to answer questions, receive consultations, or obtain training. There are also several third-party companies that exist to provide this type of help as well; however, most of the resources that are available for MySQL can be found free online. Below is a list of the help that can be obtained through online services:

- *MySQL manual*—This resource provides a comprehensive online manual for all of the current versions and editions of MySQL. These manuals provide great resources for MySQL, and can be found at *http://dev.mysql.com/doc*.

- *MySQL forums*—Forums are a great way to connect online with other users and MySQL professionals that have a wealth of knowledge to share. There are several great forums available throughout the Internet. One suggested group of forums can be found on MySQL's site at *http://forums.mysql.com*.

- *Mailing lists*—Subscribing to mailing lists is a great way to receive updates on all different types of technology. Through the MySQL mailing list, a user can ask questions and receive information on the most current updates and alerts at *http://lists.mysql.com*.

- *Bloggers*—Blogs have become a fantastic resource, especially in the technology fields. Many people who work with MySQL or have experience with MySQL blog about their experiences and share their knowledge. These blogs can be found at *http://planet. mysql.com/*.

- *Twitter*—Twitter has become a popular way to keep people informed on a minute-by-minute basis. Almost every organization has a Twitter page. It provides a quick and easy way to reach customers by sending quick updates and reminders; organizations can reach out to their customers directly via e-mail and cell phone. MySQL uses Twitter as a way for users to ask questions and for MySQL professionals to send out alerts relevant to upgrades, bugs, and other software-related support, and can be found at *http://twitter.com/MySql*.

- *Bug alerts*—MySQL, like many technical vendors, provides a Web site at *http://bugs .mysql.com* that is dedicated to obtaining information on the most recently discovered problems for all of its applications. This site can be used to report a problem or use the sophisticated search utility to find an already-known bug for a system.

Downloading MySQL

The official download site for MySQL is *http://dev.mysql.com/downloads*. This Web site contains all available versions, editions, and distribution formats of MySQL. When it comes to MySQL, you have two separate options for download: Community and Enterprise.

The Community Edition of MySQL is the most popular edition available as open source and is referred to throughout this chapter. The Enterprise Edition of MySQL provides additional assistance for monitoring and analyzing the performance of your database server.

Although it is not necessary to purchase the Enterprise Edition of MySQL server, it is recommended for large organizations. Providing tools such as MySQL Enterprise Monitor and MySQL Query Analyzer, an administrator is likely to find that the cost of this edition will override the short- and long-term benefits for larger enterprise organizations.

The Enterprise Edition also offers support, training, and consultation directly from MySQL developers. For large organizations, this in itself may be worth the cost. MySQL downloads are often combined and packaged as platform-dependent formats such as .tar, .rpm, .zip, and gz. Therefore, additional applications are often necessary to extract the files from within these packages. For example, for Windows, a .zip-compressed package is downloaded that contains the files to run the Windows platform compatible with MySQL.

 To extract these files after download, the compatible decompression and unpacking tool named WinZip is needed.

Once MySQL is downloaded and before it is installed, steps can be taken to verify the integrity of the files included within the package. The verification checks listed below are used to ensure that a package has not been tampered with and is free from Trojans:

- *MD5 Checksum*—Each package that is downloaded from MySQL is assigned an MD5 checksum, or a hexadecimal code. This code appears on the downloaded pages of MySQL, as well as within the installed package itself. The code retrieved from the downloaded pages can be compared with the code retrieved from within the package to determine a match. If the two codes match, then the application is verified. If the two codes are different, then the file should be discarded and a new file should be downloaded. How the code is retrieved from within the package is dependent on the operating system that is being used. For example, in most UNIX-based operating systems, the program md5Sum is used to extract the MD5 code from the package, while Windows uses a variant of the md5sum called the Microsoft File Checksum Integrity Verifier to extract the code.

- *GnuPG*—MySQL uses Gnu Privacy Guard to add digital signatures from which authenticity can be determined. A **digital signature** is code that uses cryptography to verify the authenticity of a source of information. Therefore, MySQL users can obtain a key to the encrypted digital signature in order to verify that the package came from MySQL, the trusted source. Digital signatures and cryptography are discussed in later chapters.

Verification of your downloaded package takes very little time, and can help to maintain the confidentiality, integrity, and availability of a database application. You can find more information regarding MySQL's package verification at *http://dev.mysql.com*.

3

Installation

Once a user has downloaded and verified a copy of MySQL in the distribution format edition and version that best fits the needs of the environment, installation can begin. This section will include the steps for installing MySQL on both Windows- and UNIX-based machines. The instructional steps provided in this section are intended to provide steps for installing the binary distribution formation of the Community Edition of MySQL 5.5.

Installing on Windows

The Windows Operating System is a popular platform on which MySQL is installed. This is partly due to its availability for Windows. MySQL is available for virtually all Windows Operating Systems active today, and both 32-bit and 64-bit versions are supported. The following section will provide information and instructions on binary installations of MySQL on Windows.

 NT-Based systems (e.g., NT, 2000, XP, 7, Server 2003, and Server 2008) can run MySQL as a service, allowing it to start and stop with a system boot up and shut down.

Installing MySQL on Windows Using an Installer Package MySQL offers three different binary packages for the Windows operating system. This makes it easy for users by automatically installing and configuring MySQL so that once installed, the application can be used immediately. There are two automatic installer packages: the Essentials Package and the Complete Package, and one Noinstall Archive. The installer packages make for easy application since they include installation wizards that automatically load the server binary configuration wizard. The configuration wizard automatically creates the option files and initial user's accounts.

Here is a brief description of these packages:

- *The Essentials Package*—As its name implies, this package includes only the essential or necessary files for binary installation. A configuration wizard is provided and optional features are not included. This package is ideal for almost any environment because it allows for a lighter installation of MySQL.

- *The Complete Package*—As its name also implies, this package provides the complete installation, which includes both necessary and optional files and features. This package should only be used if an optional component is necessary, which in most cases it is not.

- *The Noinstall Archive*—Unlike the other two packages, this package does not include the automatic installation or configuration wizard. This package contains the same components as the Complete Package, yet it requires manual installation and configuration, making this package the most difficult to apply.

It is necessary to run these installers from within an administrative account on the operating system to avoid any issues during the installation. In Windows Vista and Windows 7, a port within the Windows firewall must be added to be able to configure the server after the installation. Use the following steps to add a MySQL port in Windows Vista and Windows 7.

 The instructions provided in the following section are intended for default installations of Windows Vista and Windows 7, and are best suited for environments where the database administrator maintains administrative security rights on the system. Adjustments to these instructions may be necessary and collaboration with the network security team for your organization may be necessary in environments that are restrictive or atypical.

Adding a MySQL Port in Windows Vista

1. Click **Control Panel** found on the Start menu of Microsoft Windows.
2. Click **Security**.
3. Click **Windows Firewall**.
4. Click **Allow program through Windows Firewall**.
5. Click **Add Port**.
6. Provide a name in the Name text field. Pick a name that is descriptive enough that it will remind you what this port has been created for (e.g., MySQL).
7. Provide a port in the Port Number text field (the suggested port is 3306).
8. Click **TCP Protocol**.
9. Click **OK** to confirm your choices.

Be aware that opening ports in your firewall provides all computers access to MySQL through your firewall. For security reasons, it is suggested that access to MySQL is limited. This can be accomplished by changing the scope of the port. In Windows Vista, you can change the Port Scope, or group of computers that are able to use this port opening by clicking the Change Scope option before clicking OK (Step 9 above). This will limit the number of computers and users that have access to this port opening.

Adding a MySQL Port in Windows 7

1. Click **Control Panel** found in the Start menu of Microsoft Windows.
2. Click **System and Security**.
3. Click **Windows Firewall**.
4. Click **Advanced settings** on the left pane.
5. In the **Windows Firewall with Advanced Security** dialog box in the left pane, click **Inbound Rules**. In the far-right pane, click **New Rule**.

6. Click **Port** from the New Inbound Rule Wizard dialog box and click **Next.**

7. Apply the rule to TCP.

8. Specify the port in the Port Number text field (the suggested port is 3306).

9. Click **Next.**

10. Click **Allow the connection it is secure.** This is only compatible with Windows Vista and later versions of Windows.

11. Click **Next.**

12. Add the list of allowed user connections, as well as exceptions (if applicable).

13. Add the list of allowed computer connections, as well as exceptions (if applicable).

14. Click **Next.**

15. Select whether computers will be connecting to the server from within the domain, a private location, public location, or all locations. The public setting is not recommended unless completely necessary. It allows users and computers from public networks to connect to the MySQL server.

16. Provide a name in the Name text field. Pick a name that is descriptive enough that it will remind you what this port has been created for (e.g., MySQL).

17. Click **Finish** to confirm your choices and add the port.

Windows 7 offers additional customization features when specifying the type of connection for a port (Step 9). Explore these features for enhancement of the security of your database.

Installation Instructions

The installation package installed in this section is the binary distribution file for the Essentials Package, version MySQL 5.5.1 m2, downloaded from *http://dev.mysql.com/downloads/*.

1. Locate the downloaded file. If necessary, unzip the setup file using a compression utility tool. Double-click the **Microsoft Windows Installer** (MSI) file to execute (Figure 3-1).

How you start this wizard depends on the installation package that you download. Some packages require extraction and contain a **setup.exe** file rather than an **MSI** file. If this is the case, double-click **setup.exe** to execute the installation.

2. A security warning may appear that prompts the user to confirm that the system request is approved and intentional. This window may appear several times throughout the installation and configuration process. Click **Run** to begin the installation (Figure 3-2).

You may also encounter an End User License Agreement that you must read and accept to continue the installation.

3. The first window encountered will provide a general overview of the MySQL server release that was downloaded. Verify the accuracy of this window and click **Next** to continue (Figure 3-3).

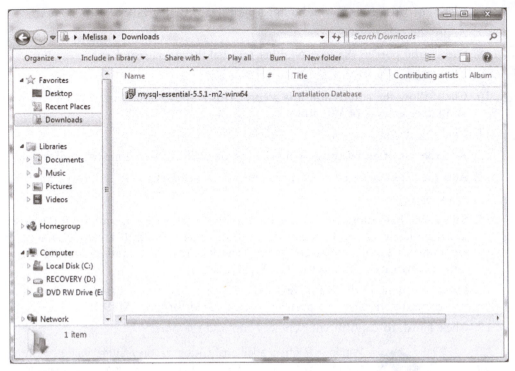

Figure 3-1 Locate the downloaded file
© Cengage Learning 2012

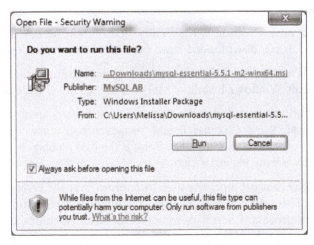

Figure 3-2 Security warning
© Cengage Learning 2012

4. There are three installation types that are available in the Essential and Complete packages: typical, complete, and custom. The type of installation chosen will depend on the needs of the environment:

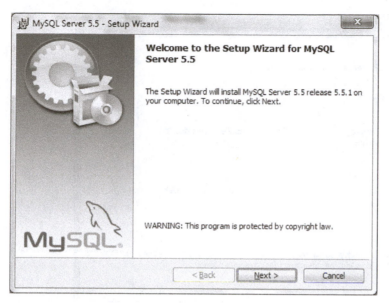

Figure 3-3 Setup welcome
© Cengage Learning 2012

- *Typical*—Installs the MySQL Server and various command-line utilities for managing the server.
- *Complete*—Installs the full package, which includes the embedded server library, a benchmarks suite, support programs, and documentation.
- *Custom*—Gives the administrator or user full control over the packages installed and the location of the files installed.

Select either **Typical** or **Complete** (Figure 3-4). Click **Next**. Once the choices made have been verified, click **Install** to begin installation (Figure 3-5).

Clicking **Custom** will bring up the Custom installation screen (Figure 3-6). The Custom installation screen lists the components available for installation. If these components are not selected for the current installation, they are marked with an X, as shown in Figure 3-6 for the feature description **C Include Files/Lib Files**.

5. Changes can be made to the way these features are installed by clicking the icon next to the component name. For example, if a user would like to change the installation state of the Client Programs, they would click the icon to the left of the name and pick an option from the drop-down list that appears (Figure 3-7).

6. If the user would like to change the directory in which the client program is installed, they can do so by highlighting the name of the component that the directory needs to change and click **Change** to customize the folder name and directory path of the installed component (Figure 3-8).

In this window (Figure 3-8), type the new directory in the Folder Name field or use the Look In list arrow to choose the custom installation directory from a drop-down menu. Once any changes to the path have been made for that component, click **OK** to return to the Setup Wizard dialog box.

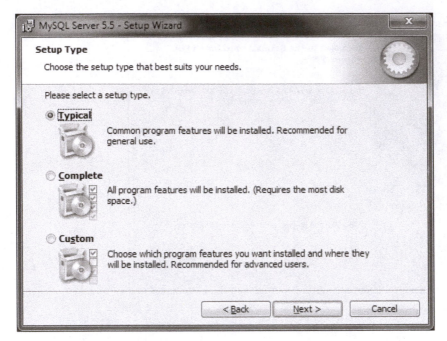

Figure 3-4 Installation type
© Cengage Learning 2012

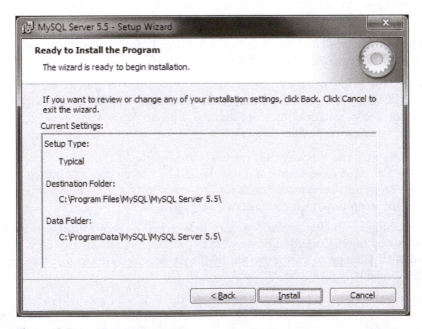

Figure 3-5 Verify installation
© Cengage Learning 2012

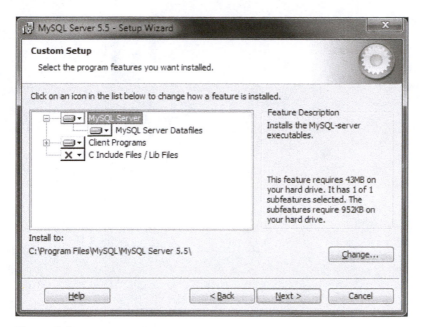

Figure 3-6 Custom installation
© Cengage Learning 2012

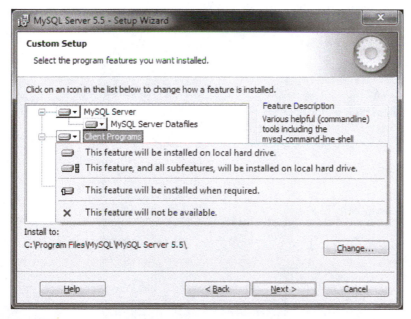

Figure 3-7 Select program features to be installed
© Cengage Learning 2012

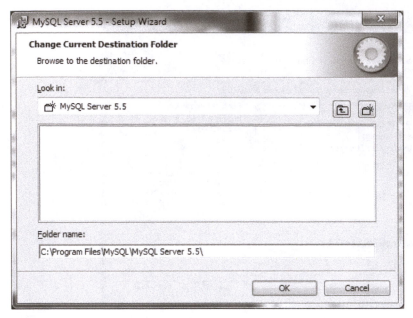

Figure 3-8 Change current destination folder
© Cengage Learning 2012

7. Once the desired installation customizations are complete, click **Next** on the Setup Wizard to advance to the verification screen (Figure 3-9). The verification screen displays all of the current installation selections for review. If everything on this screen is correct, click **Install** to begin the installation.

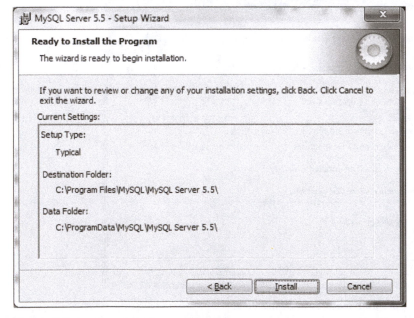

Figure 3-9 Ready to install
© Cengage Learning 2012

Installing on UNIX

UNIX-based systems are also popular platforms on which MySQL is installed. These include Sun Solaris, AIX, BSDi, FreeBSD, HP-UX, IBM, Linux, etc. There are a number of different variations of UNIX-based server package formats to install on these systems. The instructions for installing MySQL on UNIX-based systems are essentially the same, and it is suggested that binary distribution should be used, if possible. The following section will provide information and instructions on installing binary packages for UNIX-based systems.

3

Installing UNIX Binary Distributions

It is quite simple to install binary distributions on a UNIX-based system. As mentioned earlier, MySQL downloads are often combined and packaged into platform-based formats. This is especially true for UNIX-based operating systems.

 GNU tar and GNU gunzip are needed to extract the files. These tools are most often included with UNIX-based systems; however, copies of GNU gunzip and GNU tar can be obtained at *www.gnu.org*.

Installating Tar.gz

1. The initial step in installing MySQL on UNIX-based operating systems is to create users and groups. If users and groups are not created, a default user "mysql" and group "mysql" will automatically be created when installing the package. The following commands are executed as root by typing the following:

```
groupadd mysql          #Creates a group "mysql"
useradd -g mysql mysql  #Creates a user "mysql" and places that
                            user in
                        #the group "mysql"
```

2. Next, input the commands that change the directory where MySQL database files are to be extracted and the tar utility is used to unzip and unpack the distribution file. This can be done using the following commands:

```
cd/usr/local                              #Changes the directory
tar xvfz /tmp/mysql-pathname.tar.gz  #Unpacks the files
```

On the workstation, the word "pathname" would be the actual file and pathname of the file. For Solaris machines, `tar` would be replaced with `gtar`.

3. The final step is to place the appropriate files into the directory in which the machine expecting these files to be located. This is done by making the subdirectory created by tar during the unpacking link with the directory in which UNIX is expecting the software and data to be located. To do this, the following commands are used:

```
ln -s /usr/local/version /usr/local/mysql
```

In this example, `version` would be replaced with the name of the subdirectory created by `tar`. There are a few discrepancies between UNIX-based machines as to where the data and the software are expected to be, so be sure to check MySQL's site for this information.

At this point, the database is essentially installed. It now only requires the granting of privileges and tables, as well as changes in the ownership of the data files and programs. This can be completed by executing the following commands:

```
cd/usr/local/mysql
./scripts/mysql_install_db
chown -R mysql /usr/local/mysql
chgrp -R mysql /usr/local/mysql
```

MySQL server binaries for UNIX area called mysqld.

Installing Linux Binary Distributions Using RPM

MySQL using RPM packaging is a very fast and simple way to install MySQL on a UNIX-based machine, and for this reason it is the suggested avenue for installing MySQL on a Linux operating system. MySQL is compatible with all versions of Linux that support RPM packages and use the glibc2.3 library. There are both server and RPMs available that should be installed. MySQL downloads are often combined and packaged as platform-dependent formats such as **.tar**, **.rpm**, **.zip**, and **.gz**. Therefore, additional applications are often necessary to extract the files from within these packages. The installation package installed in this section is the binary distribution file for the RPM package. Like the Windows packages, it can be downloaded from *http://dev.mysql.com/downloads/*.

There are two categories of RPM packages, those that are platform-specific and those that are non-platform specific.

- *Platform specific*—Linked dynamically to libraries that are found on the specific platforms for which they are built.

- *Non-platform specific*—Statically linked to Linux threads.

Installing RPM

1. The initial step in installing MySQL in UNIX-based systems is to create users and groups. If users and groups are not created, a default user "mysql" and group "mysql" will automatically be created when installing the package. The following commands are executed as *root* by typing the following:

```
groupadd mysql           #Creates a group "mysql"
useradd -g mysql mysql   #Creates a user "mysql" and places that
                         #user in
                         #the group "mysql"
```

2. It is important to ensure that no other packages of MySQL are installed on the system. If another MySQL installation is found on a system, an upgrade must be completed. The command for locating other RPM packages is

```
rpm -qa  # This will list all rpm files installed on the system.
```

3. Next, we need to install the client and server packages for database connectivity and use. Two simple commands are used to install the RPM distributions of these packages. To install, type the following command into a terminal:

```
rmp -i MySQL - server- VERSION.glibc23.i386.rpm
rmp -i MySQL -client- VERSION.glibc23.i386.rpm
```

There are also additional options available for this command to allow monitoring such as –v, which provides a more informative output useful for troubleshooting installation errors, and –h, which displays the progression of the installation. Two packages of the same type can be installed at the same time, but the filenames should be separated with spaces:

```
rmp -i MySQL - server- VERSION.glibc23.i386.rpm MySQL -client-
VERSION.glibc23.i386.rpm
```

At this point, the database is essentially installed and data is placed in the **/var/lib/mysql** directory. Data directories and tables now need to be set up. Once complete, you should be able to connect to the server to see if everything works. Test your configuration by running:

```
MySQL -u root
```

Configuration

After installation, MySql must be configured. In Windows, the server type and role need to be identified, and resources need to be allocated for storage engines and the server in general. A root password and file ownership properties must be identified as well. Both Windows and UNIX-based systems (msqld) use a central configuration file to configure MySQL on startup. This file is called **my.cnf**, and in Windows it can also be called **my.ini**. When a server starts up, it looks for this file in several different areas of the file structure. There is a very intentional order in which the operating system looks for this file in order to complete the configuration-related tasks. This section will provide the initial and detailed configuration tasks for both Windows and UNIX.

Configuring MySQL on Windows

The MySQL Server Instance Configuration Wizard creates a custom configuration file (**my.ini**) immediately after installation. As shown in Figure 3-10, the wizard prompts the user at the end of installation to begin the initial configuration of a server. If the user accepts the option to configure the machine, the wizard begins and the custom configuration file comes into fruition.

The first choice that is presented to the user is in regard to configuration types. There are two types of configuration that can be conducted using the Configuration Wizard, detailed and standard:

- *Detailed configuration*—Gives the user more control over the configuration of the server and provides the user the opportunity to set up an ideal server for the given environment. There are several more options available for users to customize the server within the detailed configuration.

- *Standard configuration*—Meant for initial configuration only, and very little decision-making is left up to the users. With the exception of services and security configurations, the standard configuration runs automatically, setting up and conducting the necessary configuration tasks. The standard configuration type is to be relied on by users who need a quick install, are installing MySQL for the first time, and plan to reconfigure the server manually at a later time.

Standard Configuration Using the Windows Configuration Wizard

The following steps are for a typical initial standard MySQL configuration using the Windows Configuration Wizard.

1. Check **Configure the MySQL Server now** (Figure 3-10) on the confirmation window at the end of the MySQL installation. Click **Finish** to complete the installation.

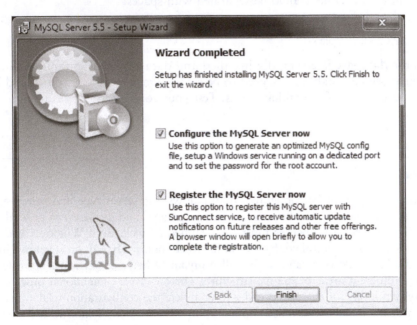

Figure 3-10 Setup Wizard completed
© Cengage Learning 2012

2. Select **Standard Configuration** (Figure 3-11) and click **Next**.

3. The Configuration Wizard automatically creates a service called MySQL (using mysqld) that launches with the start of the machine. From the following screen, users can change the name of the service, disable the service from installing, or disable the service from starting up with the machine. It is suggested that MySQL be installed as a service and automatically initiated at startup. For this example, check **Install As Windows Service** and **Launch the MySQL Server automatically** (Figure 3-12). Click **Next** to continue.

4. To maintain the security of your database server, it is important that the user password is created for the root user, that remote access is denied, and that anonymous accounts are disabled. The root user has full privileges on a MySQL server. Skipping this setting could provide intruders with easy access to the most critical components of your database. Anonymous accounts are often mistakenly left enabled on a system, therefore giving public access to the system without requiring a username and password. This provides an open door into the database for unwanted intruders. Root access allows

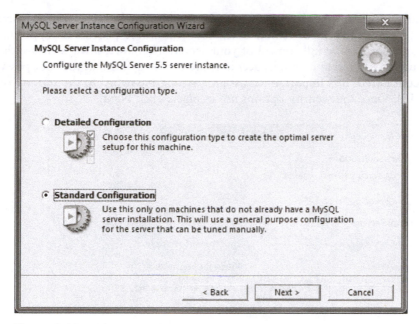

Figure 3-11 Select configuration type
© Cengage Learning 2012

Figure 3-12 Windows options
© Cengage Learning 2012

administrative access to the database server. Unless absolutely necessary, root access should not be given to outside remote machines. This would provide an opportunity for a remote intruder to take full control of your server. Therefore, always ensure that remote route access and anonymous accounts are disabled and that the root password is carefully considered. It is important to assign a strong password to the root account (Figure 3-13). Once the security options are in place, click **Next**.

Figure 3-13 Instance configuration security options
© Cengage Learning 2012

5. The confirmation screen allows a user to save the options to the configuration file (**my.ini**). Click **Execute** on the confirmation screen to save the options to the configurations (Figure 3-14).

6. Now that the **my.ini** file has been created and configured and the root password and security options have been applied, click the **Finish** button on the confirmation screen.

Detailed Configuration Using the Windows Configuration Wizard

The following steps are for a typical initial detailed MySQL configuration using the Windows Configuration Wizard.

1. Check **Configure the MySQL Server now** on the confirmation window at the end of the installation of MySQL (Figure 3-15). Click **Finish** to complete this installation.

2. Select **Detailed Configuration** and click **Next** to continue (Figure 3-16).

3. Three server types are available from which to choose to configure the MySQL machine: developer, server, and dedicated. The choice depends on the role of the machine, the number of other applications that will reside on it, and also will have an impact on the amount of RAM the hard drive space and the CPU will be allotted for the database.

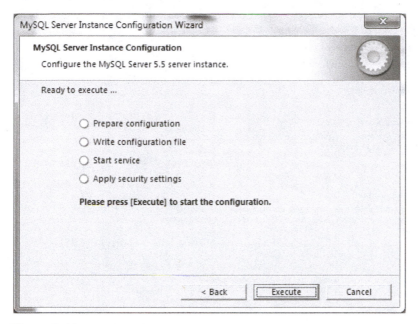

Figure 3-14 Execute instance configuration
© Cengage Learning 2012

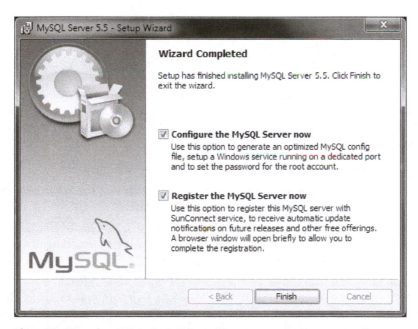

Figure 3-15 Setup Wizard exit screen
© Cengage Learning 2012

- *Developer*—The role of this machine is intended for developmental use and will likely house several applications. MySQL server will be allotted only the minimal amount of resources for the database. An administrator would choose this option if the machine on which MySQL is installed will be used to develop, build, and deploy applications.

Figure 3-16 Select configuration type
© Cengage Learning 2012

- *Server*—This machine is intended to house several other server applications. MySQL will be allotted a medium amount of resources. An administrator would choose this option if the machine on which MySQL is installed will act as another type of server alongside MySQL.

- *Dedicated*—This machine will be used only as a MySQL database server; no other unrelated applications or services will be housed on this machine. MySQL will utilize all of the available resources of the machine. This is the recommended setting for a MySQL database.

For this example, select **Dedicated MySQL Server Machine** and click **Next** (Figure 3-17).

4. The next step in configuring your MySQL database is to choose the way the database will be used. There are three options from which to choose:

- *Multifunctional*—This database is for general-purpose use. This option will enable both InnoDb and MyISAM storage engines to be available simultaneously. Resources will be equally distributed to both engines.

- *Transactional*—This database will also enable both the InnoDB and MyISAM engines; however, MyISAM does not support transactions. InnoDB will be used more extensively than MyISAM. This is the suggested setting to ensure that the InnoDB obtains more resources and acts as the main storage engine.

- *Non-Transactional*—This database is only used for simple Web applications and monitoring capabilities. InnoDB is disabled with this option. All resources are allocated to the MyISAM.

For this example, select **Transactional Database Only** and click **Next** (Figure 3-18).

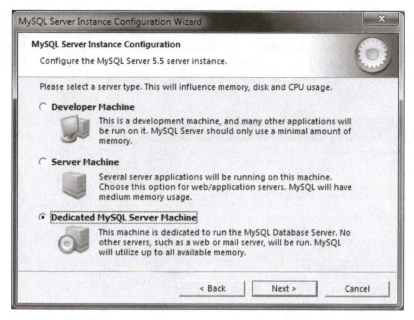

Figure 3-17 Select server type
© Cengage Learning 2012

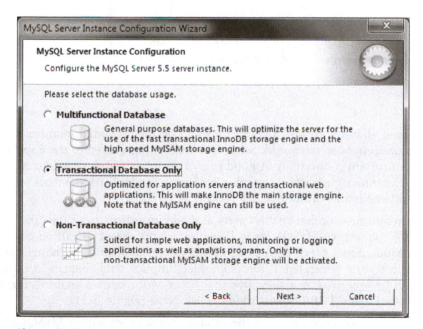

Figure 3-18 Database usage
© Cengage Learning 2012

5. The InnoDB tablespace information is stored inside a file called **ibdata1**. The information saved in this file should be saved on the drive with the greatest amount of storage and speed. This screen allows users and administrators to move the

InnoDB tablespace files to a different location. The drop-down menus provide alternative places to store the files and the screen provides information regarding each of the drives as you select them. For this screen, leave the default unless your machine contains a faster drive with more storage in which to save the tablespaces. Click **Next** (Figure 3-19).

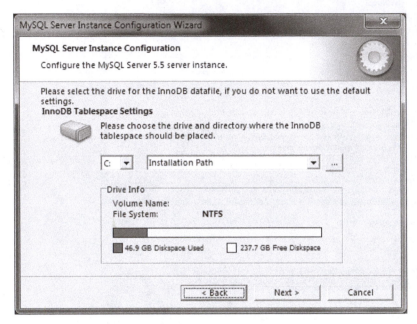

Figure 3-19 InnoDB tablespace settings
© Cengage Learning 2012

6. The next screen allows users and administrators to set the maximum number of concurrent connections in the msqld. Select **Manual Setting** and enter the approximate number of concurrent connections. A good rule of thumb is to use the number of agents that you are monitoring multiplied by two. Resources available on the machine should also be considered in this decision. Click **Next** (Figure 3-20).

7. This next configuration option enables users and administrators to change the port in which TCP/IP connects to MySQL, as well as disables the use of TCP/IP in general. Click **Strict Mode**. Strict Mode ensures that there are no implicit data changes and if one occurs, an error is generated. If this is disabled, implicit data changes can occur and no errors will be generated. It is suggested that Strict Mode remain enabled. For this example, check **Enable TCP/IP Networking**. Click **Next** (Figure 3-21).

8. The next configuration encountered is the default character set within MySQL. This determines the type of characters that can be used globally in the databases and tables. Changes to this option would change the available characters. The default character set is best suited for English and West European Languages. If a database requires a different character set, a change can be made to use multilingualism by choosing from one of the many character sets available through MySQL. For this example, select **Standard Character Set**. Click **Next** (Figure 3-22).

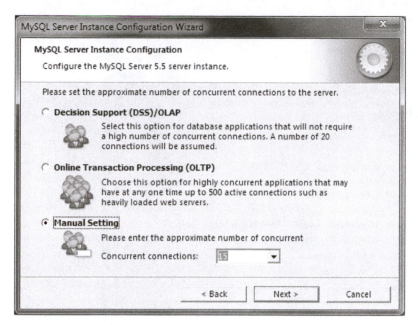

Figure 3-20 Concurrent connections
© Cengage Learning 2012

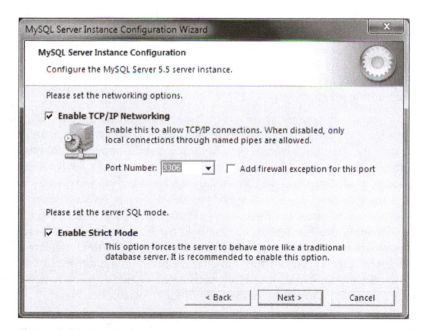

Figure 3-21 Networking options
© Cengage Learning 2012

Figure 3-22 Default character set
© Cengage Learning 2012

9. The Configuration Wizard automatically creates a service called MySQL (using mysqld) that launches with the start of the machine. From the following screen, users can change the name of the service, disable the service from installing, and disable the service from starting with the machine. It is suggested that MySQL be installed as a service and automatically initiated at startup. Click **Install As Windows Service** and **Launch the MySQL Server automatically** (Figure 3-23). Click **Next**.

10. To maintain the security of your database server, it is important that the user password is created for the root user, that remote access is denied, and that anonymous accounts are disabled. The root user has full privileges on a MySQL server. Skipping this setting could provide intruders with easy access to the most critical components of your database. Anonymous accounts are often mistakenly enabled on a system, therefore giving public access to the system without requiring a username and password. This provides an open door into the database for unwanted intruders. Root access allows administrative access to the database server. Unless absolutely necessary, root access should not be given from outside remote machines. This would provide an opportunity for a remote intruder to take full control of your server. Therefore, always ensure that remote route access and anonymous accounts are disabled and that the root password is carefully considered. Assign a strong password to your root account (Figure 3-24). Once the security options are in place, click **Next**.

11. The confirmation screen allows a user to save the options to the configuration file (**my.ini**). Click **Execute** on the confirmation screen to save the options to the configurations (Figure 3-25).

12. Now that the **my.ini** file has been created and configured and the root password and security options have been applied, click **Finish**.

Figure 3-23 Set Windows options
© Cengage Learning 2012

Figure 3-24 Set security options
© Cengage Learning 2012

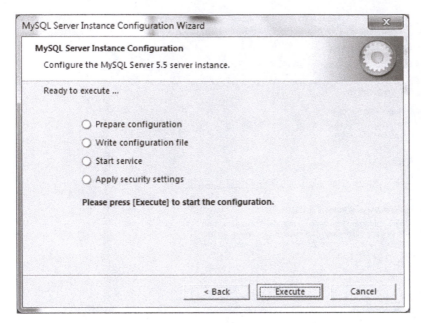

Figure 3-25 Ready to execute
© Cengage Learning 2012

Configuring MySQL on UNIX

As with Windows, UNIX-based machines require a bit of initial configuration after MySQL is installed. The configuration file for these machines is named **my.cnf.** Just as with Windows, the data directory and file permissions need to be created in order to prepare MySQL for startup. This section describes how to create the necessary initial components of a MySQL database.

Using a Configuration Script

A script called **mysql_install_db** creates the basic file directory and grant tables for user permissions automatically. In Solaris and RMP GNU/Linux installations (as with the one shown earlier in this chapter), this script is included in the installation package and therefore is run automatically. To run this script manually, navigate to the installation directory and run the script. The name of this directory depends on the way you installed MySQL:

```
For binary:
CD /usr/local/sysql
/scripts/mysql_install_db
For source installations:
CD /usr/local/sysql-5.5.1
scripts/mysql_install_db
```

Now that a data directory and initial database are in place, view the data directory by executing the following command:

```
Ls -la /path/to/datadir/mysql
```

Setting Passwords

After the **mysql_install_db** file has completed, the server prompts the user to complete other tasks, including the option to run mysqladmin:

```
PLEASE REMEMBER TO SET A PASSWORD FOR THE MySQL root USER !
>To do so, start the server, then issue the following commands:
>/usr/bin/mysqladmin -u root password 'new-password'
>/usr/bin/mysqladmin -u root -h this_host_ password password 'new-
password'
```

Just as in Windows, all initial accounts are set up without passwords and mysqladmin is a program that changes the root password. The configuration script **mysql_install-db** sets up five different user accounts. There are three root accounts: root@localhost, root@12.0.0.1, and root@hostname; and two anonymous accounts: ' '@localhost and a second account that is named the same as the server (' '@name_of_host). Each of the root accounts should be given strong passwords, and it is suggested that anonymous accounts be removed from the machine. As just mentioned in the Windows configuration section, anonymous accounts do not require unique usernames or passwords. Keeping these accounts could lead to a security breach. To remove these accounts, execute the following command from a root account:

```
DROP USER ''@localhost;
```

To find all of the anonymous users, issue the following query:

```
SELECT user.host.password FROM mysql.user WHERE user='';
```

For added security, it is recommended that the usernames of all root accounts for both Windows and UNIX-based machines be changed, as well as passwords. Changing the usernames for these accounts will further strengthen their protection.

To locate and display all databases, accounts, and access to individual database, use the following commands:

```
mysql> SHOW DATABASES;
mysql> SELECT User, Host, Password FROM mysql.user;mysql> SELECT
Host, Db, User, Select_priv FROM mysql.db;
```

Additional Security Suggestions

As mentioned throughout this chapter, MySQL is an immensely popular database application, maintaining users that vary from personal PCs to enterprise organizations. Its great popularity puts it at high risk for hacker intrusions and malware attacks. Being steadfast in security practices is important to maintaining the privacy and integrity of information networks. An attack against an organization's database can be quite damaging to its reputation and overall business success. This section addresses the basic security concerns in relation to the installation and early administration of MySQL.

Passwords

As mentioned throughout the chapter, root passwords are left blank by default. Root passwords allow execution of every command available in MySQL; therefore, they should be changed and replaced with strong passwords.

Usernames can be just as important as passwords. Default root usernames as installed on all operating systems are easy to find online. Changing the usernames of root passwords can provide additional security against intruders attempting to discover access.

Never store passwords in plain text format. When a password is stored within the MySQL database, apply strong encryption techniques. If a machine becomes compromised and the password stored is in plain text, the intruder can take full advantage and further compromise a site.

Account Access and User Privileges

MySQL provides great power and control over user privileges. Take advantage of this control. Always follow the principle of least privileges, ensuring the protection of sensitive data. For example, do not share root access. If an individual needs special access, provide privileges based on need.

Remove or disable all anonymous accounts that reside on the system. Anonymous accounts do not require credentials, providing easy access into the database infrastructure.

Implement different logins for each application. If an intruder breaches the system, having different logins for each application can isolate and minimize the damage.

Network Connection Administration

Database administrators often overlook network connections when creating a security plan to secure a database server. Network connections interface with the outside world. Therefore, it is vital for administrators to take the necessary precautions for maintaining privacy. The following are best practices for protecting network connections:

- *Disable remote access*—If not possible, secure the MySQL server behind a firewall. Remote access provides a window for intruders to access the application and acts as an ideal way to implement denial of service attacks.

- *Do not leave your ports wide open*—Although this chapter instructs the reader to open port 3306 on the Windows firewall, it is necessary to restrict this port to only those hosts with permission to access it. Another option is to close the port altogether, only opening it when needed. Ports are the intruder's preferred access to any network.

- *Use IP addresses to restrict access to the database*—MySQL provides administrators with the tools to define allowed access based on IP addresses. This will ensure that only approved persons can obtain information from the database.

- *Encrypt your connection to the server using SSH or SSL*—By default, MySQL is not encrypted, which can lead to communication being intercepted and your data compromised.

Chapter Summary

- Prior to installing MySQL, an administrator must determine which distribution format, version, and edition of MySQL to install.

3

- MySQL is an open-source application under the GNU public license. Users are encouraged to download, test, and modify the actual source code of the software for free.

- MySQL offers a great number of resources as extensions to its main Web site, including MySQL manuals, product downloads, training and technical support, bug and fix tools, and developer information.

- There are two different ways you can install MySQL: using its prepackaged binary files or by installing and compiling the source code manually.

- Different versions of MySQL are available at different stages of its development. One can download a version of MySQL in its beta form (while it is still being tested and debugged), as a release candidate (somewhat stable and tested), or as a general-availability product (fully tested and debugged).

- MySQL has adopted a milestone model, which improves the release cycle process and allows users to better predict any new versions that will be available. The milestone model dictates that new RC releases will be available every 3–6 months, while new GA releases will be available approximately every 18 months.

- Help with MySQL comes in many different forms. Besides those channels available on MySQL's Web site, users can find help within forums, from bloggers, on Twitter, and through mailing lists.

- The installation packages for Windows operating systems offer wizards to aid users in installing and configuring MySQL.

- UNIX-based servers offer several different platform-dependent installation packages from which to choose.

- Installing MySQL using the RPM binary is the suggested mode of installation for all Linux servers that use glibc2.3 library.

- MySQL can configure a machine to be either a developer machine, a server machine, or a dedicated MySQL server machine.

- Anonymous accounts are created in both Windows and UNIX. These accounts should be removed from the system as an extra security precaution.

- Passwords stored within the database should be encrypted to ensure their safety in case of a breach.

- The principle of least privilege should be followed when choosing access and privilege rights of users within the MySQL database.

- It is important for database administrators to use best practices in the process of protecting network connections.

Key Terms

binary code installations Binary files that are packaged and ready to be installed without the need for compiling the code to enable it to be run as an executable file on a particular machine.

binary file A file that contains code that can be read by machines and run as an executable file.

compile The act of converting source code that is written in one language into a different programming language or machine language.

digital signature Code that uses cryptography to verify the authenticity of a source of information.

programming language A type of synthetic language developed with a specific syntax and semantic rules that allows individuals to create statements or functions to interface and control the behavior or functionality of a machine.

source code A group of statements or functions written using a specific programming language and that are combined to create a specific type of application or utility.

source code installation Allows a user to download the actual MySQL source code, change it, and compile it into a binary file for installation execution.

Review Questions

1. List the considerations a network administrator should take prior to database installation.

2. Identify two main installation formats that can be used to install MySQL.

3. Explain why installing a source code installation format can be time consuming.

4. Explain the importance of reviewing the available versions of a database application prior to installation.

5. Identify and define the four phases of maturity for a release of MySQL.

6. Identify the main goals of the milestone model.

7. What is the recommended version of MySQL to install for the first time?

8. List six online sources of help for MySQL.

9. Explain the main difference between the two different editions of MySQL available for downloading and installation.

10. List two ways to verify that a package has not been tampered with and is clean of Trojans.

11. List two security practices employed regarding root passwords. Failure to employ these practices can result in what consequences?

12. List five practices to follow to ensure the protection of sensitive data.

13. List four best practices for the protection of network connections.

Case Projects

Case Project 3-1: MySQL Bugs

Search MySQL's bug home page and compile a list of three known MySQL bugs for both UNIX-based and Windows platforms.

Case Project 3-2: MySQL Releases

Using MySQL's download page, list all available binary versions of MySQL and include their filenames. Identify the most current release of MySQL.

Case Project 3-3: UNIX MySQL Script

Using the Internet as a resource, research and define the mysql_secure_installation UNIX MySQL script. Include the security-related tasks that it performs.

Case Project 3-4: Researching Changelog

Using the Internet as a resource, research the changelog pages of MySQL. Identify the content that can be found within them and describe the reason you would use these pages.

Case Project 3-5: Implementing Security Measures

Suppose that you are a security-conscious database manager for Haphazard, Inc. Outline the security measures that you would implement to protect a new installation of MySQL.

Hands-On Projects

HANDS-ON PROJECTS

Hands-On Project 3-1: Install an Archive Package on a UNIX-based Server

Haphazard, Inc. has hired you as a database administrator for their organization. You are instructed to install MySQL on their existing UNIX-based server using a noinstall archive package. Identify the steps that are necessary to do the following:

1. Download the file

2. Install MySQL

3. Configure the server

4. Apply necessary security

Hands-On Project 3-2: Install an Archive Package on a Windows Server

Haphazard, Inc. has hired you as a database administrator for their organization. You are instructed to install MySQL on their existing Windows server using a noinstall archive package. Identify the steps that are necessary to do the following:

1. Download the file

2. Install MySQL

3. Configure the server

4. Apply necessary security

chapter 4

Database Installation 2: Microsoft SQL Server

After reading this chapter and completing the exercises, you will be able to:

- Identify the considerations that an administrator must take into account prior to installation
- Install the Microsoft SQL Server 2008 for Windows operating systems
- Configure Microsoft SQL Server 2008 Services for Windows platforms
- Secure the installation and configuration of Microsoft SQL Server 2008

Security In Your World

Both Luke Werner and Jason Lucarelli work for Questionable Meds Pharmaceuticals, a midsized pharmaceutical sales organization that has shown tremendous growth over the last few years. Luke has been overseeing the technical development as the company's IT manager for the past five years, and from this experience he has learned a great deal about the organization's data storage needs.

Jason was recently hired as the database administrator (DBA) for Questionable Meds. Although he has only been employed for five months, he has been administrating databases for over 15 years and has developed a strong understanding of the data needs for large organizations. Armed with a midsized budget, together Jason and Luke seem to be the perfect team to tackle the task of developing and implementing a Microsoft SQL Server database environment.

Not far into the project's implementation, their different agendas began to cause problems. Luke and Jason were not seeing eye-to-eye regarding the many decisions that needed to be made for the company's data storage needs. From as early as the planning stage, their differences began to take a toll on the overall project, causing delays in development.

One major subject of disagreement was the budget. After assessing the network and mapping the organizational data, Jason believed that three separate editions of Microsoft SQL Server (Standard, Developer, and Web) were necessary to custom manage the organization's current and future data storage needs effectively.

Luke, on the other hand, felt that purchasing three separate and different licenses was excessive. He felt that the Enterprise Edition could handle the majority of data manipulation and storage for the organization.

In view of the company's recent growth, Luke proposed that the budget would be best utilized by replacing all of the network servers and PCs, confident that this would ensure they exceed Microsoft hardware recommendation requirements and ensure quality performance far into the future.

Jason adamantly disagreed. He affirmed that only the network servers needed to be updated, and that anything else would be unwarranted and excessive.

Another source of conflict was security, with Luke and Jason disagreeing on the type and amount of security needed. Luke suggested that additional firewalls be added to surround the new servers in order to isolate the database from the rest of the network. Jason felt that this configuration would be too cumbersome and unmanageable for both administrators and users. He was certain that applying different administrative passwords for different components of the database would suffice in keeping the data isolated. He argued that his approach coupled with policy management, would be

(continued)

necessary for their new environment to remain secure. He further explained that limiting access to tables and objects using groups and accounts could be just as efficient as adding expensive firewalls.

Both Jason and Luke make valid points, and their arguments represent the difficult decisions that need to be made when implementing a Microsoft SQL Server environment in the real world. Awareness of the needs of your environment and the features available within your chosen database management system are prerequisites for creating the ideal solution. SQL Server is known for its many customizable features and installations. This chapter will introduce you to these features, explore the different concerns that should be addressed when considering an installation of SQL Server, and present a step-by-step installation.

Planning for a Microsoft SQL Server Installation

Over the last decade, Microsoft SQL Server has become a significant database enterprise solution for many organizations. Improvements in its scalability and performance, combined with its ease of use and low cost, has made it an attractive solution for processing, storing, and securing data within large enterprise networks.

Installation of Microsoft SQL is as simple as any other Microsoft application installation; however, administrators must make several important decisions to ensure that the system best meets the needs of an organization. Proper planning is the key to success for any new system installation. Understanding the requirements, available versions, and available features of the system is required in order to design the most effective solutions for an organization.

In this section, we will explore the hardware, software, and networking requirements for SQL Server. We will review the different editions currently available for SQL Server, as well as the major features that these editions offer. Supported platforms will also be explored along with licensing and help resources.

Meeting the Requirements

Before installing Server 2008, administrators need to verify that the hardware, software, and network compatibility of the system on which SQL Server will be running. Supported platforms must also be considered. This section will cover the hardware, software, and network requirements of Microsoft SQL Server.

Hardware Requirements

Hardware requirements for SQL Server 2008 include processor type, processor speed, hard drive storage, and main memory storage amounts. The minimum requirements for 64-bit versions of SQL Server are: 1.4 GHz processor, 350 MB of hard drive space, and 512 MB of RAM. The minimum requirements for 32-bit versions of SQL Server are 1.0 GHz processor, 350 MB of hard drive space, and 512 MB of RAM.

Table 4-1 provides the hardware requirements for the core editions of Microsoft SQL. It is suggested that SQL Server not be run on machines that only have the minimum hardware requirements. These requirements are the lowest possible resources necessary to run the application. Attempting to run SQL Server on a machine with the minimum hardware requirements available will result in poor performance and unpredictable functionality. Microsoft recommends that SQL Servers be run on machines with at least 2.0 GHz processors, and that 2 GB of RAM must be available to function properly.

Hard drive space recommendations are not as cut and dried. In order to determine the hard drive space necessary, the current data that the organization and database need to function, combined with estimated future growth of data storage needs, should be calculated and used to determine hard drive storage space requirements. The size of the database will also differ depending on which features of SQL Server 2008 are installed. Table 4-2 displays the amount of storage used by each feature within SQL Server 2008.

Edition	Minimum CPU type	Minimum CPU speed/ recommended	Operating systems	Minimum memory/ recommended memory/maximum memory
Enterprise IA64	Itanium	1.0 GHz/ 2.0 GHz	Windows Server 2008 64-bit Itanium Windows Server 2003 64-bit Itanium Data Center Windows 2003 64-bit Itanium Enterprise	512 MB/2 GB/ Operating system maximum
Enterprise X64	AMD Opteron, AMD Athlon 64, Intel Xeon EM64T, Intel Pentium IV EM64T	1.4 GHz/ 2.0 GHz	Windows Server 2008 64-bit x64 Standard Windows Server 2008 64-bit x64 Data Center Windows Server 2008 64-bit x64 Enterprise Windows 7 Ultimate Windows 7 Enterprise Windows 7 Professional Windows 7 64-bit x64 Ultimate Windows 7 64-bit x64 Enterprise Windows 7 64-bit x64 Professional Windows Server 2003 64-bit x64 Standard SP2 Windows Server 2003 64-bit x64 Data Center SP2 Windows Server 2003 64-bit x64 Enterprise SP2 Windows Server 2008 64-bit x64 Web	512 MB/2 GB/ Operating system maximum

Table 4-1 SQL Server software and hardware requirements (*continues*)

Edition	Minimum CPU type	Minimum CPU speed/ recommended	Operating systems	Minimum memory/ recommended memory/maximum memory
Standard x64	AMD Opteron, AMD Athlon 64, Intel Xeon EM64T, Intel Pentium IV EM64T	1.4 GHz/ 2.0 GHz	Windows Server 2008 64-bit x64 Web Windows Server 2008 64-bit x64 Standard Windows Server 2008 64-bit x64 Datacenter Windows Server 2008 64-bit x64 Enterprise Windows 7 Ultimate x64 Windows 7 Enterprise x64 Windows 7 Business x64 Windows Vista Ultimate x64 Windows Vista Enterprise x64 Windows Vista Business x64 Windows XP Professional X64 Windows Server 2003 64-bit x64 Standard SP2 Windows Server 2003 64-bit x64 Data Center SP2 Windows Server 2003 64-bit x64 Enterprise SP2	512 MB/2 GB/ Operating system maximum
Enterprise X86 (32-bit)	PIII	1.0 GHz/ 2.0 GHz	Windows Server 2008 Enterprise Windows Server 2008 Web Windows Server 2008 Data Center Windows Server 2008 64-bit x64 Standard Windows Server 2008 64-bit x64 Enterprise Windows Server 2008 64-bit x64 Data Center Windows Small Business Server 2003 Standard Windows Small Business Server 2003 Premium Windows Server 2003 Standard SP2 Windows Server 2003 Enterprise SP2 Windows Server 2003 Premium SP2 Windows Server 2003 64-bit x64 Standard SP2 Windows Server 2003 64-bit x64 Data Center SP2 Windows Server 2003 64-bit x64 Enterprise SP2	512 MB/2 GB/ Operating system maximum

Table 4-1 SQL Server software and hardware requirements (*continues*)

4

Edition	Minimum CPU type	Minimum CPU speed/ recommended	Operating systems	Minimum memory/ recommended memory/maximum memory
Standard X86 (32-bit)	PIII	1.0 GHz/ 2.0 GHz	Windows Server 2008 Enterprise Windows Server 2008 Web Windows Server 2008 Data Center Windows Small Business Server 2008 Windows Server 2008 64-bit x64 Standard Windows Server 2008 64-bit x64 Enterprise Windows Server 2008 64-bit x64 Data Center Windows 7 Ultimate Windows 7 Enterprise Windows 7 Professional Windows 7 64-bit x64 Ultimate Windows 7 64-bit x64 Enterprise Windows 7 64-bit x64 Professional Windows Vista Ultimate x64 Windows Vista Enterprise x64 Windows Vista Business x64 Windows XP Professional SP2 Windows XP Professional X64 SP2 Windows Server 2003 32-bit Standard Windows Small Business Server 2003 Standard Windows Small Business Server 2003 Premium Windows Server 2003 Standard SP2 Windows Server 2003 Enterprise SP2 Windows Server 2003 Premium SP2 Windows Server 2003 64-bit x64 Standard SP2 Windows Server 2003 64-bit x64 Data Center SP2 Windows Server 2003 64-bit x64 Enterprise SP2	512 MB/2 GB/ Operating system maximum

Table 4-1 SQL Server software and hardware requirements (*continued*)

Feature	Storage cost
Complete Data Engine Core	250 MB
Complete Analysis services and data files	90 MB
Complete Reporting and Reporting Manager services	120 MB
Complete Integration Services	120 MB
Complete Client Components	240 MB
Complete Server Books Online	240 MB

Table 4-2 Storage used by SQL Server 2008 features

For a complete list of the recommended hardware requirements for editions of Microsoft SQL Server, refer to the SQL Server Books Online.

Supported Platforms

Although SQL Server 2008 supports a number of different operating systems, not all editions support the same operating system. For this reason, the platform choice should not be taken lightly. Deciding on the most appropriate operating system should involve much more than mere preference or experience of the administrator. A mistake can be quite damaging to the performance and scalability of the system. The operating system on which SQL Server will be installed will determine the features that will be available, so finding the perfect match could make the difference between a robust data management machine and an inflexible storage component.

64-bit and 32-bit

When choosing an appropriate operating system, you first must decide on either a 32-bit or a 64-bit platform. To fully leverage the capability of a 64-bit operating system, only 64-bit versions of SQL should be used. When a 32-bit version of SQL is placed on a 64-bit operating system, the platform is forced to run the database server in 32-bit mode, thus disabling many of its valuable features.

Operating System Requirements

As just mentioned, different versions of SQL Server require different operating systems. In general, SQL 2008 can be placed on different versions of Windows Server 2008, Windows Server 2003, Windows 7, Windows Vista, and Windows XP. Table 4-1 provides a basic overview of the operating systems compatible for core SQL Server 2008 editions.

It is important to take note of the service packs and processor stipulations for each operating system. Compatibility is specific to the service packs and processors listed in Table 4-1.

Other Software Prerequisites

Before installing SQL Server onto a Windows Machine, a few important prerequisites must be met. The SQL Server installation wizard will verify that these prerequisites have been satisfied prior to installation. An administrator installing SQL Server will be prompted to either install missing items manually or to give permission for the wizard to install them automatically. The following software requirements must be in place to enable the installation of all 32-bit and 64-bit Microsoft SQL Server editions:

General software

- NET Framework 3.5 SP11
- Microsoft Windows Installer 4.5 or later
- Internet Explorer 6 SP1 or later
- Latest version of PowerShell
- Microsoft Data Access Components (MDAC) 2.8 SP1 or later

Network software

- Shared Memory
- TCP/IP
- Named Pipes
- Virtual Interface Adapter Via Protocols

Network Resource Requirements

The network is a vital component in a database success story. After all, what is a database without a network on which to share the information? SQL Server data is stored, retrieved, and manipulated within a client-server architecture. The effectiveness of the communication and connections established on this network will be determined by network hardware and software within a Microsoft SQL Server 2008 environment.

Network design and architecture play a large role in the reliability and efficiency of a client-server environment. Although these topics are beyond the scope of this book, it is important to identify concerns related to network design and efficiency.

Changes to the network's hardware and software may be necessary with the implementation of Microsoft SQL Server. An environment being prepared for an initial installation of Microsoft SQL should be tested to ensure that it can handle the amount of data that will be transferred across segments of the network. Check network cards, switches, cables, and other hardware devices to determine how well they operate under heavy traffic conditions.

Making the Difficult Decisions

Difficult decisions are a part of any database system installation planning stage. Customization is one of SQL Server's greatest selling points, so its software includes a few more choices than most. SQL Server currently offers several different editions of its database, each with its own set of features from which to pick and choose. This section will cover the important decisions that a DBA must make when choosing to implement SQL Server into their environment, such as SQL Server editions, features, and licensing options.

Choosing an Edition

New editions have made improvements in the server's scalability and performance for developers and administrators, adding the flexibility needed to fit in virtually any organization. Microsoft has added features that offer a variety of different user interfaces and editions which are focused on a specific business database purpose. These provide a way to meet the needs of varying data storage scenarios at low cost and with little to no overhead caused by extra unnecessary features. For example, an organization may need a database that can handle a lot of online activity, such as an e-commerce environment, while another may need to implement a solution that enables the use of their mobile handheld devices.

Microsoft has created editions of SQL Server to meet both of these specific needs independently. Becoming familiar with what each edition has to offer is critical to choosing the right solution for your particular environmental needs.

- *SQL Server Express Edition*—A free, lightweight version of SQL Server 2008, this edition replaced the SQL Server desktop engine. It is recommended for personal and individual use. SQL Server Express is available for download at *http://msdn.microsoft.com/express*.

- *Compact 3.5*—A skinny version of SQL Server 2008, this free edition is created for mobile devices and for mobile application developers. SQL Server Express is available for download at *http://msdn.microsoft.com/express*.

- *Workgroup Edition*—Intended for a department or small business use, this edition is ideal for environments that require small user data storage or Web applications that have minimal usage, such as remote branch office access scenarios.

- *Web Edition*—Built for a large amount of traffic, this edition is ideal for full Web hosting.

- *Developer Edition*—Providing the same features as the full Enterprise version, this edition is to be used for development and testing only, and is not intended for production.

- *Standard Edition*—Ideal for most applications, this edition can be used in small to large organizations where server redundancy is not required, but usage is significant and integration services are needed.

- *Enterprise Edition*—The complete feature set of the product that provides the most scalability, and is intended to support the largest organizations. This version is ideal for large workloads and frequent usage, including features for high availability, enterprise security, data warehousing and business intelligence. The Enterprise Edition of SQL Server includes a great number of features that are tailored to an enterprise environment, and are not offered in the standard version. Features included are partitioned table parallelism, database mirroring, online indexing, online page restore, extensible key management, failover clustering, transparent database encryption, resource governor, text mining, and performance data collection.

Table 4-3 provides some SQL Server editions and hardware requirements, but for a complete list of the features available in each edition of Microsoft SQL Server, refer to the SQL Server Books Online.

Edition	CPUs supported	Maximum addressable memory	Maximum database size
SQL Server Express (x86, x64)	1	1 GB	4 GB
SQL Compact	OS maximum	OS maximum	4 GB
SQL Server Workgroup (x86 and x64)	2	4 GB on a 64-bit OS and the OS maximum on a 32-bit one	No maximum
Web (x86, x64)	4	OS maximum	No maximum
SQL Server Developer (x86, x64, and IA64)	OS maximum	OS maximum	No maximum
Standard (x86, x64)	4	OS maximum	No maximum
Enterprise (x86, x64, and IA64)	OS maximum	OS maximum	No maximum

Table 4-3   **SQL Server editions and hardware requirements**

SQL Server Features and Components

Server features have experienced quite a number of significant changes throughout history, yet each change has had a noteworthy impact on the application in its current form. Refer to Table 4-4 for a complete history of Microsoft SQL Server releases and added features.

Microsoft SQL Server is made up of a number of features administrators can choose to include or leave out of an installation. The goal of this modular packaging is to provide an organization with a customizable, lightweight server built with environment-specific capabilities.

Choosing the right fit for an organization first and foremost requires familiarity with what optional components are available in Microsoft SQL Server. In this section, the major server and management tools of SQL Server are explored. For a complete listing of features available in Microsoft Server 2008, refer to the SQL Server Books Online.

Server Tools   Server management tools represent the fundamental tools available with an installation of Microsoft Server 2008, and include the Database Engine Services, Reporting Services, Analysis Services, and Integration Services.

- *Database Engine Services*—This is the heart of the SQL Server database. This service is responsible for data storage, retrieval, manipulation, and security. It provides access control and fast transaction processing. There are two subcomponents of the Database Engine Service: Replication and Full Text Search. **Replication** (the act of sending copies of one database to another database within a network) is the component responsible for managing database replication within a network. The replication of a database is the process of sharing recent changes made to a database with all other network databases in hopes of remaining consistent and in sync with one another. It is also used to support load balancing, fault tolerance, and data distribution. Full Text Search is the component that maintains the indexes and full text catalogs, making searches more simple by allowing full word and phrase searches.

- *Reporting Services (SSRS)*—Provides different ways for presenting and delivering data in Microsoft SQL Server 2008. The Database Engine sends the data to the

Year	Version	Comments
1987	Sybase SQL Server	Released for UNIX
1988	SQL Server	A joint effort between Sybase and Microsoft, included support for use on OS/2 Capable of storage and handling of personal and small department use
1989	SQL Server 1.0	Fine-tuned, focused support for OS/2 Capable of storage and handling of personal and small department use
1990	SQL Server 1.1	Added support for Windows 3.0 Capable of storage and handling of personal and small department use
1993	SQL Server 4.2	Integrated with Windows NT; capable of storage and handling of personal and small department use
1994		Microsoft and Sybase split; Sybase continues to focus on UNIX database systems while Microsoft focuses on Windows
1995	SQL Server 6.05	First version to be written solely by Microsoft; database engine rewritten to support small business and e-commerce applications
1996	SQL Server 6.5	Gaining prominence
1998	SQL Server 7.0	Database engine rewritten to support small-to-medium-sized businesses Additional features include analysis services and data transformation services
2000	SQL Server 2000 enterprise database	First version to support enterprise environments; database engine was enhanced for improved performance and scalability; provided full support of online operations of businesses, improved development, and analysis tools
2005	SQL Server 2005	Engine rewritten to include integration services, .NET Framework giving the user the ability to create NET SQL Server-specific objects
2008	SQL Server 2008	Additions to 2005 to include additional data types, use of Language Integrated Query (LINQ), and XML; enhanced support of large installations

Table 4-4 Timeline of Microsoft SQL Server releases

reporting services for formatting and creating a graphical representation of the data into reports.

- *Analysis Services (SSAS)*—Provides online analytical processing (OLAP) and data mining for a database. It is designed for the fast and frequent processing of data and queries to be used in OLAP-appropriate environments.

- *Integrated Services (SSiS)*—Joins together and normalizes data from different sources. **Integrated Services** is a valuable tool in data warehouses where different types of data need to be joined together for reporting and extrapolation.

Management Tools The management tools available in Microsoft SQL Server 2008 are those features available to aid in the administration and customization of the server:

- *SQL Server Configuration Manager*—This tool is used to configure the installation of SQL Server. It provides administrators the ability to configure network protocols used by the application to manage services associated with the SQL Server and to configure native client connectivity.

- *SQL Server Management Studio*—This component is the primary administrative interface to the SQL Server database. This tool enables administrators to configure and interact with the database from a single console.

- *Business Intelligence Development Studio*—An environment for application development, allowing developers to create custom applications and forms to meet business needs. These forms can include built-in analysis, as well as integrated and reporting services to improve their functionality.

- *Client Tools Connectivity*—A group of tools that enable communication between a client and a server.

- *Server Profiler*—The service that provides the graphical user interface (GUI) to the computer monitor for an instance of the database.

Licensing Options

During installation of Microsoft SQL Server 2008, administrators are prompted to choose a licensing option. Once this option is chosen, it cannot be changed, so it is important that these options are fully understood prior to the installation of the database application.

Express and Compact editions of Microsoft SQL Server 2008 are free for download, yet typically the cost of the server will depend on the server edition as well as the number of features included within that edition. The more features available within an edition of SQL Server, the higher the licensing costs.

Microsoft licensing can be negotiable for larger organizations, software vendors, and educational institutions. Contracts for these type of organizations may be flexible, yet for the most part, licensing for Microsoft SQL Server 2008 is available under three specific terms: Per Processor Licensing, Per Server Plus Device CAL, and Per User Plus Device CAL.

Per Processor, or Per Server licenses, provide access for an unlimited number of users and devices, so individual user and device Client Access Licenses, or CALs, are not necessary. A **Client Access License (CAL)** is a unique license that allows users or devices access to gain a licensed Microsoft SQL Server 2008 server. There are two types of CALs:

- *SQL CAL*—In this agreement, it is stated that any SQL CAL can be used with any licensed SQL Server regardless of the type of platform.

- *Workgroup CAL*—In this agreement, it is stated that Workgroup CALs can only be used with a licensed Workgroup Server.

The Developer edition of SQL Server 2008 can only be purchased and used by application developers. Therefore, this edition is sold only to individuals, and cannot be registered on production servers.

- *Per Processor Licensing*—In this contract, organizations and individuals pay for each available processor intended for a Microsoft SQL Server 2008 install.

- *Per Server Plus Device CAL license*—In this contract, a license is required for each server, plus a CAL is required for each device accessing the SQL Server within the organization.

- *Per Server Plus User CAL license*—In this contract, a license is required for each server. In addition, a CAL is required for each user accessing the SQL server.

In per-processor licensing, the term *processor* refers to the physical processor only. This essentially means that those processors deemed multi core (e.g., Dual Core, Quad Core), which enable the installation of several instances of SQL Server on one machine, are only considered to be one physical CPU by Microsoft licensing standards. This specification allows organizations ways to save costs if taken into consideration when designing the environment's Microsoft SQL Server installation strategy.

4

Locating Help

As with any major or minor hardware and software installation, being able to locate help is vital to the success of the installation as well as the future reliability of your environment. The Internet continues to provide an opportunity for an endless amount of peer and expert support, yet there is no better resource than that found within the product manufacturer's main site. This section will identify the major Web sites and resources available for Microsoft Server 2008.

Help Resources

As with all other Microsoft products, help resources are plentiful and rich. Several levels of technical support are offered with the licensing of SQL Server. Contracts can be formed to provide help in many different areas. Whether help is necessary over the phone, in person, or online, you can find resources for a variety of different concerns (e.g., technical support, database consultation, and object development). The resources are endless. Searching online is often the most common first step in obtaining support with any concern. Following are several major Web sites and resources available for Microsoft Server 2008:

- *SQL Server Books Online*—A detailed set of online documents that help you find information regarding all aspects of SQL Server 2008 functionality. The categories include, but are not limited to: Database Engine, Analysis Services, Integrated Services, Replication, and Reporting Services. You can find these documents within SQL Server as well as on the Web at *http://msdn.microsoft.com/en-us/library/ms130214.aspx*.

- *Web sites*—A number of Microsoft SQL Server Web sites are available online. Web sites offer a great amount of information through forums, knowledge bases, blogs, vlogs, and digital libraries. One of the most useful Web sites for Microsoft SQL 2008 is the Microsoft SQL Server Development Center. This site offers the greatest number of resources for SQL Server 2008. The site features links to the Microsoft SQL Library, software downloads, searches of the Microsoft SQL knowledge base, SQL Server communities (including blogs, newsgroups, and forums), self-paced and instructor-led courses, product demos, and training videos. You can view the Microsoft SQL Server Development Center at *http://msdn.microsoft.com/en-us/sqlserver/default.aspx*.

- *The Microsoft Online Books*—This resource provides a comprehensive online manual for all of the current versions and editions of MySQL. These manuals can be found at *http://dev.mysql.com/doc/*.

- *Microsoft SQL release notes*—The benefits of the release notes are that they contain the newest information not necessarily provided in the online book.

- *Microsoft SQL Forums*—Forums are a great way to ask questions and share ideas with other users and Mircrosoft SQL Professionals online. Several great forums are available on the Internet. One suggested group of forums can be found at the Microsoft SQL Server Development Center, which is located at *http://msdn.microsoft.com/en-us/ sqlserver/bb671050.aspx*.

- *Bloggers*—Blogs have become a fantastic resource, especially for the technology fields. Many people who work with Microsoft Server 2008 or have experience with the application, blog about their experiences and share their knowledge at this blog site: *http://msdn.microsoft.com/en-us/sqlserver/bb671054.aspx*.

- *Twitter*—Twitter has become a popular way to keep people informed on a minute-by-minute basis. Sending quick updates and reminders, organizations can reach out to their customers directly via e-mail and cell phone. Microsoft uses Twitter as a way for users to ask questions and for Microsoft SQL professionals to send out alerts relevant to upgrades, bugs, and other software-related support at *http://twitter.com/ sqlserver*.

Installation

Once a user has obtained the desired copy of MySQL, verified that the hardware and software requirements have been met, and decided on its purpose and design (by choosing the desired edition and features), installation can begin. If prerequisites have not been met, SQL Server will require updates before the installation process.

The Server Installation Center

The server installation center, illustrated in Figure 4-2, is the first window that appears once your prerequisites have been satisfied and before installation begins. It is important to become familiar with the different resources available here. This section will explore those tools and resources.

The Planning Page   The planning page provides all of the resources and tools necessary for planning a Microsoft Server 2008 installation. This window provides links to the following resources:

- *Hardware and Software Requirements*—This document displays the hardware and software requirements for the current SQL Server 2008 installation.

- *Security Documentation*—Documentation displays security considerations for a SQL Server 2008 installation.

- *Online Release Notes*—These notes provide the most up-to-date information for the most current release of SQL Server 2008.

- *System Configuration Checker*—A tool that checks the system for anything that might interfere with or prevent the current installation.

- *Install Upgrade Advisor*—This tool is for update installations. The Install Upgrade Advisor will check older versions of SQL already installed on the current machine and fix any known issues with these versions prior to the upgrade.

- *Online Installation Help*—Documentation that provides step-by-step installation instructions as well as information for troubleshooting an installation.

- *How to Get Started with SQL Server 2008 Failover Clustering*—Documentation that provides instructions on setting up and preparing for failover and clustering strategies using Microsoft SQL Server.

- *Upgrade Documentation*—Documentation that provides step-by-step upgrade installation instructions as well as information for troubleshooting an upgrade.

The Installation Page

On this page, you will find the launch tools to begin stand-alone installation, to start a failover cluster installation, and to add a node for failover cluster installations. Links to product updates and upgrades are also available on this window.

- *New SQL Server stand-alone installation or add features to an existing installation*—This link launches a wizard to provide administrators a way to add features to an existing installation of SQL Server or to initiate a new installation.

- *New SQL Server failover cluster installation*—This link launches the single-node failover strategy wizard.

- *Add node to a SQL Server failover cluster*—Launches a wizard for adding nodes to existing failover installations.

- *Upgrade for SQL Server 2000 or SQL Server 2005*—Launches the upgrade wizard.

- *Search for product updates* —Takes user to the Microsoft server update site located at *http://www.update.microsoft.com*.

The Maintenance Page

On this page, you will find various maintenance options available to upgrade, repair, and remove features from SQL.

- *Edition Upgrade*—This link launches a wizard to change your edition of SQL Server 2008.

- *Repair*—This link launches a wizard to repair damaged versions of SQL Server 2008.

- *Remove node to a SQL Server failover cluster*—This link launches a wizard for removing nodes from existing failover installations.

The Tools Page

On this page, you will find various tools available for SQL Server.

- *System Configuration Checker*—A tool that checks the system for anything that might interfere with or prevent the current installation.

- *Installed SQL Server features discovery report*—Compiles a report of all previously installed versions and features of SQL Server.

- *Upgrade Integration Services Package*—Launches a wizard for upgrading SQL Server integration packages to 2008.

The Resources Page

On this page, you will find links to various resources for SQL Server. Here is a list of resources found in this area:

- Books Online
- TechCenter
- Developer Center
- Product Evaluation Web site
- License Agreement
- Register your copy of SQL Server 2008 Express
- Microsoft Privacy Statement
- Community
- CodePlex samples Web site

The Advanced Page

On this page, you will find various advanced tools available for SQL Server.

- *Install-based configuration file*—A tool that enables the administrator to use an existing configuration file to install SQL Server 2008.
- *Advanced Cluster Preparation*—A wizard to prepare SQL Server failover cluster installation.
- *Advanced Cluster Completion*—A wizard to create a failover cluster from existing cluster instances.

The Options Page

On this page, you can specify which edition architecture of SQL Server to install (e.g., x86, x64, ia64) and the installation media root directory. This option is available for installations that will be applied from someplace other than the CD.

Step-by-Step Installation

This section will include the steps for installing Microsoft SQL Server on a Windows 64-bit machine. In order to ensure a successful installation, the machine on which the installation will take place must meet the minimum hardware and software requirements described earlier in this chapter. The instructional steps provided in this section are intended for installing the Enterprise Edition of Microsoft SQL Server 2008.

1. Insert the CD into the CD or DVD drive. From the main folder, double-click the **setup executable file** (Figure 4-1).
2. If all of the necessary hardware and software prerequisites have been met, the Planning page of SQL Server Installation Center will appear (Figure 4-2). On the menu at the left, click **Installation** to gain access to the Installation Page (Figure 4-3).

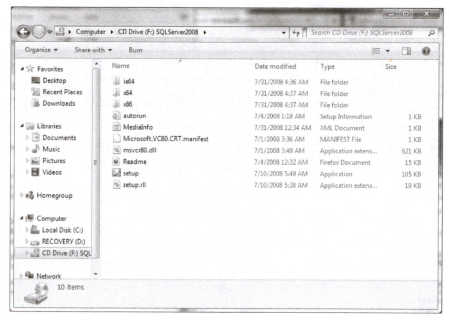

Figure 4-1 Locating the setup file
© Cengage Learning 2012

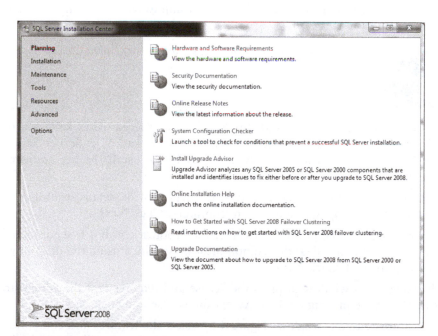

Figure 4-2 SQL Server Installation Center—Planning page
© Cengage Learning 2012

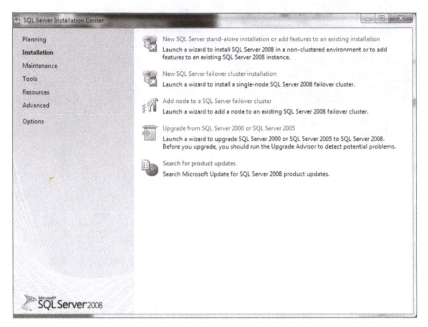

Figure 4-3 Installation page
© Cengage Learning 2012

3. On the Installation Page of the Server Installation Center, click **New SQL Server stand-alone installation or add features to an existing installation.** The Configuration Checker will run (Figure 4-4). Click **OK.**

The Show details button will display the Configuration Checker log.

4. The Installation Wizard will install the SQL Server prerequisites software (e.g., NET Framework 3.5 SP1, SQL Server Native Client, and SQL Server Setup Support Files) if this was not already completed. To install the prerequisites, click **Next.**

5. The System Configuration Checker (Figure 4-5) will provide details regarding the system state of the computer before setup continues. Click **Next.**

6. The administrator will be prompted to enter the product key. If a free edition of SQL Server 2008 is being installed, this edition must be specified using the drop-down list provided (Figure 4-6). Click **Next.**

7. The Licensing terms window displays the license and requires that the administrator accept the license terms (Figure 4-7). Accept the license and click **Next.**

8. On the Feature Selection window (Figure 4-8), select the features and components to customize your installation. A description for each component will appear in the right pane once a feature is selected.

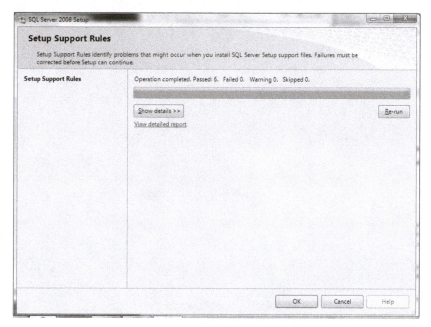

Figure 4-4 System Configuration Checker
© Cengage Learning 2012

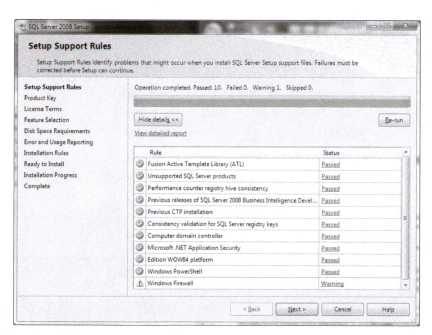

Figure 4-5 System Configuration Checker Details
© Cengage Learning 2012

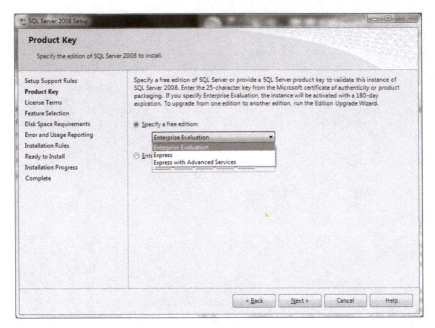

Figure 4-6 Product Key window
© Cengage Learning 2012

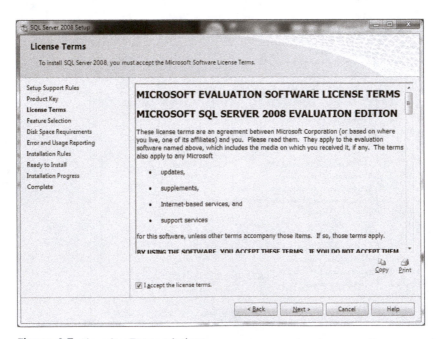

Figure 4-7 Licensing Terms window
© Cengage Learning 2012

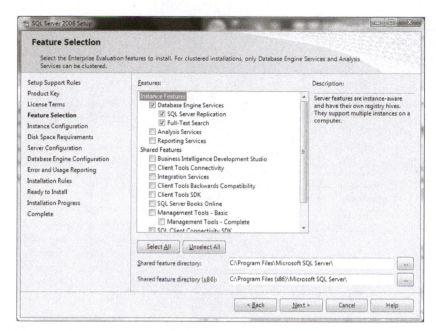

Figure 4-8 Feature Selection window
© Cengage Learning 2012

Any number or combination of features can be included within the installation. The administrator can choose to select all or none of the features using the available buttons, Select All and Unselect All. Shared directories can also be customized for the specific network environments by clicking the browse button (depicted as '…') and selecting the location for the shared features directory. Once features are selected, click **Next**.

9. On the Instance Configuration window (Figure 4-9), the administrator can specify whether to use a default instance or a custom named instance and instance directory. The name that is specified will also be used as the Instance ID by default. The Installed instances field displays instances that are already installed on the computer within the root directory. Click **Next**.

10. The Disk Space Requirements Window (Figure 4-10) calculates the required disk space for the features that were specified earlier in the installation. Click **Next**.

The remaining instructions may differ since they are dependent on features that you specified earlier in the installation.

11. For security reasons, some services require a username and password. On the Service Accounts window, the administrator will specify login accounts for SQL Server services (Figure 4-11). Change the names by clicking the Account Name and Password fields for each corresponding server feature, and insert the required information into these fields. These services can be assigned the same username and password or each service can be assigned its own unique username and password. For security purposes, provide a separate logon for each service, ensure that the passwords for these accounts are strong,

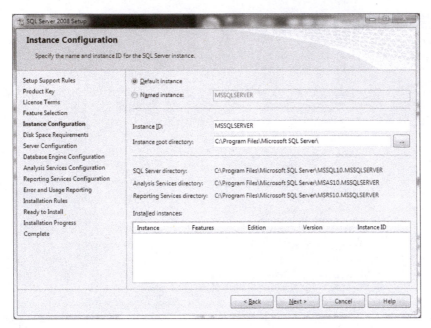

Figure 4-9 Instance Configuration window
© Cengage Learning 2012

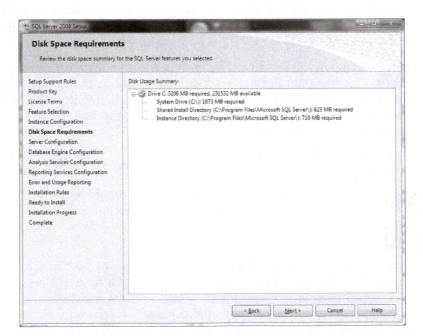

Figure 4-10 Disk Space Requirements window
© Cengage Learning 2012

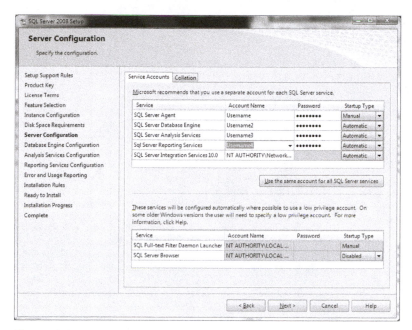

Figure 4-11 Service Accounts window
© Cengage Learning 2012

and that accounts are enabled for least privilege. Services can also be disabled, set to start up automatically, or set to start up manually. For security reasons, do not set services to start automatically unless completely necessary and secured. When finished specifying login information for the services, click **Next**.

12. The Database Engine Configuration window helps ensure that security measures are taken for the initial installation of a server (Figure 4-12). For server administrators, the Account Provisioning page specifies the security mode and the server administrator. The security mode can be set to either Windows Authentication or Mixed Mode Authentication for an instance. Mixed Mode Authentication requires either server or windows authentication, but requires the transmission of login names and passwords over the network. It is recommended that you choose Windows Authentication for installation. The server administration section requires at least one system administrator for the server instance. To add the account under which SQL Server Setup is running, click **Add Current User**. To add or remove accounts from the list of system administrators, click **Add** or **Remove,** and then edit the list of users, groups, or computers that will have administrator privileges for the instance of SQL Server. When the list is finished, click **OK**. Verify the list of administrators in the configuration dialog box and click **Next**.

13. The Analysis Services Configuration window allows administrators to specify users or accounts that will have administrator permissions for Analysis Services (Figure 4-13). At least one system administrator for Analysis Services must be specified. To add the account under which SQL Server Setup is running, click **Add Current User**. To add or remove accounts from the list of system administrators, click **Add** or **Remove**, and then edit the list of users, groups, or computers that will have administrator privileges for

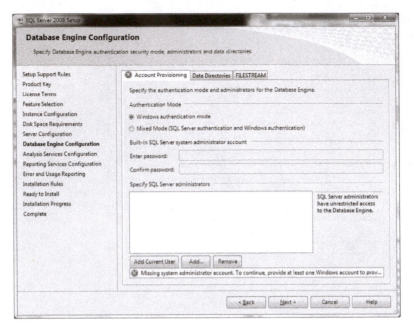

Figure 4-12 Database Engine Configuration window
© Cengage Learning 2012

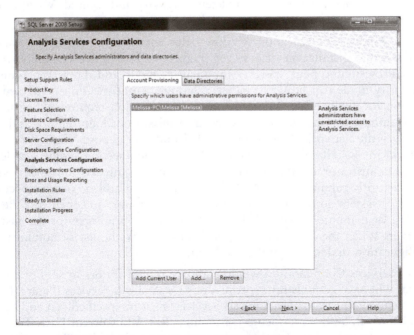

Figure 4-13 Analysis Services Configuration window
© Cengage Learning 2012

Analysis Services. Once complete, click **OK**. Verify the list of administrators in the configuration dialog box and then click **Next**.

14. The Reporting Services Configuration window enables administrators to specify the kind of Reporting Services installation to create (Figure 4-14). There are three different types of Reporting Services from which to choose:

    - *Native Mode*—Setup will install the Report Server and configure it using default values.

    - *SharePoint Integrated Mode*—Setup will install the Report Server database using SharePoint integration default modes.

    - *Not Configured*—Setup will install but not configure the Report Server Software.

    Select **Native Mode** and click **Next**.

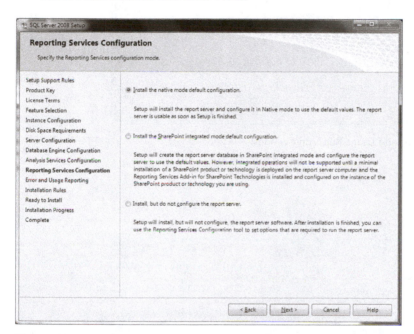

Figure 4-14 Reporting Services Configuration window
© Cengage Learning 2012

15. The Error and Usage Reporting window specifies the information that you want to send to Microsoft that will help improve SQL Server (Figure 4-15). By default, options for error reporting and feature usage are enabled. Click **Send Windows and SQL Server Error Reports to Microsoft or your corporate report server**. This setting only applies to services that run without user interaction. Click **Next**.

16. The System Configuration Checker will run once again to validate your configuration (Figure 4-16). Once complete, click **Next**.

17. The Ready to Install window (Figure 4-17) shows a tree view of installation options that were specified during setup. Click **Install**.

18. After installation, the Complete window (Figure 4-18) provides a link to the summary log file for the installation and other important notes. To complete the SQL Server installation, click **Close**.

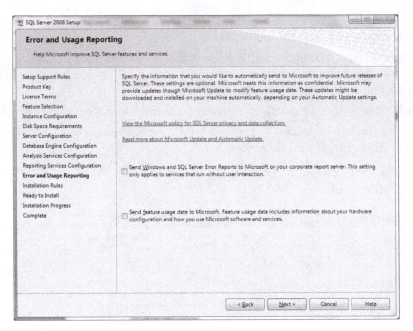

Figure 4-15 Error and Usage Reporting window
© Cengage Learning 2012

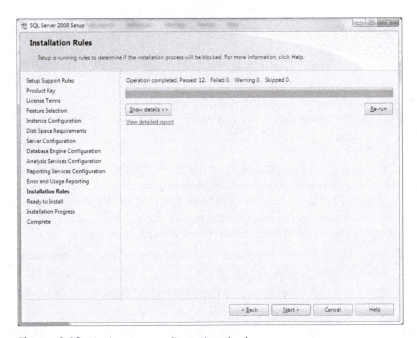

Figure 4-16 Final system configuration check
© Cengage Learning 2012

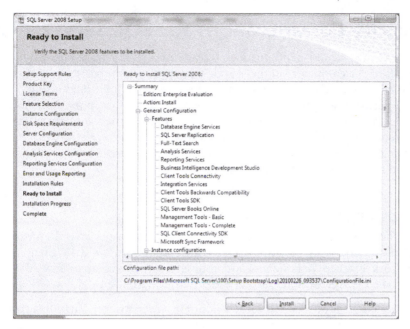

Figure 4-17 Ready to Install window
© Cengage Learning 2012

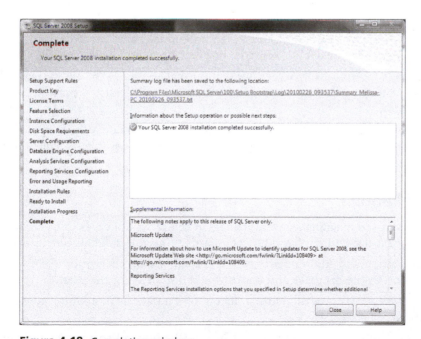

Figure 4-18 Completion window
© Cengage Learning 2012

Additional Security Considerations for SQL Server 2008

Microsoft has been a household name for many years, and its software currently resides on close to 90% of all of the computers in the world. This type of popularity is the reason it currently creates the most sought-after applications and platforms among the hacking and cracking community. Microsoft SQL Server is no exception to this. As its popularity continues to increase, so do the security attacks. An attack against an organization's database can be quite damaging to its reputation and overall business success, so taking early security measures is vital. This section addresses the basic security concerns in relation to the installation and early administration of Microsoft SQL Server 2008.

Security Steps Prior to Installation

As mentioned earlier, security must be addressed promptly. Even prior to the installation of SQL Server, administrators and network architecture designers should be planning a best-practice strategy to keep their organization's database secure. Here are a few best practices when considering the security of SQL Servers prior to installation:

- Place servers behind firewalls and locked doors in order to keep intruders from gaining access both inside and outside of the organization.
- Use multiple firewalls (both internal and external); create subnets, and require strict authentication.
- Isolate database servers from public networks such as the Internet and eliminate all connections to unnecessary segments of the network.
- Use a very selective strategy when deciding which users to give permission to access the database.
- Configure ports on a computer, and on an individual basis. Avoid group range exceptions whenever possible. Never leave ports open and unmanaged.
- Choose servers for your SQL Server installation that use an NTFS file system. They provide extra security through encryption and access control list permission implementation.
- Encrypt your connection to the server using SSH or SSL. By default, Microsoft SQL Server is not encrypted, which can lead to communication being intercepted and compromised data.

During Installation

- Apply policy-based management and manage it centrally. Polices help to enforce naming conventions and configuration standards to keep a database safe.
- Utilize Encryption and Auditing services. Transparent data encryption (TDE) enables the encryption of the database and backups without affecting the user.
- Enhanced auditing features allow the tracking of data access in addition to data modification.
- As mentioned in the chapter, passwords should be applied to services individually and uniquely. Different passwords limit the access of those who may intrude.

- Choose Windows authentication over Mixed authentication to avoid login names and passwords being sent across the network.

- Passwords should always follow a strict and strong policy. The more complex the password, the better defense against it being cracked.

- Administrative usernames can be just as important as passwords. Change default usernames whenever possible, as they are easy to find online. Changing the usernames of root passwords can provide additional security against intruders attempting to discover access.

After Installation

- Never store passwords in plain text format (udf files). When a password is stored within your SQL Server database, apply strong encryption techniques. If a machine becomes compromised and the password is stored in plain text, the intruder can take full advantage and further compromise your site.

- Take a multitiered approach to access. Create specific roles at the server, application, and database layers.

- Just as one should assign separate passwords to separate SQL Services, these services should run under separate Windows accounts that are local or that have minimum rights.

- Always apply the principle of least privilege when creating accounts and providing access to database objects and services.

- Keep up to date with security updates and patches from Microsoft.

- Configure auditing services to enable login auditing at both the Operating System and SQL Server level. Frequently review the logs for any clues.

- Disable all guest accounts within Windows.

- If possible, group database users on a different global group, separate from all other user groups.

- Make use of your error logs and ensure their security as well.

- Never use the administrative account to run the database service engine; log on with a user account having the least privilege possible for these intended tasks.

- Make sure all the file and disk shares on the SQL Server computer are read-only whenever possible.

Chapter Summary

- Microsoft SQL Server offers flexible installations that require a number of decisions to be made during the planning phase.

- There are 32-bit and 64-bit versions of SQL Server 2008 available.

- Supported platforms for Microsoft SQL Server are dependent on their edition. Overall, Microsoft SQL Server 2008 is supported in Windows XP, 2003 Server, Vista, 2008 Server, and Windows 7.

- Microsoft SQL Server 2008 cannot be installed on computers without NET Framework 3.5 SP2, Microsoft Windows Installer 4.5, the newest version of PowerShell, and MDAC 2.1 SP1.

- The network software required for SQL Server to communicate are Shared Memory, TCP/IP, Named Pipes, and Virtual Interface Adapter via Protocols.

- Changes in the network design and architecture may be necessary with the installation of SQL Server. This change will depend on the amount of data and the amount of users adding traffic to the network.

- There are seven editions of Microsoft SQL Server 2008: Express, Compact, Workgroup, Web, Standard, and Enterprise. The main core editions are Express, Standard, and Enterprise.

- The number of CPUs permitted, maximum memory that can be utilized, and the maximum database size are determined by the edition of Microsoft SQL Server.

- Components or features in SQL Server are optional, allowing for customizable installations that are based on specific network scenarios.

- Database Engine Services, Reporting Services, Analysis Services, and Integrated Services are examples of optional server tools available within SQL Server 2008.

- Configuration Manager, Server Management Studio, Business Intelligence Development Studio, Client Tools Connectivity, and Server Profiler are examples of optional management tools in SQL Server 2008.

- Licensing options for SQL Server enable users to choose to pay per server, processor, or user.

- Microsoft offers a number of online and offline help sources that can provide consulting, development, or technical support.

- Microsoft Online Books are the most comprehensive and popular resources available both online and within the application.

- Forums, blogs, and tweets are great ways to share knowledge and get answers from SQL Server experts.

- The Server installation center is the main administrator interface within SQL Server. It provides access to resources for planning, management, installation, and tools within SQL Server.

- Strong security is vital to the success of SQL Server since its popularity makes it a major target for potential intruders.

- Prior to installation, security design decisions such as firewalls, subnets, encryption, and file systems should be considered.

- During installation, administrators should choose secure usernames and passwords, apply policy-based management, and utilize encryption and auditing practices.

- After installation, logs and auditing techniques should be put into place and authentication should be applied using several tiers.

Key Terms

Client Access License (CAL) A unique license that allows users or devices access to gain a licensed Microsoft SQL Server 2008 server.

integrated services A valuable tool in data warehouses where different types of data need to be joined together for reporting and extrapolation.

replication The act of sending copies of one database to another database within a network.

4

Review Questions

1. List the decisions a network administrator should make prior to database installation.

2. Explain the difference between a 32-bit and 64-bit operating system.

3. Explain why installing the mimum hardware requirements is not suggested.

4. Explain how server hard drive storage requirements and network hardware components are similar to the way an administrator determines requirements.

5. Explain what must be considered when choosing the appropriate supporting platform for an edition of SQL Server 2008 being installed on a machine.

6. Explain how editions of Microsoft SQL Server are able to provide customization for specific network and environment scenarios.

7. How do the Compact and Express editions differ from all other editions of Microsoft SQL Server 2008?

8. List the online resources that are also accessible within the pages of SQL Server.

9. Identify and define at least six different features of Microsoft SQL Server available for downloading and installation.

10. Identify and define at least three different ways Microsoft SQL Server is licensed.

11. Explain why it is better to install a unique username and password for each installed feature, compared to one general username and password for all features.

12. List three security practices to follow during installation of Microsoft SQL Server 2008.

Case Projects

CASE PROJECTS

Case Project 4-1: Microsoft SQL Server Identify the Edition

Write a paragraph providing a rationale for identifying the server component best used for the following business scenarios:

a. Questionable Meds Pharmaceuticals has been collecting sales data for five years. Sales have tremendously increased over the last two years. Jason is asked to look for trends to explain the increase.

b. Jason of Questionable Meds Pharmaceuticals must provide sales information to the senior managers on a weekly basis. Senior management has requested that they receive the information in the same format and using the same organization each week.

Case Project 4-2: Microsoft SQL Server Community

Using SQL Server Books Online, list all of the available resources currently provided within the Microsoft SQL Server community. Choose one resource, explore it, and explain one thing that you have learned.

Case Project 4-3: Implementing Security Measures

Suppose that you are Jason for Questionable Meds Pharmaceuticals. Outline the security measures that you would implement to protect a new installation of MySQL.

Hands-On Projects

Hands-On Project 4-1: Installing a Sample Database

Go to *http://www.codeplex.com/*. Describe the purpose of this Web site, find one sample, provide the name of that sample, and install it.

Hands-On Project 4-2: Researching and Applying Authentication Mode

Using the Internet, further research the Authentication Mode. Describe the steps that you would take to show an example of Authentication Mode when authenticating through Windows.

chapter 5

Database Installation 3: Oracle

After reading this chapter and completing the exercises, you will be able to:

- Identify the considerations that an administrator must take into account prior to installation
- Install Oracle for Windows and UNIX-based operating systems
- Configure Oracle 2008 Services for Windows and UNIX-based platforms
- Secure the installation and configuration of Oracle

Joseph Michael has worked in the database management field for over 15 years and has witnessed a number of enormous changes over the last decade. A data storage engineer at heart, he has had to make large adjustments to his database administration strategy in order to accommodate the industry shift toward database security. His position has become much more demanding, yet he has remained flexible and eager to learn. Recently, Joseph was promoted to Senior DBA of his company's enterprise data architecture, and was asked to lead a major overhaul of the organization's data storage solution.

The plan was to deploy new Oracle database servers to accommodate the growing organization's data storage and management needs. After many hours of researching, planning, testing, and meeting with practically every person in the organization, the day finally came for the installation and deployment to take place. Joseph, very diligent in his process, decided to take advantage of the Enterprise Edition of Oracle. Meticulous, he carefully took an inventory of the environment to ensure that every device and application on the network would satisfy the requirements of this edition. He put forth great effort in planning the data storage needs, choosing the features and optional components that would best suit the complex environment. He familiarized himself with the privacy laws and ethical standards for his organization, and in a collaborative effort with the networking team, he ensured that the network and data architecture was in full compliance.

In the end, Joseph made informed and effective security decisions. He added more firewalls to isolate the servers, closed all unnecessary ports, hardened the operating systems, and planned encryption for the data in storage and in transit. He applied all of the necessary security patches and created security policies for passwords and data access. He also implemented the most restrictive and limited access control possible. While most administrators would create an account using a general predefined set of privileges, Joseph decided to build accounts using most-restricted access first, only adding additional access when the need was justified.

The migration was planned for off-hours, and due to Joseph's diligence, the data migration was executed seamlessly. Although everything seemed to be working fine, he knew that the real test would come during work hours the following day.

He arrived at work early and in good spirits, feeling confident about the work that he had done, yet unfortunately for Joseph, the employees were not feeling as confident and excited as he. The restrictive nature of the database access caused much frustration and chaos. Users, unable to access their data, caused productivity to drop to an all-time low. Frustrated and angry about the newly implemented restrictions,

(continued)

individuals at every level of the organization were calling Joseph to complain and reject the new database. Despite his attempts to explain the importance of security, the employees expressed their disapproval and concerns with the new system. Many even went as far as to question Joseph's knowledge and experience.

Joseph didn't necessarily take a wrong approach here. Although this is the ideal situation from a security standpoint, the ideal security solution is rarely the ideal business solution. Even the most comprehensive packages and strategies can result in disaster.

Oracle provides a comprehensive, multifaceted suite of solutions for applying security throughout an organization, yet, as we can learn from Joseph, choosing the right security measures is a delicate task that should not be taken lightly. Understanding these tools and what solutions they offer can help us close in on our security and business needs.

This chapter will discuss the different applications and features available within the Oracle suite, as well as provide a step-by-step approach to installing Oracle Database on Windows and UNIX-based machines.

Planning for an Oracle Deployment

Throughout its history, the Oracle Corporation has taken a comprehensive approach to offering business data solutions, but nothing displays this more than its progression over the last five years. Refer to Table 5-1 for a complete history of Oracle. Oracle has greatly extended its primary database focus and expanded its business support by developing products that interact at each layer of an infrastructure. It has broadened its range of support from applications that are integrated at the user level to hardware developed to sustain the performance and clustering of servers. A number of different solutions can be purchased and integrated to create a robust business solution.

Year	Version	Comments
1977		Software Development Laboratories founded
1979	Oracle 2	Was renamed Relational Software, Inc., and released their first database for VAX machines; included IBM's SQL and did not support transactions; OS support did not extend beyond Digital Equipment's -VAX/VMS
1982	Oracle 2.3	Renamed Oracle Corporation, and extended support of computers to include DEC VAX-11, PDP-11, and IBM mainframes
1983	Oracle 3	New version written in C language, supported COMMIT and ROLLBACK for transactions, included support for UNIX and any hardware with a C compiler
1984	Oracle 4	Read consistency support added, as well as a broader range of hardware and software compatibility

Table 5-1 **History of Oracle** (*continues*)

Year	Version	Comments
1985	Oracle 5	Support for client-server environments as well as the increased development of customized interfaces to support a variety of business needs; this includes its first spreadsheet application
1986	Oracle 5.1	Distributed query support and clustering were added to allow for larger environmental support
1988	Oracle 6	Relational Database Management System; supported PL/SQL within forms for more flexibility, added row/level locking and real-time backups; business support being developed to keep up with the growing commercial networks
1989	Oracle ERP	Oracle released its first ERP product and finds a place in the commercial world
1990	Oracle Applications release 8	Oracle business support applications are released, including its first client/server application and GUI support for PCs and Macs
1992	Oracle 7	Referential integrity, stored procedures, and triggers are added to the database as database administration features; application development tools and security components are offered
1994		Oracle introduces the first media server on the market, which included an array of tools for multimedia objects
1997	Orace 8	Support of object-oriented development and multimedia applications are integrated
1999	Oracle 8i	The *i* stands for Internet, Oracle's attempt at making the database better integrated with the Internet and online processing; Oracle JVM is included
2000	Oracle E-Business Suite 11i	Applications developed for enterprise organizations to support their business needs
2001	Oracle 9i	400 added features to support the Internet and business, including XML support, RAC, and clustering
2003	Oracle Database 10g	The *g* stands for grid computing and architecture that the current versions of Oracle are built upon
2005	Oracle 10 Release 2	Announces Oracle Enterprise Linux, also known as the unbreakable Linux project for improved support and reliability for enterprise environments
2007	Oracle 11g	Released for Linux and Microsoft Windows users
2009	Oracle Middleware 11g	Acquired BEA a year before, adds BEA products and introduces Oracle Fusion Middleware 11g
2010	Oracle 11g release 2	Oracle acquires Sun Micrososystems

Table 5-1 History of Oracle (*continued*)

With variety come cost and complexity. Many organizations cannot pay the price for a fully integrating Oracle solution that spans every level of the business architecture, so administrators and designers must find a solution that meets both business and budget needs. Effective planning is vital to the success of any data maintenence strategy, but due to its cost and complexity, understanding the requirements and available components of Oracle is even more important in developing the most efficient and cost-effective solution.

In this section, we will explore the hardware, software, and networking requirements for the Oracle database. We will review the different editions currently available, as well as the major features that these editions offer. Supported platforms will also be explored along with licensing and help resources.

Checking the Requirements

Before an installation of an Oracle database server, administrators need to verify the hardware, software, and network compatibility on which the Oracle Server will be running. Supported platforms must also be considered. This section will cover the hardware, software, and network requirements of an Oracle database server.

Hardware Requirements

Hardware requirements for an Oracle database server include processor speed, hard disk storage, main memory, and virtual memory (swappable memory) storage amounts. The minimum requirements for an installation of Oracle on 64-bit version platforms are: AMD64 or EM64T processor, 5.22 GB of hard drive space of which 150 MB must be available within the temporary directory, 1 GB of RAM, and 2 GB of virtual memory (or double the RAM). The minimum requirements for an installation of Oracle on 64-bit version platforms are: 550 MHz processor (800 MHz on Windows Vista), 4.76 GB of hard drive space of which 200 MB must be available within the temporary directory, 1 GB of RAM, and 2 GB of virtual memory (or double the RAM). These requirements are the lowest possible resources necessary to run the basic application. Attempting to run Oracle using the minimum requirements will cause a number of services to fail. Many variables must be considered when choosing the hard drive space, memory space, and CPU speed necessary to run an Oracle database. Here are a few of the variables that must be considered:

- *Hard Disk Space*—The needs of the hard drive will depend on the size of the operating system, the databases data files, redo files, archived redo files, and control files. Although the size requirement of the operating system can be pretty straightforward, the control files, redo files, and archive redo files are dynamic and often fluctuate as changes are being made to the database. The dynamic nature of these files can make it very difficult for their size to be estimated. In terms of the size of the data files, the database engineer must have a good idea of how much data will be stored within the tables of the database. This size is often greatly underestimated since it requires knowledge of each row of data as well as the number of rows of data that will be included. Therefore, hard drive space cannot be limited and it is better to overestimate than it is to underestimate the required storage.

Oracle provides a number of best-practice recommendations for the storage and placement of files during installation and configuration. These recommendations have been grouped together and named Optimal Flexible Architecture (OFA). During configuration, the Database Configuration Assistant (DBCA) uses the OFA automatically. One of the recommendations within the OFA is that the database files are placed separately from the file system of the operating system. These recommendations are made to ensure optimal performance and can be found within the Oracle database support documentation.

- *The Main Memory or RAM*—This area is the most utilized within the database architecture. It is here that the system stores space for users' connections, query executions, and SQL statements reused by the system. Retrieving data from this memory is much faster and more efficient than reading and writing to the hard disk files, and therefore, the reason for Oracle's strong performance and speed. The utilization of this memory is dependent on the number of queries, data objects, and user connections, so it is difficult to determine how much memory is necessary.

- *The CPU*—This will be determined by the number of simultaneously used instances and applications at any given time of the day. This is another set of variables that is difficult to determine prior to the system launch and should be carefully considered during the planning stages.

Another consideration regarding hardware is the maximum resources allotted for each specific edition of Oracle Database. The edition of Oracle that is deployed defines the hardware capabilities. For limitations as to how large a database can be, how many CPUs can be used, and how much addressable memory is available per user, refer to Table 5-2. More detail regarding each edition of Oracle is provided later in the chapter.

Edition	CPUs supported	Maximum addressable memory	Maximum database size
Oracle Express	1	1 GB	4 GB
Oracle Standard One	2 Sockets	OS maximum	No maximum
Oracle Standard	4 Sockets	OS maximum	No maximum
Oracle Enterprise	No maximum	OS maximum	No maximum

Table 5-2 **Oracle editions and hardware limitations**

Operating System Requirements

Oracle supports a number of different operating systems, yet the operating system on which it resides determines the features and optional components that the database can deploy. For this reason, the platform choice should be considered carefully and should be in line with the overall database goals. If the operating system of the machine on which Oracle is installed is overlooked, necessary components may not function, and as a result the business's needs will not be met. Just as with MySQL and Microsoft SQL Server, careful consideration of the operating system could make the difference between a robust data management machine and an inflexible storage component.

64-bit and 32-bit

Oracle Database is available in both 32-bit (x86) and 64-bit (x64) versions. This is the case for both Windows and UNIX-based systems. Choosing the correct version is important to the functionality of the database. A 32-bit version of Oracle can run on either 32-bit or 64-bit platforms, while a 64-bit version of Oracle can only run on a 64-bit platform. Keep in mind that installing a 32-bit version of Oracle on a 64-bit operating system will not increase its performance and will result in limited capability. To fully leverage the capability of Oracle, it is recommended that the 64-bit version be installed on a 64-bit platform and a 32-bit version on a 32-bit platform operating system. Table 5-3 displays the supported platforms for all editions of Oracle Database.

Windows-based platforms	Linux-based platforms	Other UNIX-based platforms
32-bit	32-bit	Solaris
• Windows 2000 with Service Pack 1 or later	• Asianux 2 SP2	• Solaris 9 Update 7 or later
• Microsoft Windows 2000	• Asianux 3	• Solaris 10
• Windows Server 2003	• Oracle Enterprise Linux 4	HP-UX
• Windows Server 2003	• Oracle Enterprise Linux 5	• HP-UX 11i V1 (11.11) PA-RISC
• Windows XP Professional	• Red Hat Enterprise Linux 4	• HP-UX 11i v2 (11.23)
• Windows Vista (Business, Enterprise, and Ultimate)	• Red Hat Enterprise Linux 5	• HP-UX 11i v3 (11.31)
64-bit	• SUSE Enterprise Linux 10	AIX
• Windows Server 2003 (all x64 editions)	64-bit	• AIX 5L version 5.3, TL 05, Service Pack 06
• Windows Server 2003 (all x64 editions)	• Asianux 2 SP2	• AIX 6L version 6.1, TL 00, Service Pack 04 or later
• Windows XP Professional x64	• Asianux 3	
• Windows Vista x64 (Business, Enterprise, and Ultimate)	• Oracle Enterprise Linux 4	
	• Oracle Enterprise Linux 5	
	• Red Hat Enterprise Linux 4	
	• Red Hat Enterprise Linux 5	
	• SUSE 10	

Table 5-3 Oracle supported platforms

NOTE

It is important to take note of the service packs and package requirements for each operating system. Compatibility is specific to the service packs and packages. For a complete list of supported operating systems, including service packs and package requirements, please see Oracle's installation documentation at *http://www.oracle.com/technetwork/indexes/documentation/index.html.*

Other Software Requirements

Before installing Oracle Database, a few additional software requirements must be considered. The software requirements for Oracle will be dependent on the operating system on which the database will be installed, along with any additional components that are chosen to fulfill the purpose of the database. For example, Linux and Windows will require different software compilers for an Oracle database installation because they are different types of operating systems. The type of compiler isn't dependant on the type of operating system alone. The purpose of the database plays a role as well, so two Windows installations can require different compilers if both installations individually required different Oracle components to fulfill their purpose within the environment. Therefore, an administrator should check Oracle's supporting installation documentation for the specific operating system and any additional installed option components for prerequisites.

Network Resource Requirements

Consideration must be given to network requirements. A database ultimately shares its data over a network and the effectiveness of the communication and connections established on this network will be determined by network hardware and software that is installed. Changes in network hardware and software may be necessary to accomodate the increased activity that an implementation of Oracle database server will cause. An environment that is being prepared for an initial installation of Oracle should be tested to ensure that it can effectively handle the amount of data that will be transferred across segments of the network. Check network cards, switches, cables, and other hardware devices to determine how well they operate under heavy traffic conditions. Network software must also be considered; for example, Oracle requires TCP/IP with SSL and named pipes in order to communicate with other devices on a network.

Preinstallation Decisions

Hardware and software needs are not the only considerations when implementing a database into an environment. There are several other equally important components to planning a database architecture. This section will explore these components and help to ensure that decisions are made that best serve a specific environment's needs. Topics will include Oracle Database editions, additional database features, licensing packages, and support contracts.

Choosing an Edition

Just as with MySQL and Microsoft SQL Server, Oracle packages its software in different editions. Oracle database is available in four main editions. These editions have been created with specific deployment scenarios in mind. It is important to note that Oracle offers more than just software editions to provide a solution for specific environments. Similar to Microsoft, Oracle has a number of optional features that offer a way to specifically meet the needs of a variety of environments. This section will review the different editions of the Oracle database server.

 Oracle has established itself as the most comprehensive and powerful database solution available on the market by including the development of middleware applications and hardware components built and designed specifically to support the Oracle database server application. These additional components, when combined with the Oracle database server application, provide for the most efficient and reliable use of resources within an environment.

Becoming familiar with what each edition has to offer will ensure the best, most cost-effective solution to meet a particular environment's needs.

- *Express Edition (XE)*—This edition is intended for beginning users and first-time database deployment. It provides an easy, user-friendly approach to installation and development. Express Edition offers a solution for small environments and individuals looking for a database solution that is easy to deploy at no cost to the user.

- *Oracle Database Standard Edition One (SEO)*—Oracle SEO offers a viable solution for single-server environments looking to implement a simply managed, full-featured database at low cost. Although recommended for smaller departments and Web development environments, it easily scales in environments where there is an increased demand.

- *Oracle Database Standard Edition (SE)*—Oracle SE is a full-featured database that offers support for all types of environments. Although suggested for small to midsize organizations, Oracle SE provides a highly scalable secure solution for enterprise networks as well.

- *Enterprise Edition*—The Enterprise Edition of Oracle is designed for environments that require high-volume, query-intensive, mission-critical data management. Oracle EE includes all of the components available within the Oracle Database as well as many features that are not available within all other editions. These additional features are described below and are undoubtedly the reason EE is a viable solution for high-demand networks.

  - *Virtual Private Database (VPD)*—Also known as Row Level Security or Fine Grained Access Control, this feature provides a method for applying security to specific rows of a table. Used when privileges associated with objects are not strict enough, VPDs allow policies to be created that identify access control for specific rows and tables of a database.

  - *Advanced Replication*—A tool that allows for bidirectional copying of database objects, procedures, and indexes. Advanced Replication enables updatable snapshots and improves performance and availability of applications by allowing faster replication and more objects to be replicated.

  - *Transparent Application Failover (TAF)*—Redirects user connections to surviving databases in cases where the connections fail. TAF reduces failover time and improves availability through transparent redirection.

  - *Fast Start Fault Recovery*—Shortens the time it takes to write a change from buffer to disk. Fast Start Fault Recovery reduces the time for recovery from failure by reducing the amount of data that hasn't been written to disk.

  - *Oracle Data Guard*—Enables the creation of failover databases for instances of failure. Data Guard improves the availability of the system by offering secondary servers for failover.

  - *Online Index Rebuild*—Eliminates the need for processes participating in online operation to maintain exclusive access to tables. Online Index Rebuild increases performance and reliability by allowing the rebuild of an online index while updates and configuration changes are occurring.

  - *Transportable Tablespaces*—Enables data to be moved by copying datafiles and integrating tablespace structural information only, increasing performance by speeding up the process of moving data.

  - *Materialized View*—Tool that allows for the precomputing of data and prejoining of tables, increasing performance by improving query performance.

  - *Bitmap Indexes*—A unique, two-dimensional index structure for fast combinations of low-cardinality data columns that improves performance by increasing response time of complex queries.

  - *Oracle Parallel Query (OPQ)*—A divide-and-conquer approach to large-table and full-table scans. OPQ improves performance by increasing the response time of complex queries.

  - *Parallel DML*—Allows for updates and changes to a database at the same time, improving data loading and manipulation speeds.

5

- *Parallel Indexing Rebuilding*—Rebuilds table indexes in a very short time, increasing the response times for data manipulation and retrieval while only requiring a single CPU system.

- *Parallel Index Scans*—Allows simultaneous full-index scans and reads of data blocks, increasing the response times for data manipulation and retrieval.

- *Parallel Backup and Recovery*—Allows backups to happen concurrently, tremendously increasing the speed of backups in large databases.

- *Oracle Connection Manager (CMAN)*—Provides scalability by supporting large volumes of concurrent user connections.

- *Oracle Streams*—A tool that provides synchronization of replicated databases, it improves performance and availability by enabling high-speed system replication, data sharing, and failover software.

Oracle Extra-Cost Enterprise Edition Options

In addition to the editions noted in the previous section, Oracle offers many optional extra-cost components for the Enterprise Edition of the database. These can be purchased separately from the Enterprise Edition features listed in the previous section and they provide an option for the added tools necessary to create a more robust database management architecture. The cost of these additional options ranges from $20 to $41,500. First and foremost, choosing the right fit for an organization requires familiarity with what optional components are available.

- *Oracle Real Application Clusters (RAC)*—An application that provides increased scalability and fault tolerance by enabling a single Oracle Database to run on a cluster of servers.

- *Oracle RAC One Nod*—An application that adds to Oracle RAC by including the ability to integrate multiple databases into one cluster, further enhancing the scalability and fault tolerance of the architecture.

- *Oracle Advanced Compression*—Tools that have been designed to provide advance compression services for all types of currently active and previously archived data objects.

- *Advanced Security Option*—An application that offers encryptions and authentication tools to keep data confidential and secure both inside the database and while in transit.

- *Oracle Data Mining*—Sophisticated suite of artificial intelligence tools designed to locate trends and predictive behavior within stored data.

- *Oracle Data Profiling and Quality*—A group of tools that verify the quality, reliability, and integrity of a database.

- *Database Vault*—Helps organizations comply with regulatory mandates (e.g., HIPAA) by providing tools that safeguard from internal threats. These sets of tools use internal controls (e.g., access rules and policies) to avoid exposure of data within the environment.

- *Label Security*—A set of tools designed to provide multitiered security capabilities for protecting data by classifying data for which access rights and privileges are then assigned and monitored.

- *Oracle In-Memory Database Cache*—Improves application transaction response times by providing enhancements in cache technology that minimize communication delays that are often due to computer hardware and processes.

- *Oracle Partitioning*—Designed for very large databases (100 GB or larger). This application partitions large tables and indexes, dividing them into smaller, more manageable components.

- *Oracle OLAP*—An online analytical processing server that provides centralized management and advanced analytical capabilities (e.g., budgeting, forecasting) for data within an environment.

- *Oracle Active Data Guard*—Improves performance and ensures data recovery by maintaining a replica of a main database to act as a secondary database for workload sharing and failsafe.

- *Oracle Real Application Testing*—Designed to ensure availability of a server by testing the potential effects that a new application will have on an environment before that application is installed.

- *Oracle Total Recall*—Designed to enable the tracking of the history of a table, for auditing and compliance purposes.

- *Oracle Spatial*—Designed to support spatial 3-D data for integration into Web and enterprise applications.

- *Oracle Change Management Pack*—Aids in the change management needs of an organization. The change management pack provides version and update control as well as manages and monitors changes on a network.

- *Oracle Configuration Management Pack*—Obtains configuration information from the network systems, and uses this information to monitor and identify the configuration of the environment, greatly lessening problem resolution time.

- *Oracle Diagnostic Pack*—Provides a set of tools that monitor and diagnose issues with the performance of the databases of an environment.

- *Oracle Provisioning and Patch Automation Pack*—A set of tools designed to provide seamless application patch deployment across an organization.

- *Oracle Tuning Pack*—Online tools providing an automatic solution to tuning of the schema structure and data usage of the Oracle database.

Licensing Options

As mentioned earlier, Oracle deployment can be quite a costly venture. A separate license is required for each edition of the Oracle Database, and the cost is dependent on the number of users utilizing the application. If the number of users cannot be identified or counted, or the cost per user is much greater than the cost of the processor, the number of processors can be used for licensing. In addition, an edition can be licensed for a specific time period. You can license an edition of Oracle Database for either one to five years or perpetually. Refer to Tables 5-4 and 5-5 for a cost comparison of the different user and processor licenses. Additional costs are required for any of the optional features described in the previous section. The specific terms of each license are provided in this section.

- *Express Edition (XE)*—This edition is free for use and distributed on a Windows or Linux platform. It is developed for servers with only one CPU, and is restricted to using 4 GB of user data and only 1 GB of RAM.

Edition	1-year license	2-year license	3-year license	4-year license	5-year license	Perpetual
Standard One	$36.00	$63.00	$90.00	$108.00	$126.00	$180.00
Standard	$70.00	$123.00	$175.00	$210.00	$245.00	$350.00
Enterprise	$190.00	$333.00	$475.00	$570.00	$665.00	$950.00

Table 5-4 Licensing cost per user

Edition	1-year license	2-year license	3-year license	4-year license	5-year license	Perpetual
Standard One	$1160.00	$2030.00	$2900.00	$3480.00	$4060.00	$5800.00
Standard	$3500.00	$6125.00	$8750.00	$10,500.00	$12,250.00	$17,500.00
Enterprise	$9500.00	$16,250.00	$23,750.00	$28,500.00	$33,250.00	$47,500.00

Table 5-5 Licensing cost per processor

- *Oracle Database Standard Edition One (SEO)*—This edition is licensed on a per-user or per-processor basis. It was developed for servers that use one to two processors. If the number of CPUs on a server exceeds two, the user must upgrade to the Standard license. There are no restrictions placed on memory usage or user data storage. To qualify for a license for this edition, there must be at least five or more users.

- *Oracle Database Standard Edition (SE)*—This edition is licensed on a per-user or per-processor basis. It was developed for servers that use four processors or fewer. If the number of CPUs on a server exceeds four, the user must upgrade to the Enterprise license. There are no restrictions placed on memory usage or user data storage. To qualify for a license for this edition, there must be at least five or more users.

- *Enterprise Edition*—This edition is licensed on a per-user or per-processor basis. It has been developed to run on servers that use four or more processors. There are no restrictions put on memory usage or user data, but it this edition requires the most cost per unit. To qualify for a license for this edition, there must be at least 25 or more users.

In per-processor licensing, the term processor is defined differently for different editions. In the Standard and Standard One editions of the database, the term *processors* refers to the number of sockets or physical CPUs. This essentially means that those processors deemed multi-core (e.g., Dual Core, Quad Core), which enable the installation of several instances of SQL Server on one machine, are only considered to be one physical CPU or socket by the Oracle licensing standards for these editions. On the other hand, the Enterprise Edition depends on the hardware being used. The core is multiplied by a specific CPU type factor. For example, to determine the licensing cost of an AMD multi-core processor, one would multiply the number of users by a factor of .50. For more information regarding Enterprise Edition's licensing by processor, see the Oracle support documentation online.

Free Unlimited Downloads of Oracle

Oracle offers a free download of all editions of the Oracle Database for purposes of education, testing, or development. Personal information (e.g., name and organization) or a license key are not required to download. The downloads permit unlimited usage of full versions of the software, and there are no restrictions on the usage of these applications. This may seem like a poor decision for Oracle, yet similarly to open-source applications, these free downloads have contributed to the development and success of Oracle. The free dowloads can be found at *http://www.oracle.com/technology/software/index.html.*

Locating Help

5

As with any major or minor hardware and software installation, being able to locate help is vital to the success of the installation as well as the future reliability of your environment. Oracle has built a well-established community consisting of users, administrators, developers, CFOs, and more. There are several opportunities to share Oracle knowledge. The Oracle community spans forums and blogs. This section covers a few of these areas.

- *Technical Support*—Several levels of technical support are offered with the licensing of Oracle. Contracts can be formed to provide aid for any product available. Whether help is necessary over the phone, in person, or online, you can find resources for a variety of concerns (e.g., technical support, database consultation, and object development). For more information regarding Oracle's technical support policy, go to *http://www.oracle.com/us/support/index.htm.*

- *Oracle Community*—The Internet continues to provide an opportunity for peer and expert support, yet there is no better resource than that which can be found within the product manufacturer's main site. The Oracle Community site maintains a number of the largest interactive member areas in the world. Here one can find forums specific for partners, CFOs, programmers, and customers. Also available on this site are blogs, user groups, and general technical support discussion areas. The Oracle Community can be found at *http://www.oracle.com/us/community/index.htm.*

- *Oracle University*—This is the No. 1 resource for educational information regarding Oracle products. This site provides videos, tutorials, self-paced courses, and instructor-led training on all things Oracle. The Oracle University can be located by going to *http://education.oracle.com.*

- *Oracle's Knowledge Center*—This resource provides a comprehensive collection of online manuals, installation guides, and release notes for all Oracle Products. Oracle's Documentation Library is located at *http://dev.mysql.com/doc/.*

- *Metalink*—Metalink is a support service provided to all Oracle customers free of charge. It is a warehouse of knowledge that users can search to find well-known issues and to obtain bug reports.

- *Bloggers*—Blogs have become a fantastic resource, especially in the technology fields. Many people who work with Oracle or have experience with the application blog about their experiences and share their knowledge at this blog site: *http://blogs.oracle.com.*

- *Twitter*—Twitter has become a popular way to keep people informed on a minute-by-minute basis. Microsoft uses Twitter as a way for users to ask questions and for Oracle professionals to send out alerts relevant to upgrades, bugs, and other software-related support at *http://twitter.com/ORACLE.*

Installation

Once a user has obtained the desired copy of Oracle, verified that the hardware and software requirements have been met, and decided on the best purpose and design (by choosing desired edition and extra-cost options) that fit the needs of the environment, installation can begin. If prerequisites have not been met, Oracle will require updates before the installation process.

The Oracle University Installer

The Oracle University Installer (OUI) is a Java-based application that provides a graphical user interface to help ease the installation of some of the most complex Oracle deployments. The OUI guides an administrator through installing Oracle using a step-by-step wizard. Using the OUI enables an administrator to record selections made within a typical Oracle installation. These recordings are placed in a file called the response file. A **response file** holds the specifications of a typical Oracle installation for the purpose of creating silent installations.

A **silent installation** is an installation of an application that completes without prompting a user for setting specifications. Silent installations use the settings recorded within response files and enable administrators to add Oracle to user machines without interruption or user interference. The OUI's silent files and response files help administrators install Oracle on a large number of machines quickly and consistently. Before performing a silent installation, administrators should familiarize themselves with the settings in the response file template for that specific Oracle product.

 For Windows installations, the OUI can be run from the system's administrative account, using the system's administrative privileges. With UNIX-based systems, an administrator must create a privilege **NOTE** from where to run the OUI.

Step-by-Step Installation for Windows

This section will include the steps for installing the Oracle Database Server on a Windows 64-bit machine. The instructional steps provided in this section are intended to provide steps for installing the Enterprise Edition 64-bit edition server using the Oracle University Installer. For this installation, the DVDs or a downloaded version of the DVD for Oracle Database are needed. In this section, the installation will derive from the downloaded version of Oracle Database 11g.

From the directory where the downloaded files were unzipped, double-click the directory setup.exe file to start the OUI (Figure 5-1).

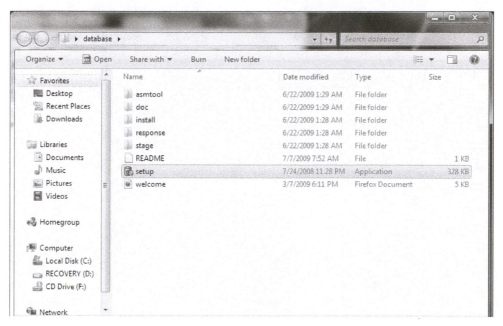

Figure 5-1 Locating the setup file
© Cengage Learning 2012

1. There are two different types of installations for the Oracle Database, basic and advanced. The basic installation creates a default database quickly and with minimal user involvement. The advanced option is for custom installations that require very specific software and database configurations. For instance, the advanced installation allows administrators to choose components of the database individually, whereas the basic installation automatically chooses the typical components, yet provides a list of non-default components from which an administrator can choose. These instructions will display a basic installation. Therefore, on the OUI welcome screen, choose the Basic Installation (Figure 5-2). The windows that appear following this selection will depend on the type of installation chosen.

The advanced installation is recommended because it limits the number of unnecessary features that are installed on a system, creating an easier environment to control and secure. The advanced installation is not shown here because the possibilities are too numerous to present, but it is highly recommended that specific features are chosen and installed individually. To see a list of available components within the custom or advanced installation of the database, choose advanced installation and then choose Custom from the Installation Type window.

The OUI welcome screen also prompts the user to provide a global name and system password for the intended database. To ensure a secure installation, be sure to create a strong database password, as Oracle will allow weak passwords for this account. For the purpose of this installation tutorial, input the database name as SecureData and the password

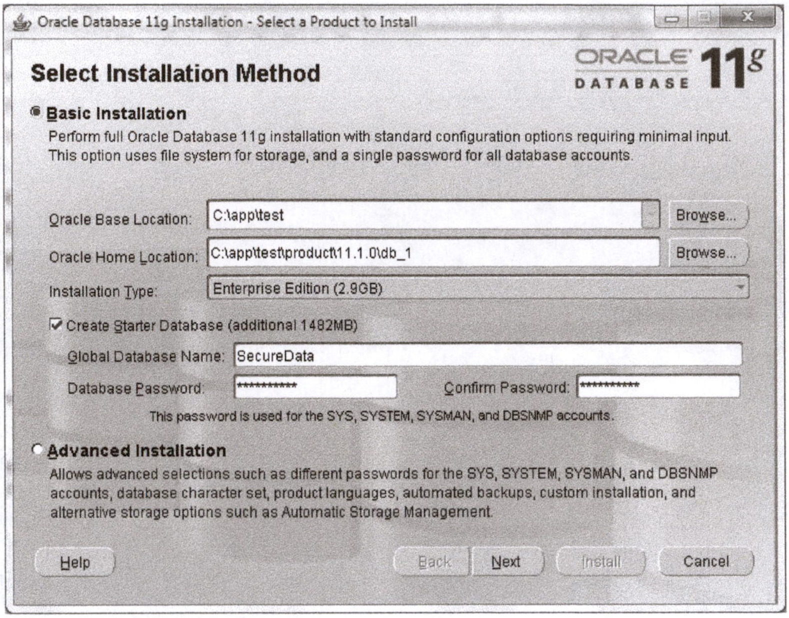

Figure 5-2 OUI welcome screen
© Cengage Learning 2012

as SecurePass. Once the installation type has been chosen and the database has been given a name and a password, click **Next**.

1. The following screen is for obtaining and receiving security and configuration updates and alerts, as well as for creating a Metalink account. Administrators are given the option to provide an e-mail address from which to be informed of security and configuration issues or to use their Metalink for these alerts (Figure 5-3). See the security section for more information regarding security and Metalink. Once this information has been input, click **Next**.

2. Oracle will now conduct a system check to ensure all prerequisites and indicate any errors found, warnings to be noted, and verification checks that were completed (Figure 5-4). If errors are found, they must be fixed before the installation can continue. Once the prerequisites have all been satisfied, click **Next**.

3. The Configuration Manager (Figure 5-5) provides an option where the administrator can have the current machine's configuration associated with their Metalink account. Click **Next** to move forward with the installation.

4. The next window displays the installation summary (Figure 5-6), a complete summary of components that will be installed on the machine. Click **Install** to begin the installation.

5. Once the installation begins, the progress window will appear, displaying the progress of the installation (Figure 5-7).

6. Once the installation completes, the Configuration Assistant Window appears (Figure 5-8) and begins the creation of the database. When complete, a

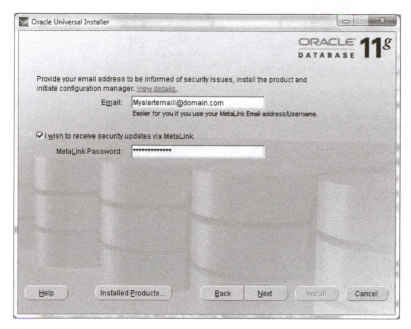

Figure 5-3 Options for receiving alerts
© Cengage Learning 2012

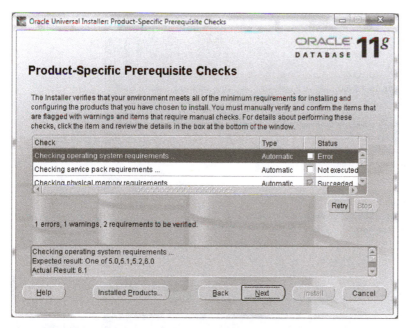

Figure 5-4 The prerequisite check
© Cengage Learning 2012

Figure 5-5 Configuration Manager
© Cengage Learning 2012

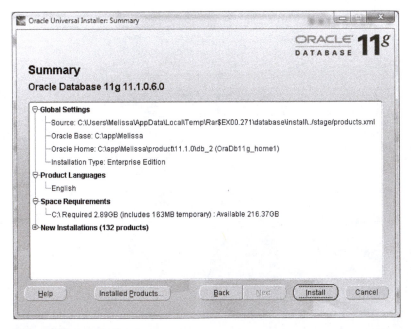

Figure 5-6 Installation Summary
© Cengage Learning 2012

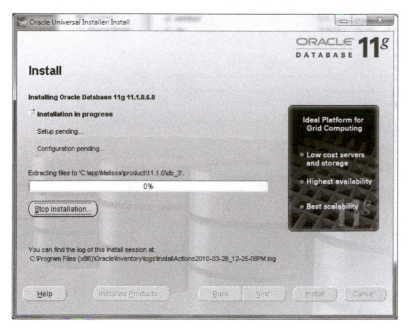

Figure 5-7 Progress window
© Cengage Learning 2012

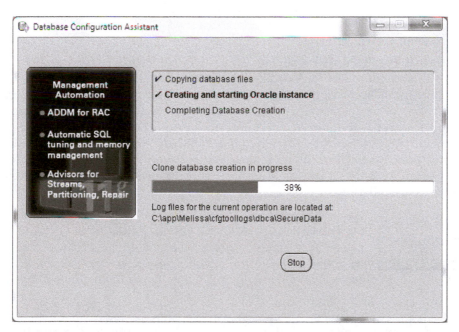

Figure 5-8 Configuration Assistant window
© Cengage Learning 2012

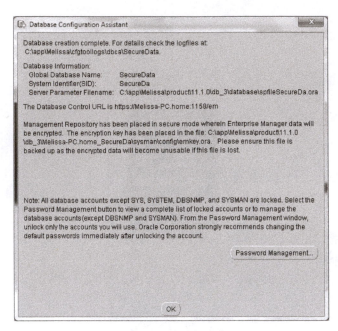

Figure 5-9 Configuration Assistant confirmation window
© Cengage Learning 2012

Configuration Assistant confirmation window will appear (Figure 5-9), providing the location of the log files, the Global Database Name, the System Identifier (SID), the server Parameter Filename, the Database Control URL, and the location of the encryption key for the Management Repository. By default, Oracle encrypts the Enterprise Management Data Repository and it is set to secure. Click **Password Management** to review the accounts that contain passwords.

7. Ensure that all unused system administrative accounts are locked (Figure 5-10). Click the cell of an account to lock it. A checkmark will be present in the column titled Lock Account? for all accounts that are currently locked. Also be sure to set strong usernames and passwords for those accounts that are left unlocked for use. It is not secure to leave default passwords for unlocked accounts unchanged. The accounts that are unlocked by default are Sys, System, DBSNMP, and SYSMAN. Once the appropriate accounts are locked or assigned strong usernames and passwords, click **OK** to return to the Configuration Assistant confirmation page and click **OK** on this page to confirm the end of the installation.

The accounts that are shown here are not locked during a manual installation of Oracle. If a manual installation of Oracle is being conducted, it is extremely important to the security of the environment that these accounts are locked and chosen to expire in correspondence with the version of Oracle that is being installed.

8. At this point, installation has completed. An installation summary and reminder page will appear (Figure 5-11). Review the information and click **Exit**, and then click **Yes** if prompted to confirm.

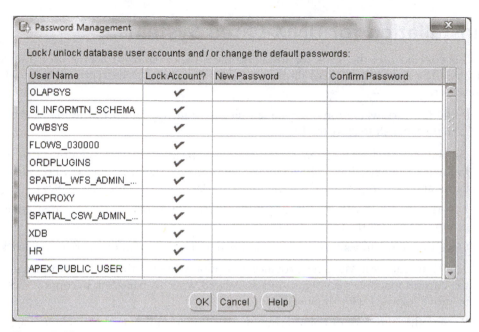

Figure 5-10 Confirm locked accounts
© Cengage Learning 2012

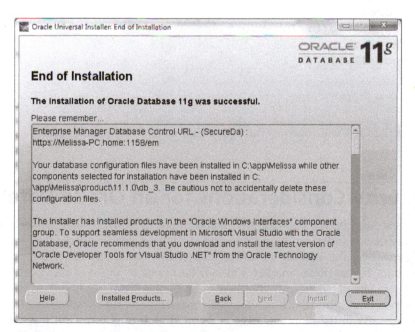

Figure 5-11 Installation summary and reminder
© Cengage Learning 2012

5

Quick Installation for UNIX-based Systems

This section includes the steps for installing the Oracle Database Server on a Linux 64-bit machine. The instructional steps displayed are for installing the Enterprise Edition 64-bit edition server.

From the directory where the downloaded files were unzipped, open a terminal window and type **./runInstaller.sh** to start the OUI.

1. On the OUI Welcome screen, choose the Basic Installation. The windows that appear following this selection will depend on the type of installation chosen. Provide a global name and system password for the intended database, and then click **Next**.

2. Ensure that the Inventory directory is the correct directory and set the operating system group name, and then click **Next**.

3. Once the prerequisites have all been satisfied and the installation is error-free, click **Next**.

4. The Configuration Manager provides an option whereby the administrator can have the current machine's configuration associated with his Metalink account. Click **Next** to move forward with the installation.

5. Review the summary of components that will be installed on the machine. Click **Install** to begin the installation.

6. Click **Password Management** to lock and assign passwords to unlocked accounts. Unlock **orainstRoot.sh** and **root.sh** as the root user.

7. Open a terminal window and type the following to verify:

```
su -
<rootpassword>
cd /u01/app/oracle/oraInventory
./orainstRoot.sh
cd ./product/11.1.0/db_1
./root.sh
exit
exit
```

8. Click **OK** on the OUI window and then click **Exit** to end the installation.

Additional Security Considerations for an Oracle Database

Maintaining a great hold on the data solution market since the early 1980s, Oracle Corporation is a well-respected and trusted organization, which accounts greatly for its success. Although less expensive and equally as efficient alternative solutions exist, Oracle holds a majority of the data management market and can be found in most of the world's largest organizations. These characteristics are the reason the Oracle database is one of the greatest commodities for potential intruders. It is vital that considerations for securing an Oracle database are addressed early in the planning stage and continue throughout the life of the system. This section addresses the basic security concerns from planning to the installation and early administration of an Oracle database.

Security Checklist

As mentioned earlier, security must be addressed in all stages of database deployment. Security planning should include administrators, network architecture engineers, and designers, as well as a best-practice strategy to keep the Oracle database secure. A multilayered approach should be considered early in the deployment stages. This section will review early Oracle security considerations at different points of deployment.

- *Harden the operating system*—Research the platform on which the database resides and identify any ports that are left open as a default setting. Close those ports that are unnecessary or not being used (e.g., FTP, Telnet).

- *Close ports for unused applications and services*—Ensure that unused applications and services of the system are not providing a channel intruders can invade. Search the system for unused applications and services and ensure that any ports that provide transit or allow communication are closed or disabled.

- *Use firewalls*—Firewalls can be used for both isolation and security for the database. It is a best practice to use firewalls whenever possible to provide an extra layer of security for the database.

- *Apply the newest security patches*—Security patches are critical to maintaining a reliable database. As security holes are found within operating systems, manufacturers create software called patches to protect these holes. Without the most up-to-date security patches, the platform is vulnerable to intrusion.

- *Restrict run time*—Run time is the system that supports the execution of a computer program. Java is an example of a run-time machine that supports the execution of Oracle. Intruders can manipulate Java (as well as other run-time machines) by redirecting the execution of a piece of malware that may be residing on the computer. Therefore, it is important that permissions are explicitly set as to who and from what location run-time systems can execute.

- *Restrict using IP address*—Just as access can be restricted using environmental object names, it also can be restricted using environmental object addresses. Minimize unwanted intruders by explicitly identifying the IP addresses or range of IP addresses that have permission through the firewall and to access the machines.

- *Include only required software*—Although this chapter has reviewed a typical installation, it is recommended that the custom installation mode is chosen within an environment. Keeping unnecessary features at a minimum will result in a less-complex environment that offers the administrator more security control.

- *Choose database security*—Newer installed versions of Oracle by default include security configuration options such as auditing and password policy settings. There is an option to disable this feature, yet doing so will limit the security options available to the administrator. Therefore, unless Security Vault is installed, do not disable security features during install.

- *Apply Oracle patches*—As mentioned, patches are extremely important to maintain a reliable platform. This is just as important to applications, so apply the newest patches to ensure that all identified security holes within Oracle have been fixed.

5

- *Use encryption to transfer*—Encryption is vital to the success of secure data transfer and storage in today's society. To apply strong security to your Oracle database, encrypt all client-to-server and client-to-client communications.

- *Use encryption to store*—Protecting the storage of your data is equally as important as protecting it in transit. Hard disks should apply encryption techniques to add an extra layer of security to the database.

- *Enforce stringent access control*—As with any discussion of security, it is important to remind readers of the importance of the principle of least privilege. In database terms, this equates to restriction of access at the row level. Row-level restriction can be cumbersome, but it will ensure that access is explicitly controlled.

- *Restrict users with operating system access*—A user with access to the operating system, or the main system directories, essentially has access to the database as well. Limiting the number of users with permission to access or modify critical operating system directories–or the paths associated with them–can greatly minimize external threats.

Take Advantage of Oracle's Security Suite

Oracle provides a number of applications to support the confidentiality, integrity, and availability of the database. Although these applications can be costly as add-ons when budgetary restrictions may limit an organization, Oracle highly suggests that careful risk-measurement studies are conducted before dismissing them altogether. Oracle's suite of security applications, such as Oracle Security, Label Security, Database Vault, Identity Management, Transparent Encryption, and Secure Backup offer a comprehensive multilayered approach to securing the environment and maintaining privacy of the data within it. These tools address each of the security items listed in this chapter by using best-practice strategies while protecting the database from both internal and external unauthorized access. Encryption, security-based data classifications, internal realms, and real-time access controls are a few of the strategies included within these applications.

Password Policies and User Accounts

During the automatic installation and configuration of Oracle Database, Oracle installs a number of preset user accounts. Measures are taken by Oracle automatically to secure these accounts. For example, unless the database is manually created, most of the default user accounts are locked and assigned passwords are set to expire. Although these measures are taken, it is necessary that administrators take steps to further secure these accounts to ensure privacy throughout the database.

A password is the first defense in maintaining a secure account. The default password for all unlocked accounts needs to be changed either during or immediately after an install. If the database is created using the interactive or progress modes, the passwords can be changed during the installation. On the other hand, if the database is created using the silent mode, the passwords are changed after the installation has completed or are specified within the specific template chosen for the database creation.

Although Oracle will allow for all administrative accounts (Sys, System, DBSNMP, and SYSMAN) to use the same password, different passwords should be specified for each. This will minimize the chance of all passwords being breached at the same time.

Whether for a user or an administrator, passwords should follow strong security standards. Oracle allows "_", "&", and "#" symbols to be used within usernames and passwords. Strong passwords use these symbols in conjunction with a mixture of letters and numbers, both lower-case and uppercase, creating a password of considerable length (8–15 characters).

Creating strong passwords for default user accounts during the installation of Oracle is only one step to ensuring secure account protection. Ensuring users in the environment follow appropriate password standards is another. This involves the creation and strict enforcement of policies within the Oracle server. Several options provided in the server environment enable administrators to develop secure policies. Here is a list of password characteristics available within the server that can be combined to develop a password policy for the environment:

- *Complexity*—A policy can be created that identifies the required length and character type combination (e.g., number, letter, upper, lower, symbols) of a password. It also determines whether a user can use common or dictionary words.

- *Failed attempts*—A password that has been attempted too many times without avail can be an indication of an intruder. Therefore, it is best to lock an account that has had too many failed password attempts. The number of failed password attempts and the way these are handled in the environment can be identified as part of the password policy.

- *Expired passwords*—This component of a password policy specifies the length of time a user can use a password before being forced to change it. This is to minimize the damage and risk that can be done if a password is breached.

- *Reused passwords*—The number of password changes that a user must wait to reuse a password is specified here.

Passwords are critical to the security of our accounts. Following best-practice guidelines such as those listed in this section, along with the creation and enforcement of policies within the Oracle server will ensure success in any environment.

Chapter Summary

- Oracle offers a number of software and hardware components that can be integrated at each level of an organization. From user interface to supporting hardware, Oracle offers a comprehensive solution to any organization.

- There are 32-bit and 64-bit versions of Oracle available. It is highly suggested that a 32-bit version of Oracle be used on a 32-bit platform, and a 64-bit version of Oracle be used on a 64-bit platform to ensure that the database applications are used to their fullest potential.

- Supported platforms for Oracle are dependent on their edition. These include all current versions of 32-bit and 64-bit Windows platforms beginning with Windows 2000. Linux Asianux 2 and 3, Oracle Enterprise Linux 4 and 5, Red Hat Linux 4 and 5, and SUSE 10 are also supported in both 32-bit to 64-bit versions. UNIX-based platforms include Solaris 9 and 10, HP-UX 11v1–3, and AIX5L and 6L. Specific service packs are required for each version of a platform.

- Four main editions of the Oracle Database are available: Express, Oracle Database Standard One, Oracle Database Standard, and Enterprise.

- Oracle Enterprise Edition is the most robust of all of the Oracle editions. This edition of Oracle includes more features embedded into the application than any other database editions available; several extra-cost options exist that extend its capability and add to its value.

- A host of tools are available as extra add-on support to the Oracle database environment. These separately installed applications can be purchased to extend the Oracle capabilities within a business architecture and include such topics as security, compression, analysis, and change management.

- Licensing can be purchased on a per-user or per-processor basis. Restrictions for Oracle applications vary based on the edition purchased. Licenses can be purchased on a yearly or perpetual basis.

- Full-featured installations of all Oracle products can be installed at no charge and without time and use restrictions by developers and users intending to learn about and test the application.

- Oracle has developed a well-established support community both online and off. A vast amount of knowledge and resources can be found to support Oracle users, developers, and administrators.

- The online Oracle Community is one of the most comprehensive and popular resources, and is a great starting point for those looking for Oracle-related tutorials, videos, blogs, and forums.

- MetaLink is a support service offered to all licensed Oracle users, providing bug reporting and technical support specific to a user's system.

- The Oracle University Installer and the Database Configuration Assistant are two tools that automate the installation of Oracle. Both of these tools can be used to create automatic or silent installations for deployment on several client or server machines at once.

- Oracle holds a majority of the data management market and can be found in most of the world's largest organizations. These characteristics are the reason the Oracle database is one of the greatest targets for potential intruders.

- Oracle offers a number of security-related applications to help organizations maintain their confidentiality, integrity, and availability. These applications also focus on privacy laws compliancy, ensuring that regulations and standards are being followed.

- Security should be multitiered and include strategies for all levels of a network and database environment. Security needs to protect an organization from both internal and external threats and include strategies for protecting network architecture, storage of data, transmission of data, and the access of information.

- Passwords are the first defense to securing a network. They should follow strict guidelines, and policies need to be created and enforced to ensure that these guidelines are being met.

Key Terms

response file A file that holds the specification of a typical Oracle installation for the purpose of creating silent installations.

silent installation An installation of an application that completes without prompting a user for setting specifications.

Review Questions

1. List the decisions a network administrator needs to make prior to Oracle database installation.

2. Explain why installing the minimum hardware requirements is not suggested.

3. The Enterprise Edition of Oracle offers both cost options and additional features. What is the difference between these two categories?

4. List the extra features and extra-cost options that are available with the Enterprise Edition of Oracle.

5. Of the additional options and features available for Oracle, identify the security-specific applications.

6. Explain the advantages and disadvantages of offering an unrestricted, freely download-able full version of Oracle Database to learners and developers.

7. List and define two support resources available through Oracle's Web site.

8. Explain how silent installations can benefit an organization.

9. Identify the differences between a basic and an advanced installation.

10. Explain two different password policies that can be enforced on an Oracle Server.

11. List three security practices to follow during installation of Oracle.

Case Projects

Case Project 5-1: Estimating Required Hardware

Write a paper defining a strategy for estimating the disk space, virtual memory, processor, and network requirements for an installation.

Case Project 5-2: Oracle University

Using Oracle's Online University, list all of the available resources currently provided within The Oracle University.

Case Project 5-3: Oracle Metalink

Explore the Metalinks resource by going to *http://support.oracle.com/CSP/ui/flash.html* and registering for a free account. Write a paper discussing the potential security risks associated with Metalink. How could hackers use Metalink to intrude into a system?

Case Project 5-4: Implementing Security Measures

Suppose that you are in charge of implementing security for a large organization. Outline the security measures that you would implement to protect a new installation of Oracle.

Hands-On Projects

Hands-On Project 5-1: Creating a Password Policy

Research all of the password variables available for a server and create a password policy to be enforced. Include characteristics such as password complexity, failed attempts, expiration, and reuse.

chapter 6

Password, Profiles, Privileges, and Roles

After reading this chapter and completing the exercises, you will be able to:

- Define authentication and then implement with SQL Server, MySQL, and Oracle
- Define authorization and then implement with SQL Server, MySQL, and Oracle
- Manage users based on security best practices using SQL Server, MySQL, and Oracle
- Identify and apply password best practices using SQL Server, MySQL, and Oracle
- Define and create roles using SQL Server, MySQL, and Oracle
- Define, grant, deny, and revoke privileges using SQL Server, MySQL, and Oracle

Tony, the database administrator for Haphazard, Inc., was desperate to redeem himself for the major loss that he had caused during the poorly executed MySQL deployment earlier this year. Hoping to regain trust and prove to his superiors that he was a security-conscious database administrator, he decided to create the most secure database environment possible.

Working many hours of overtime through the evenings and weekends, he mapped out each employee's database usage and created a plan that implemented a high level of granularity for object privileges and access control. Feeling confident that a layered approach to security was the best strategy, he opted against Windows authentication and created separate login accounts for users to access the database. Roles were developed based on privileges and the appropriate users were assigned to these roles.

Just as the final touches were being placed on the database, he received a message from his managers requesting a meeting. Excited to present his new security strategy to his managers, he eagerly accepted. Much to Tony's surprise, the meeting was set up to discuss his "early" retirement from Haphazard, Inc. Management felt that he hadn't displayed any progress with the new database and, in fact, they had been receiving a number of complaints from users regarding limited database access and excessive required logins.

To Tony's dismay, management informed him that he had been replaced. Infuriated with this decision, Tony returned to his desk to pack his things. Along with his boxes of desk toys, Tony took with him a few of the other employees' login credentials. Having opted out of Windows Authentication mode, Tony knew that his database account was separate from his Windows account and that even the most experienced database administrator (DBA) would have a difficult time removing it from the database. This meant that he only needed to aquire basic user-level Active Directory credentials to access the company's Windows system from his home computer. With this access, he would be able to log in to his own privileged database account (providing that it wasn't removed right away), giving him full reign over the Haphazard database once again. As he walked out of the building with his belongings in hand, he smiled, knowing that he would get the last laugh after all.

An endless number of disastrous scenarios come to mind when considering the implications of even one small mistake within user account management. User accounts, and the privileges assigned to them, should be carefully planned and monitored throughout any organization.

(continued)

As was discussed in previous chapters, databases often contain business-critical data, such as credit card numbers, customer account information, and company financial statistics. A loss or theft of this data can be devastating to any organization.

Thus far, we have examined steps to securely install a database and have explored ways to protect data traveling to and from the environment. The next, and arguably most important, step toward creating a safe and reliable database environment is to avoid unauthorized access. This chapter explores the steps that administrators can take to ensure proper authentication and authorization of those users attempting to access a database.

Authentication

It takes a great deal of time and effort to ensure that access to a database remains secure. Several layers of security must be put into place to ensure that data is only granted to those authorized individuals and applications. There are two main steps to controlling access to data: authentication and authorization. Authorization is discussed later in this chapter. **Authentication** is the process of confirming the identity of those individuals or applications that request access to a secure environment. Confirming the identity of a person or an application is done by verifying that the login and credentials match those that have been created within that same environment.

A **login** is an object that is mapped to a user account within each database and is associated to users by the security identifier or SID. Logins differ from user accounts in that a login is required for authentication into the environment and a user account is used to control activities performed within that environment. This is a very specific distinction because there are default logins created during the installation of a database that must be managed correctly. Consequently, there are default user accounts that must be managed correctly as well. User accounts are discussed later in this chapter.

A **credential** is a piece of information that is used to verify identity, such as a person's username and password, an application's secure ID, or a host's network name and address. The types of credentials that are used to verify the identity of a user or an application depend on the requirements and authentication processes of a particular system or environment. Although usernames and passwords might be sufficient for some environments, additional requirements, such as host addresses and security identification numbers, might be required for others.

Authentication can be verified a few times and at different levels during a single attempt at logging in to a system before permission is granted to a user. For example, SQL Server checks the authentication of a user at the server level to establish a connection to the server and at the database level to establish access to the database. Third-party applications can also be used within a database environment to further add security to the authentication of users because they often take additional steps, such as password encryption, to keep a network environment secure. This section reviews the three most common levels of authentication found in a database environment: the operating system level, the database level, and third-party support. Combined, these levels make for a secure environment, but using one alone can bring great advantages and disadvantages to the security of the environment.

Operating System Authentication

Credentials that are authenticated primarily through the operating system must have an account residing on that particular operating system and the operating system account credentials must be used to access the system. In some cases, an operating system login alone can be used to authenticate users to the database. This means that if the user has an operating system account residing on the system and these credentials are used, no other logins are necessary to access the database. Authentication through the operating system allows users to conveniently connect to the database without specifying a database username or password, skipping database login prompts altogether. This type of authentication also provides DBAs with the advantage of centralized account administration because all accounts are located in one place and each individual requires only one set of credentials to be managed.

With operating system authentication, workstations and user accounts must be monitored much more diligently. If an unauthorized individual obtains user credentials for accessing the operating system or gains access to an unattended workstation, they inherit access to the database as well. It does not take much knowledge or skill to access the database from the operating system.

Database Authentication

Credentials that are checked against the database require that the user attempting to access the system has a local database account therein. In this situation, the user may be required to access a few different systems prior to reaching the database. This means that users must keep different account credentials for different systems. This often leads to poor password practices, such as writing passwords down and choosing weak passwords, for memory's sake. Administration of this type of environment is also more difficult. Administrators must not only keep track of more than one account for each individual, but often these accounts are located in separate areas, making audit tracking a very difficult feat. On the other hand, separate accounts for separate systems can create a more segmented and secure environment. Those intruders who gain unauthorized access to a user's operating system password or machine will also need to obtain the database credentials to access it.

Network or Third-Party Authentication

Authentication for a database can also be conducted using third-party applications and at the network level of the environment. Third-party applications and network account authentication systems can be used for remote and physical environments. These users are not required to have an account created on the operating system or the database; however, they are required to have a network account or be recognized by the third-party application. For example, a type of external authentication is a smart card. Smart cards require the user to insert a PIN for authentication; this PIN is unrelated to the OS and the database. Secure protocols such as Kerberos are often used for network and third-party authentication as well. These protocols require greater technical experience and know-how, yet they add a much-needed layer of security to any database environment.

Kerberos is an authentication protocol that was built by MIT to provide secure means for authentication using symmetric-key cryptology to verify the identity of a client to a server and a server to a client. Once a client and server have used Kerberos to prove their identity, they can also encrypt all of their communications to ensure privacy throughout the transaction.

The Kerberos process begins when a user or application attempts to log in to an environment using an application or a Web form using the Kerberos protocol. When a user attempts to access the environment, a request for a ticket to get a ticket, also known as a ticket-granting ticket (TGT) is sent to a server known as the Key Distribution Center (KDC). The KDC sends the user back an encrypted response with the original password hash and the TGT embedded within a message. If the message is sent back to the KDC by the user decrypted and with the original TGT, then a service called the Ticket-granting service (TGS) located within the KDC assigns the user a service ticket. A **service ticket** is a unique key that is used to validate a person's identification (similar to a driver's license or smart card ID), for the purpose of gaining access into a secured environment. The assigned service ticket is sent to the network or database the user wants to access, and if appropriately verified, the user obtains access. It is important to note that it is only necessary for the user to log in once when using Kerberos; each resource that is requested after the original login will check the requestor's ticket as a way to authenticate that user.

Now, let's review this process again, this time using a simple example that will help you better understand what happens throughout the Kerberos process.

Let's assume that there is a secret group of individuals known as the World Bank Database Society (WBDS). Members of this society have control over the world's banking system, so obtaining access to the WBDS would provide an individual with the tools needed to attain wealth or financial security.

To acquire access to the WBDS, an applicant must first be given the secret password (a service ticket), which they can only obtain through a trusted source (the KDC), or a partner of the WBDS. So, in order to receive the secret password and subsequently use it to request membership into the WBDS, the applicant must know where to find a trusted source (KDC), obtain access to the trusted source (authentication), and request the password information needed for requesting membership into the society (TGT).

Once deemed fit for membership (authenticated through the KDC), the trusted source gives the person a photo ID that includes the encrypted version of the password, the location of the secret society, and the applicant's identification information (service ticket). The WBDS can't send the applicant the real password because it would jeopardize its secrecy, so the applicant uses a photo ID (service ticket) as a way to locate the secret society and subsequently request membership. If the society finds that an applicant has been approved by the trusted source and that the photo ID contains the correct password, decrypted, then the applicant is offered membership or access into the World Bank Database.

Network authentication can also use other security protocols to validate a person's identity. Another common security technique is known as public key infrastructure (PKI). PKI utilizes encrypted keys similar to the way in which Kerberos issues TGTs, yet it verifies a requester's identity by assigning a digital certificate to a user for authentication into secure environments. A **digital certificate** is a password-protected and encrypted file that holds the identity of a user or object. A digital certificate is essentially a digital document that is issued by a trusted central authority. Individuals and companies can obtain digital certificates for a fee through a trusted authority such as VeriSign. A digital certificate can also be assigned after an identity verification process similar to that of public key infrastructure, or PKI. It is important that network or third-party external authentication is carefully considered and that the technology used for authentication is researched thoroughly prior to its implementation because although network authentication uses sophisticated cryptology to authenticate users, it poses a greater risk to a network due to its exposure to the public network.

Third-party or external authentication is not recommended to be used alone, yet it can be combined with OS and server authentication to create an ideal security scenario for any environment.

Database Vendor–Specific Authentication Components

There are a few important differences in the way that authentication is handled between different database vendors. This section explores the differences regarding authentication modes between SQL Server, Oracle, and MySQL.

SQL Server Authentication Information
SQL Server supports two types of authentication modes, Windows Authentication mode and Mixed Mode Authentication. **Windows Authentication mode** is a form of authentication that only allows Windows authentication to be used for accessing the database; users logging in to the database must have a Windows login to access it. Windows authentication is also known as trusted authentication because of the security enforced through Windows. This is the default mode during installation and it is the recommended authentication mode for SQL Server. It is much more secure than the alternative. It uses the Kerberos protocol and requires strong passwords and password expiration (discussed later in the chapter).

Once a user is able to log in using his or her Windows account, user verification is confirmed by Windows and no further credentials are needed to access the database server. SQL Server authentication is disabled when Windows authentication is chosen. **Mixed Mode Authentication** is a form of authentication that allows both Windows authentication and SQL Server authentication to be used to obtain access into the database; therefore, the database will accept both Windows and Server logins. Yet, to access a SQL server using Mixed Mode Authentication, a user must supply two separate sets of credentials. As mentioned previously, this multiaccount approach poses a difficulty for administration and security of database users. This mode is also known as an "untrusted" connection because it is not as secure as Windows Authentication mode and because protocols such as Kerberos cannot be used. Mixed Mode Authentication is most appropriate for environments with older operating systems and mixed operating system environments.

MySQL Authentication Information
MySQL uses an authentication protocol for access to the server and it identifies users slightly differently than SQL Server and Oracle do. A MySQL user's identity is verified using three pieces of information:

- The host name for which the server is running
- The user-supplied MySQL username
- The user-supplied password

To access the database, the identity credentials must match those credentials stored in the database. The username is separate from login names that are managed by the operating system, and management of a username is separate from a login name. There is no way to synchronize this management, so they remain separate and distinct from one another. The password is also separate; there is no relationship between the MySQL password and the one used for the operating system. Host names can be given as an IP address, and the host name does not have to be provided if the host that is trying to authenticate is on the same machine as the server. These three components are stored in three user table scope columns (host, user, and password). The connection is only permitted if the host and user columns in some user table row match the client host name and username and the client supplies the password that is specified in that row.

Oracle Authentication Information Oracle supports many options for authenticating users, applications, and machines, and it provides customization options to support almost any environment. Database servers, database links, and environment passwords can all be used as credentials for authentication within Oracle 11g, and several additional applications are available to be purchased to further enhance the security of the database infrastructure.

One of the more notable services that can be purchased and added to Oracle as a way to further enhance authentication is *Advanced Security*. Advanced Security is a comprehensive security application. It offers encryption of both information transmitting across the network and stored within the database and provides strong and proxy authentication strategies that support and integrate with the industry-standard authentication methods (e.g., Kerberos, PKI, and SSL).

In addition to the applications that can be added onto the environment, Oracle offers a number of applications that are built to mediate the communication between the database environment and the external Web resource. These are known as middleware applications. Middleware applications are designed to monitor external requests that are sent to obtain access to the database, and the database environment's responses to these requests. Middleware applications that offer strong authentication and authorization include: Server Certificate Authority, Oracle Identity Federation, and Oracle Operating System Authentication Services.

The Oracle database management system itself includes many strategies that help ensure proper authentication of the database environment as well. Database linking is an example of one feature that enhances authentication support. Database links can be created in Oracle, allowing users to access data from remote servers without additional credentials. A **database link** is a link made between two databases that, when created, results in one logical data storage unit. Links are created to apply common policies and to create associations between databases. Database links can be both private and public. Private linked databases can only be accessed by the user who created the link itself; public linked databases are available to all users who have access to the databases. Database links allow two physically separate databases to be logically combined for data maintainence, storage, and retrieval. When a public database link is made between two physically separate databases, users view and access them together as one logical data storage unit.

Two authentication methods are supported between database links: *current user* and *connect to user*. A current user authentication method for a database link requires the current user's credentials (CURRENT_USER), and all users must have an account in all of the linked databases to be accessed. If the database link is created with *connect to user* authentication, the user account must exist in the remote database only.

Password Policies

Passwords are the key to opening a user account. Ask any experienced database administrator—he or she would not deny that most intrusions into a system originate from a cracked or stolen user password. An endless amount of money, time, and resources are wasted due to password vulnerability. Password policy implementation should be the first defense for any organization desiring to lower the risk of compromised user passwords. Password policies can be enforced within the database server application as well as within the workplace's written user agreements. That is, policies can be defined within the database system, or they can be written as a formal agreement of acceptable computer use between management and employees. Database server password policies that are configured within the database are enforced throughout the database management system. They are much more effective than written policy, because users cannot violate them, yet written policies can result in negative consequences (e.g., demotions, suspensions) and raise awareness of the need for security. Therefore, both written and server-defined policies should be used within any database environment for maximum effectiveness.

Database-Enforced Password Policies

Although written password policy agreements are effective, an organization should never rely solely on the confidence that users will follow written policies. Users are the weakest component within any security architecture. Mistakes happen and, far too often, users do not follow written policies as they should. As a security professional, it is best to remove user decisions and implement database server–enforced policies. Options that are available within a server for creating strong password policies are often vendor specific, yet most server applications share similar configuration settings. This section identifies the common password settings found within a database management environment. Database administrators and security professionals set the ground rules for employees defining acceptable use of equipment and technology within an organization. The following four different attributes of passwords can be enforced in almost every database server:

- *Complexity*—A policy can be created that identifies the required length and character type combination (e.g., number, letter, uppercase, lowercase, symbols) of a password. It also determines whether a user can use common or dictionary words.

- *Failed attempts*—A password that has been attempted too many times without avail can be an indication of an intruder. Therefore, it is best to lock an account that has had too many failed password attempts. The number of failed password attempts and the way in which these are handled can be identified as part of the password policy.

- *Expired passwords*—This component of a password policy specifies the length of time a user can use a password before being forced to change it. This is to minimize the damage and risk that can be done if a password is breached.

- *Password reuse*—The number of password changes that a user must make before being allowed to reuse a password is specified here.

Written Password Policies

Written policies are often included in some type of equipment usage agreement between an organization and its employees. Even though the database management system automatically restricts users' abilities, database-enforced passwords from the previous section are included within the usage agreement as well. Too often, written policies are not consistently enforced within an organization because from a business standpoint, these policies are often not viewed as critical to meeting the business needs. For example, a common policy included within a usage agreement forbids users from sharing passwords. Imagine this scenario: The vice president of the organization is attending a meeting at a remote office and realizes that she left a few files back on her office PC that are vital to the success of the meeting. The vice president calls her administrative assistant and asks him to log on to the computer to retrieve the important files. The vice president then provides the administrative assistant her username and password credentials to enable the assistant to obtain access to the PC to send the files. Although this is a clear violation of the policy, the vice president justifies the violation as being required and critical for overall success.

A usage agreement must be flexible enough to be consistently enforced throughout each level of an organization and yet strict enough to ensure that users abide by the policy.

Many different types of standards can be included within a written password policy, and these will vary depending on the organization, yet this section provides a list of common standards that are likely to be included in an equipment usage agreement between an IT group and its users:

- *Password discretion*—Usage agreements commonly include a policy that informs users not to tell their password to anyone in the organization. In some environments, users are even forbidden to tell their technical support group their password. In one organization, an intruder sent an e-mail to all employees claiming to be the technical support group. The e-mail directed users to reply back with a list of current passwords, explaining it as an ongoing effort toward increased quality control. Although some security-conscious users phoned the IT group to confirm the request, many provided a list without a second thought. This is one example of why users are instructed to keep their passwords private, despite who might be requesting them. Some organizations do not restrict users from communicating their password to the IT team, and instead use a variation of this policy by stating that users should never provide their password to IT through e-mail, through instant message, or by phone. This ensures that the user physically sees a person face-to-face before providing his or her password.

- *Password sharing*—Users must agree to never share their password with any other employee in the organization. It isn't uncommon for users to share their passwords with one another. This often occurs in cases where one employee has access to a resource that a coworker needs to use to complete a specific task. Using a coworker's access to the resource is often much faster and less bothersome than calling the IT group to have a new account created or access granted. Consider this scenario: Joan's supervisor is short on time and asks Joan to help her with her quarterly report by compiling specific data. Joan agrees, but quickly realizes that she does not have access to the database tables that she needs to gather some of the data. Knowing that her coworker Betty does have this access, she asks her for help. Both Betty and Joan agree that calling the IT group to obtain the appropriate access would be too cumbersome and take up too much time. Therefore, Betty walks to Joan's computer and logs in to the database using her own credentials so that Joan can gather the information that she needs.

- *Password storage*—Many equipment usage policies do not permit users to store a password on or around their desks and some demand that users never write passwords down. Although the justification for this is clear, it is important that policies be realistic in the demands that they place on users. The typical network environment user must keep track of an average of three to four different passwords (this number is drastically lowered if single sign-on strategies or Windows Authentication mode are implemented) within their organization. Users are asked not to write these passwords down. This is not an unreasonable request alone, yet when combined with other password policies, this can be quite a great expectation. For example, if an employee has three passwords to remember and these three passwords change every 30 days, this can be difficult. Now imagine a scenario in which a nontechnical user is required to remember three different passwords that change every 30 days and that they are required to create passwords using unrecognizable words, symbols, numbers, and uppercase letters. In addition to this, that same user can only reuse a password every 10th password change, or every 300 days. This expectation is much higher! This is one case where security can add a great deal of complexity. If password storage policies are not realistic, then an organization can be setting up a system that is doomed to fail.

Database Vendor–Specific Password Management

There are a few important differences in the way passwords are managed from one type of database to another. This section explores the differences in how passwords are managed between SQL Server, MySQL, and Oracle.

SQL Server Password Policy SQL Server can use the same password policy methods as available within Windows Server. Password complexity, password expiration, and enforcing password policy are the three password policy methods that are available. The following password complexity requirements are necessary for creating a new password in SQL Server:

- Passwords should be unique and cannot include common words, reserved words, or account usernames.

- Passwords should be between 8 and 30 characters, but can be as long as 128 characters.

- Passwords can include the underscore (_), dollar sign ($), and number sign (#) characters.

- At least one digit and one alphabetic character must be included within a password; however, a user cannot begin the password with a number.

Password policies can be reconfigured and customized for each user login using the ALTER LOGIN function.

MySQL Password Policy MySQL alone does not provide password enforcement, so for policy enforcement, MySQL database administrators must rely on the operating system and third-party applications for help. Passwords are stored in 45-bit encryption in the user table, allowing them to be verified and checked, but not reconstructed or viewed by outside resources. In other words, the existence of a password in the user table can be verified by an attacker and an attacker can obtain access to the user table, but there is no way for him to reconstruct and obtain the original text. MySQL passwords are case sensitive, can vary in length, and special characters can be used. One application created and built specifically for MySQL to aid in password enforcement is Securich, which is an open source security package. You can find Securich at *www.securich.com/*.

Oracle Password Policy Oracle passwords are stored encrypted in the DBA_USER table and they provide user authentication for a client/server environment. Oracle provides several built-in password protection services that go to great lengths to maintain the privacy of a password. Case sensitivity, password hashing, and password complexity checking are only a few of the strategies used in securing passwords in Oracle. Oracle verifies the complexity of a password using a built-in program or script, (UTLPWDMG.SQL), and passwords that do not meet the default complexity criteria are not accepted. The following are the default complexity requirements verified for Oracle database accounts:

- Passwords should be unique and cannot include simple words, server names, account usernames, server names with numbers added, or account usernames with numbers appended.
- Passwords should be between 8 and 30 characters, but can be as long as 128 characters.
- A new password must differ from the previously used password by at least three letters.
- At least one digit and one alphabetic character must be included within a password, yet the password cannot begin with a number.
- Passwords can include an underscore (_), a dollar sign ($), and a number sign (#).
- Passwords beginning with a special character or passwords containing any character other than _, $, and # must be surrounded by quotation marks.

Password verification parameters can be customized by changing the PASSWORD_VERIFY function in the UTLPWDMG.SQL script file. A **user profile**, or a set of rules that limits a user's access to database resources, can be used to set password restrictions as well. A user profile can be created using the CREATE_PROFILE command. Table 6-1 contains Oracle's password-specific functions, along with their default installation settings.

Feature	Default setting	Comments
FAILED_LOGIN_ATTEMPTS	10	Number of allowable failed login attempts before the account is locked
PASSWORD_LIFE_TIME	180	Number of days that the password is valid
PASSWORD_REUSE_TIME	Unlimited	Number of days that must pass before a password can be reused
PASSWORD_REUSE_MAX	Unlimited	Number of times a password can be reused
PASSWORD_LOCK_TIME	1	Number of days an account is locked due to failed attempts
PASSWORD_GRACE_TIME	7	Number of days ahead of expiration that the user is warned

Table 6-1 Oracle password-related functions

Authorization

Once data is authenticated, or a system has verified the identity of a user or login, a set of predefined permissions determine which databases or database objects are able to be accessed. The process for which permissions are applied to a user is known as authorization. **Authorization** is the process of ensuring that those individuals or applications that request access to an environment or an object within that environment have the permission to do so. Basically, authentication verifies the identity, whereas authorization verifies the ability of that identity. Authorization is determined prior to a user obtaining authentication credentials. In fact, early in the planning process of a database management system, an administrator analyzes the work environment and determines each user's appropriate access to the database. User management is critical and choosing the most appropriate privileges for each user in an organization helps maintain a healthy and secure database. This section reviews user management and logins, including the privileges and roles that they are assigned.

User Account Management

Proper administration of users is important in controlling the security and access of the database. The most common activities that a database administrator will perform on a database involve user management. At the bare minimum, a DBA must know how to properly add, remove, and assign privileges to the users in his environment. Another important thing that any security-conscious DBA should know is the user accounts and privileges that are created by default during the installation of a the database management system. This section explores the concerns related to adding, removing, and assigning privileges within an environment as well as explores the default users and user privileges.

Default User Accounts

In virtually every type of database, default user accounts are created with predefined user access. Most of these default users created during install are the system or administration accounts, holding access to just about anything in the database. Information about these accounts, such as default passwords and usernames, rights and privileges, and account accessibility, can be easily found conducting a simple search online. Therefore, leaving these accounts untouched can provide a way for intruders to access and have free reign over your data. This section identifies the default passwords created in SQL Server, MySQL, and Oracle.

Default Users Installed with SQL Server During the installation of SQL Server, three main default logins and user accounts are created and configured. Two administrator accounts, *SA* and *BUILT-IN\Administration*, and one general PUBLIC account, *Guest*, are created. As you may recall from earlier in this chapter, we discussed the difference between a login and a user account. As you read this section and explore the default logins for SQL server, keep in mind that a login is mapped to a user account and is used to authenticate, whereas user accounts are used to authorize.

- SA is the system administrator login and it holds great power on the database. SA uses SQL Server Authentication, so if Mixed Mode Authentication is chosen during the installation of SQL Server, a strong password must be set to complete the installation process. If Windows Authentication mode is chosen during setup, SA is created, but is disabled because it will not be needed.

- The BUILT-IN\Administration login is mapped to the user account dbo, the only actual user created with the database install. The dbo stands for database owner, which means that it holds ownership of the database's default schema. The database owner Guest is another specialized user of the database and, by default, is a member of the PUBLIC role (discussed later in this chapter). The Guest account is not needed and should be removed whenever possible.

Default Users Installed with MySQL During the installation of MySQL, four default accounts are created, two root accounts and two anonymous-user accounts. Initially, no passwords are set for any of these accounts and to remain secure, passwords should be assigned immediately during installation. The root accounts allow administration of the database, so it is especially important that this account is given a password right away.

When installing MySQL on Windows, one of the root accounts is used for local connections only, whereas the other is configured for remote access. Conversely, one anonymous account is for connections from the local host, with no global permissions, whereas the other has all privileges for any test databases.

Default Users Installed with Oracle The number and type of default accounts created during an Oracle installation can vary greatly, as they depend on the options, features, and additions that are chosen to be installed. Three different types of accounts can be created—administrative, nonadministrative, and sample user—and each of these types has several types of user accounts. Thankfully, most of these accounts are created to expire and be locked after installation. Only three accounts are created during installation and open for use automatically after installation: SYS, SYSMAN, and SYSTEM. The SYS account is similar to the sa account found in SQL Server; it permits administrative tasks to be performed within the database. The SYSMAN account also allows database administration, but specifically for Oracle Enterprise Manager; any administrative duties in relation to this feature are done using this account. SYSTEM is the default generic database administrator account for Oracle databases. SYS and SYSTEM are automatically granted the DBA role, but SYSTEM is the only account that should be used to create additional tables and views that are used by Oracle. SYS owns the base tables and base views for the database, yet tables should never be modified by the SYS user. Default passwords are created for these three accounts; however, they are generic passwords that can be found online, so it is extremely important that you change these account passwords.

Adding and Removing Users

Adding users to a database is a fairly straightforward process if the database administrator has planned appropriately and is prepared with user privileges and accessibility predefined. During the creation of a user account, security and access rights are also applied. Without proper documentation and careful consideration, a user account can expose the database to many types of security risks and violations. Always change the default password of a new user or force the change of a password prior to server entry. As a best practice, save user passwords in an encrypted file and enforce strong password policies to keep the database safe. Whenever possible, use different logins and passwords for different applications. This helps to minimize a user's access to unnecessary information and limits an intruder as well. Before providing access to the database, ensure that a user receives, reads, and agrees to the organization's policies on appropriate database usage. Policies hold great power in the security of a network.

Removing a user can be a bit more complicated. When user accounts are removed from a system, so are all of the objects for which that specific user had ownership; depending on the user's role in the company, this can be quite a disaster. Before removing any user from a database, perform a careful inventory of the user's created objects and back up the user account. It is strongly recommended, whenever possible, to disable a user account—instead of deleting it—and always document removals of database user accounts.

The most important component when adding and deleting accounts is documentation. Organizational policies should exist that include standardized steps for adding and removing users and all changes or additions to user accounts should be documented thoroughly.

User Privileges

The smallest unit of authorization is a privilege. A **privilege** is the ability to access a specific database resource or to perform a specific action within a database. Examples of privileges include deleting a row, creating a table, or executing a procedure. Users can either be given or denied privileges, or privileges can be grouped together creating a specific role for which users can be a member. Privileges should be planned out well in advance and early in the planning stages of the database. A critical review of the database environment's user needs is necessary to properly assign privileges. Privileges should be carefully considered and follow the principle of least privilege. The **principle of least privilege** is a security standard by which each user added to a system is given the minimum set of privileges that he or she requires to conduct legitimate business within that system. User privileges can be managed by granting, denying, or revoking them within a database:

- *Granting a privilege*—The act of providing a user with permission to access or perform an action within a database

- *Denying a privilege*—The act of explicitly preventing a user from accessing or performing an action within a database

- *Revoking a privilege*—The act of taking away or reversing a previously granted or denied privilege

Privileges can be managed at different levels of the environment. The granularity at which privileges can be managed depends on the database vendor. Privileges should be allocated to individuals on a need-to-use basis only to protect the data integrity of a system. There are two ways to grant a privilege:

- *Fixed*—Fixed privileges are predefined by the server. They are often grouped together as one group to which users are assigned.

- *Single statement*—Single statement privileges are assigned individually to individual specific users of the database.

Which one of these techniques is used is dependent on the need of the database. As you will see in the next section, grouping together privileges can be very handy and efficient when assigning permissions on a system. Such grouping saves a great deal of time and resources.

Assigning Privileges in SQL Server   Three levels of permissions can be granted within SQL Server: server-level, database-level, and object-level. Server-level privileges allow users access to certain tasks at the server level. These are fixed, which means that they are predefined and grouped by the SQL server to fit the needs of specific user accounts. Fixed, server-level privilege groups cannot be altered or removed and are only meant for specific accounts that exist on the server; it is important that administrators become familiar with these privileges to avoid redundancy within the server. For example, sysadmin is a default account that is created in SQL Server during installation. This account is assigned a fixed group of privileges meant to meet the needs of the system administrator. Changes to the sysadmin account cannot be altered. Database-level privileges are granted in one of two ways, fixed and single statement. Privileges granted at the database level can be fixed, and similar to fixed server privileges, they are grouped together and predefined by SQL Server to fit the needs of a specific user account. Privileges can also be single statements, which are granted manually to specific users. Object-level permissions are granted using the GRANT, REVOKE, and DENY statements. You can grant object permissions to individual users or roles (roles are discussed in the next section).

To grant a permission:

GRANT *privileges* ON *object* TO *user*

To grant single statement permission using Enterprise Manager:

1. Open the Enterprise Manager interface.
2. Choose the plus sign to expand the server that contains the database in which you want to grant the single statement permissions.
3. Open the properties box for the database.
4. Click the Permissions tab.
5. Place a check mark in the permission that you would like to grant.
6. Click OK.

Assigning Privileges in MySQL MySQL uses tables and columns for storing and organizing privileges. Columns that hold privileges always end with the _priv name; tables in which these columns can be found vary, and are dependant on the level of privilege. Five levels of privileges can be granted within MySQL:

-   Global privileges apply to all databases and are stored in the mysql.user table. Global privileges should be avoided when possible, as one mistake can cause a great security breach on the database.

    To grant global privileges:

    GRANT *privilege_list* ON *.*

-   Database privileges apply to all objects of a specific database. These are stored in the mysql.db and mysql.host tables.

    To grant database privileges to all users for all tables on a specific database:

    GRANT ALL on *db_name*.*

-   Table object privileges apply to all columns in a given table. These are stored in the mysql.tables_priv table.

    To grant table privileges for all columns on a specific table of a database:

    GRANT ALL on *db_name.table_name*

-   Column object privileges apply to one or more columns in a given table of a specific database. These are stored in the mysql.columns_priv table.

    To grant SELECT privileges on two columns (col1 and col2) to a user on the table located in the database user_db:

    GRANT SELECT (col1.col2) ON user_db.table_name
    TO 'user'@'hostaddress';

- Routine privileges apply to stored routines (functions and procedures), such as CREATE ROUTINE, ALTER ROUTINE, EXECUTE, and GRANT. These can be granted at the global and database levels. These are stored in the mysql.procs_priv table.

 Where global privileges provide access for all objects of a database, object privileges are more specific to certain database objects. Object privileges are more time and resource intensive, but they are more secure.

For MySQL, the GRANT command is used to provide access to a privilege; it will also create a new user at the same time you are giving that user privileges. For example, if a statement is created to GRANT a nonexistent user a privilege, that user will be created and the privilege will be granted at the same time. The ability to grant privileges is limited to those that are already owned by the person trying to grant privileges. In other words, no user can grant a privilege that he or she does not already hold.

MySQL uses tables to hold various administrative tasks and privileges. These tables are called grant tables. Table 6-2 displays an overview of these tables as well as their privileges.

Table name	Privilege
user	Contains global privileges and specifies which users can access MySQL Server and from what servers they can access it
db	Specifies which users can access the MySQL database
host	For those not listed in db, provides information on which host names can access the database
tables_priv	Identifies which users can access which tables in a database
column_priv	Identifies which users can access which columns of a table
Procs_priv	Identifies which users are permitted to execute individual stored procedures

Table 6-2 **Grant tables for privilege administration**

Assigning Privileges in Oracle Two levels of privileges can be granted in Oracle: system-level and object-level. Only administrators or those who have been given permission by an administrator can grant system privileges to others, whereas object privileges can be granted to a user by the schema owner of that object. A user account created within Oracle holds no privileges, not even enough to connect to the database. Privileges are granted based on need, which is the recommended approach for all database design. Privileges can also be granted to PUBLIC. A privilege granted to PUBLIC grants the privilege to all database users on the database. It is recommended never to use PUBLIC when assigning privileges; granular approaches are the most secure and reliable. One wrong PUBLIC privilege can cause a great security breach on the database.

To grant permissions in Oracle using PL/SQL:

```
grant privileges on object to user;
```

To grant permissions in Oracle using the Enterprise Manager security tool:

1. Open Enterprise Manager and select the database.
2. Click the Users link and select the user for whom you want to grant permissions.
3. Click the Object Privileges link and choose the privileges that you want to grant.
4. Click OK.

Roles

Related privileges can be combined to create a role, used to centrally manage a group of objects or users within a database. A **role** is a set of related privileges that are combined to provide a centralized unit from which to manage similar users or objects of a database. Consider an enterprise telemarketing company, CallsRus, that recently hired 2000 salespeople in their sales department to fill the position of *cold call salesperson*. Based on the job duties of the *cold call salesperson*, the DBA determines that he will need to grant these individuals privileges to read and update tables for when they speak to customers, and he will need to deny them privileges to delete tables so that they cannot delete customers from the company database. The DBA is aware that individually assigning these privileges would take quite a bit of time and resources and that if individually assigned, any future management of these privileges will be very cumbersome. So, the DBA creates a role named CLDCLL_SALES_ROLE that includes the set of privileges that meets the needs of the salespeople and then assigns each salesperson as a member of this role. This is less time and resource intensive and ensures that any future adjustments to the database requirements of the salespeople only require an adjustment of the CLDCLL_SALES_ROLE.

Roles can be created for users, objects, and applications alike and they offer many advantages to database administration by saving time and resources and by providing a central location for administration. A user can be assigned many roles and a single role can be assigned to many users. Roles can also be assigned other roles and inherit their privileges, which works well for application roles. For example, suppose the company CallsRus decides to split the sales department into two separate groups, cold call salespeople and call back salespeople. Suppose the call back salespeople need to be able to delete tables from the database for those customers who call back to cancel their orders. These salespeople cannot be assigned to the CLDCLL_SALES_ROLE because the privilege to delete tables is denied in that role. Further, the CLDCLL_SALES_ROLE cannot be adjusted to allow the deletions because this would not follow the standard of least privilege, as the cold call salespeople would then have access that they do not legitimately need. CallsRus uses the same application for both sales groups. So, the DBA creates a new role with the privilege to delete tables titled CALBAK_SALES_ROLE and adds all of the call back salespeople to this group. Now, the database application that is used by the sales team must be available and given access to the database as well. The applications require the same privileges to the database as both CLDCLL_SALES_ROLE and CALBAK_SALES_ROLE to provide the services that both groups require. In this case, there are two choices. Create a new role and reassign all of the privileges that both groups hold individually, or create the new role SALES_DEPTAPP_ROLE and assign the two already existing roles to the new role. The most efficient choice is the latter, which allows for centralized administration and requires less time and resources. For example, if changes need to be made to the call back salespeople's privileges, only one adjustment needs to be made and this is to the

CALBAK_SALES_ROLE. Because the SALES_DEPTAPP_ROLE is assigned to CALBAK_SALES_ROLE, privileges are inherited, so any change made in one will automatically be assigned in the other. In addition to the advantages already mentioned, an administrator can password-protect a role and develop applications to enable a role only when the correct credentials are supplied. Overall, assigning roles to users, objects, applications, and other roles provides better access management and, therefore, a more security-conscious database environment.

No two roles can be assigned the same name. Although this section discusses a hierarchical structure, the roles are not actually contained within each other, so two roles with the same name can cause a database to fail.

Defining Roles in SQL Server Within SQL Server, roles are defined at either the server or database level. Server roles grant rights to manipulate the server environment. These rights are granted to login accounts. Database roles grant access to database objects and grant these rights to user accounts. Five types of roles are available within SQL Server: fixed server roles, fixed database roles, user-defined roles, application roles, and public roles.

Fixed server roles include a set of predefined privileges that are combined by SQL Server to create a role for a specific user account. As with fixed privileges, these cannot be changed or deleted, yet users can be added to them. These roles provide server-level privileges. For example, the ysadmin account is assigned a fixed role that includes privileges that are predefined by SQL Server to fit the system administrator user account. Table 6-3 displays a list of predefined fixed server roles for SQL Server; it is important that an administrator familiarize herself with these roles for proper permission granting and management of the server.

User account	User permissions
sysadmin	A system administration account that holds the rights to perform any action at the server level
securityadmin	A system administration account that holds the right to manage and configure the server's security settings (e.g., passwords, logins, auditing, and read error logs)
serveradmin	A system administration account that holds the right to change server configuration settings
setupadmin	A setup administration account that holds the right to manage linked servers, replication, and stored procedures
processadmin	A process administrator account that holds the right to manage the processes running in SQL Server
dbcreator	Database creator accounts that can create, alter, and resize databases
diskadmin	A disk administration account that holds the right to manage disk files

Table 6-3   Fixed server roles for SQL Server

Like fixed server roles, fixed database roles are predefined by SQL Server to fit the needs of a user account. These roles cannot be altered, yet users can be added to them. Whereas fixed server roles give users access to the server, those who are included within a fixed database role have privileges that are specific to the database. Table 6-4 provides a list of fixed database roles within SQL Server; administrators should familiarize themselves with these roles to avoid redundancy when creating roles.

User account	User rights
db_owner	Members of the db_owner role hold the rights to perform any action at the server level
db_accessadmin	Members of the db_accessadmin role can add or remove database groups and users
db_datareader	Members of the db_datareader role can see all data from all user tables and have SELECT permission
db_datawriter	Members of the db_datawriter role can add, change, or delete data from all user tables and have INSERT, UPDATE, and DELETE permissions
db_ddladmin	Members of the db_ddladmin role can make any database definition language commands
db_securityadmin	Members of the db_securityadmin role can manage roles and object permissions
db_backupoperator	Members of the db_backupoperator role hold the right to back up the database and force checkpoints
db_denydatareader	Members of the db_denydatareader role are unable to read any data, but they can perform other actions, such as INSERT
db_denydatawriter	Members of the db_denydatawriter role cannot change the data in the database

Table 6-4   **Fixed database roles for SQL Server**

User-defined roles are built at the database level and are created to control the access of objects within the database. Although the built-in database roles handle permissions for common database management tasks, a best practice is to group users who have access to perform and require the same database functions. The example provided in the previous section for *CallsRus* displays an example of user-defined database roles and the reason for which they would be created. User-defined roles can be nested to simplify the process.

Application roles are SQL Server roles that are created to support the security requirements of applications. They do not represent a set of users, but are intended to grant permission to software. An application role contains a password, which users must provide to gain access to the privileges of the role, providing more complex security management.

The PUBLIC role is a special role in which every SQL Server database user is a member and cannot be removed. Every SQL Server database has a role named PUBLIC and it provides a way for all users to be assigned a privilege at the same time and in the same manner. PUBLIC should be used with great caution, keeping in mind that any privilege added to the PUBLIC role applies to everyone in the database.

Defining Roles in MySQL   Although MySQL offers a sophisticated privilege and access system, roles are not included as an ability in MySQL Server alone. Roles can be created in MySQL with the help of scripting and third-party applications. As discussed earlier in the chapter, Securich is a third party that offers security and password support. Securich also provides support for creating roles in MySQL. Again, Securich can be found at *www.securich.com*.

Defining Roles in Oracle Oracle comes with several predefined, built-in roles that are available to administrators and users alike. These built-in roles are automatically defined for Oracle databases when you run the standard scripts that are included during database creation and if additional options or features are installed, more roles may be created as well. Just as with Oracle privileges, roles provide privileges at two levels: system and object. Roles can be granted to other roles to further manage the access of users and applications. Table 6-5 provides a list of common default Oracle roles, yet note that there are 33 roles for the Oracle database alone.

Role	Information
DBA	Holds access to all areas of the database; this role is provided for compatibility with previous releases of Oracle Database and it is recommended that administrators create their own security-based roles
JAVA_ADMIN	Provides administrative permissions to update policy tables for Oracle Database Java applications
SCHEDULER_ADMIN	Allows the grantee to execute the procedures of the DBMS_SCHEDULER package; it includes all of the job scheduler system privileges and is included in the DBA role
WM_ADMIN_ROLE	Provides all Workspace Manager permissions and includes the grant option; by default, the DBA is granted the WM_ADMIN_ROLE role
XDB_WEBSERVICES	Allows the grantee to access Oracle Database Web services over HTTPS
XDB_WEBSERVICES_OVER_HTTP	Allows the grantee to access Oracle Database Web services over HTTP
MGMT_USER	Provides administrative privileges to perform various activities with Oracle Enterprise Manager
OEM_MONITOR	Provides privileges needed by the Management Agent component of Oracle Enterprise Manager to monitor and manage the database

Table 6-5 **Common predefined Oracle roles**

It is also possible to grant roles to PUBLIC, yet this is not recommended and would defeat the reason for needing to create a role altogether. Oracle provides several dictionary views to help you find out what roles are assigned and to whom they have been assigned. Table 6-6 displays a list of the most common views used for locating roles in Oracle.

View	Contained
DBA_ROLES	All of the roles within the database
DBA_ROLE_PRIVS	All of the roles that are assigned to a user
ROLE_ROLE_PRIVS	All of the roles that are granted to other roles
ROLE_SYS_PRIVS	All system privileges that have been assigned to a role
ROLE_TAB_PRIVS	All object privileges assigned to a role
SESSION_ROLES	A list of roles that are enabled in the current session

Table 6-6 **Locating roles in Oracle**

Inference

Inference is a way that unauthorized users can obtain sensitive information by making assumptions based on the database's reactions or query responses to nonsensitive queries. Based on the knowledge obtained about the database, the unauthorized users can use their own reasoning and deduction (e.g., SQL syntax, data structure) to draw conclusions about the database that enable them to acquire knowledge or further develop their understanding of the data within it. Inference poses a great security threat to any database management system because it is difficult to predict, detect, and eliminate. Inference can be achieved by internal users, which are those who have some legitimate level of access and authority to the database, or by external users, which are unauthorized outsiders attempting to capture data from Web applications and forms. This section explores the primary means by which internal users obtain unauthorized information using inferences and discusses a few ways in which security professionals and database administrators can detect and minimize the potential for inference. External users and inference are discussed in later chapters.

Examples of Inference

Inference is possible in any way that a user can apply logic to a database's response to a query. This section explores two primary examples and means by which inference takes place within a database environment: those that use logic and those that use statistics. These examples are meant to provide an understanding of the sheer complexity of these likely security hazards as well as display the struggles that security professionals and database administrators must manage every day in their attempts to maintain a secure environment.

Logic, Relationship, and Constraint Inference Database management systems are built in a way that enables the efficient storage and retrieval of data. Tables that are well organized, logical, and object oriented are very efficient, yet it is these same characteristics that make them so vulnerable to inference. Once a user obtains enough experience using a particular database, he can use his own logic and his own understanding about object relationships or constraint-driven responses to make inferences about data within a database.

Consider a high-class hotel in Hollywood, California. Each time a person registers for a night, a record is added to a table in the hotel's database that includes his or her customer ID, room number, last name, first name, and profile level. The customer ID acts as the primary key in this table and can be used as a reference to locate other information held in the database related to a particular person, such as date of arrival, home address, and payment information. Table 6-7 represents what the table might look like for the 40th floor of the hotel.

CustID	Room	LName	FName	Profile
120209	4000	Jones	Michael	Low
120210	4001	Lopez	Jennifer	High
120211	4002	Franks	Peter	Low

Table 6-7 Guest table view

For this particular hotel, the DBA has created a special security rule or constraint to ensure that only hotel managers can view information about rooms that are occupied by high-profile guests. Let's assume that the hotel desk attendant gets a call from a potential guest inquiring about room availability on the 40th floor of the hotel. She queries the database and obtains the view shown in Table 6-8.

CustID	Room	LName	FName	Profile
120209	4000	Jones	Michael	Low
120211	4002	Franks	Peter	Low

Table 6-8   **Secured available room view**

Assuming that room 4001 is available, the desk attendant tries to book the room for the inquiring caller. However, the attempt fails due to another rule that is set up to ensure that no room is booked by two people at the same time. Without much thought, the desk attendant can now infer that the room is occupied by a high-profile client. Further exploration using the customer ID can potentially help the desk attendant acquire more unauthorized information about the guest in room 4001. This is one example of how even in a multilevel, secured database, rules, relationships, logic, and constraints all give clues that can lead to database inference.

Statistical Inference   Statistical database inferences present another great problem in database security. Statistical queries are often overlooked as potential security breaches because they do not return any actual data from the database. These queries are used to analyze the data in a database for auditing users and finding trends. For example, a statistical database can be used to identify the average amount of user activity over a given time period or to identify the number of queries per user in a specific day. These queries seem harmless and in many ways benefit an organization, yet they can be easily manipulated to retrieve sensitive information such as employee salary and company sales.

For example, let's assume that Sally works in data entry for Haphazard, Inc. and has found out that another data entry worker, Shawn, who has less seniority than herself, has recently been given a raise. Frustrated, and considering leaving the company, she wants to find out how much Shawn makes in comparison with herself. Sally, like most typical database users, does not have the security privileges to query her coworker's private records, but she does hold the rights to perform basic query operations. She discovers that if she can obtain the average of her salary and Shawn's salary combined and apply basic arithmetic, she can figure out exactly how much Shawn makes. This example shows that the statistical database has potentential to be compromised, and an unauthorized individual can retrieve sensitive company stats by obtaining collective or aggregate data and applying basic mathematical formulas to it. Like all other types of inferences, those drawn from statistical databases can be done from inside the company as well as from outside the company. Finding the salary for someone outside the company would only require a few more queries and comparisons, but the information is certainly attainable.

Minimizing Inference

As with all other approaches to security, there is no guaranteed assurance in securing against inference. As was mentioned earlier in this section, inference is difficult to predict, identify, and eliminate. There isn't an automatic scan that will help here, yet there are a few techniques that can have a great impact on limiting a person's ability to infer. This section identifies a few primary strategies to help minimize inference capabilities within database storage and management environment.

Polyinstantiation Polyinstantiation is a strategy that allows the database to contain multiple instances of a record, all pointing to the same primary key, but which contains and displays different values to users of different security classifications. For example, review our Hollywood hotel example from earlier. Polyinstantiation allows two records to exist for the hotel room 4001, both of which point to the same customer ID, as shown in Table 6-9.

CustID	Room	LName	FName	Profile
120209	4000	Jones	Michael	Low
120210	4001	Lopez	Jennifer	High
120210	4001	Smith	Paul	Low
120211	4002	Franks	Peter	Low

Table 6-9 Polyinstantiation view

This strategy enables two separate records to exist and be retrieved and manipulated separately. Those who attempt to view, modify, or delete the record with the correct privileges will have access to the correct record of the guest residing in room 4001, whereas those who attempt to view, modify, or delete the record without the correct privileges will only have access to the "fake" record of the guest in room 4001. If the security classifications are set up correctly, the unauthorized user isn't aware that they have access to a false record and the sensitive record remains safe and secure. Jennifer Lopez can rest easy, knowing that her true identity will not be discovered.

Polyinstantiation is an excellent strategy for keeping sensitive information hidden, yet like all security strategies, it has its downfalls. Many have criticized this technique for being morally wrong because it involves the falsification of records, yet some state that this falsification is greatly justified. Another issue with this strategy is that it leaves a database inconsistent, which can cause great confusion if not properly documented and managed. For example, think of the consequences of confusing the real files with the false ones.

Finally, the redundancy required for this strategy will consume a much greater amount of resources, especially if your security classifications are very granular. All in all, this is a great technique if you have the time and resources to make it work and you feel morally okay with the decision.

Other Ways to Minimize Polyinstantiation is an effective technique for keeping sensitive information hidden, yet a number of efforts can be made are less disruptive to the database environment. This section provides a few examples of ways in which inference can be minimized with or without polyinstantiation. These examples do not by any means represent an exhaustive list. If there is anything that we learned about security thus far, it's that it should be multilayered. This list represents a few tasks that focus on inference and that can be included in one of the many layers of security within the environment:

- *Log, monitor, and alert of events*—Activity logging is an important task for any security administrator. Almost every type of activity can be monitored actively within a database environment. Even queries can be monitored in real time. Both statistical and logical inference can be identified by monitoring and analyzing unusual queries and by setting a baseline and threshold alert for unusual user activity. Alerts can be sent directly to an administrator's cell phone for instant action; in addition, a great amount of insight can be found by capturing and analyzing the database activity logs.

- *Limit user capability*—It should be somewhat apparent by now that limiting a user's capabilities within a database is extremely important. This is especially true for minimizing statistical inference. For example, only allowing aggregate operators and limiting a user's query size can be great strides in minimizing inference attempts.

- *Limit query responses*—Limiting query responses can be just as helpful as limiting a user's capabilities. If you feel as though polyinstantiation isn't morally correct, limiting a query response can be almost as effective. For example, when it comes to the extremely sensitive data such as an employee's income, return classes and ranges instead of exact numbers. This helps to maintain morality of the database while minimizing inference.

Chapter Summary

- Authentication is the process of verifying the identity of a user attempting to access a resource, whereas authorization is the process of verifying the user's permission to access a resource.

- A login account is used to verify the identity of a user for authentication purposes and user accounts are used to determine privileges of a user for authorization purposes.

- Credentials are used to authenticate and authorize a user or application. Credentials can be required a few times throughout the login process, and can require a different set of credentials each time to positively identify a user.

- Credentials can be required at different levels of an environment, as authentication can be verified at the operating system, database, and network layer. Third-party applications can also be used to authenticate a user.

- Operating system authentication requires that the user has an account that resides locally on the server's OS, and only this account is necessary to access the database, despite its location.

- Database authentication checks the user's credentials against an account that resides within the database. Two sets of credentials (operating system and database) are required to log in to the database when database authentication is used.

- Third-party applications can be used to verify a user's identity. These applications use security protocols such as Kerberos and PKI.

- Authentication varies from one database vendor to another. For example, SQL Server supports only two different types of authentication, whereas Oracle supports many.

- Intrusions into a system can originate from a user's password; all of the security measures in the world will not make a difference if your passwords are found out. Therefore, server-enforced password policies are vital to the security of your organization's data.

- Server password policies can be in written form or they can be defined and enforced within your servers. When combined, they offer the most effective way to maintain the privacy of your database environments.

- Database servers can enforce different types of password policies. Variables such as the complexity and the number of failed attempts of a password help to ensure accurate authentication.

- User management is one of the most important duties of an administrator. Any security-concious DBA knows how to effectively assign privileges and understands the default users that come installed with a specific database.

- User privileges can be granted, denied, or revoked, and administrators should use these functions while following the principle of least privilege.

- For effective access management, related privileges can be combined to create roles, from which users can be added or removed. Roles allow for centralized management and security of the database.

- Inference can be used to gain unauthorized information from a database either intentionally or unintentionally, from both internal users and external intruders. Inference is very difficult to detect, predict, and control.

Key Terms

authentication The process of confirming the identity of those individuals or applications that request access to a secure environment.

authorization The process of ensuring that those individuals or applications that request access to an environment or an object within that environment have the permission to do so.

credential A piece of information that is used to verify identity, such as a person's username and password, an application's secure ID, or a host's network name and address.

database link A link made between two databases that when created results in one logical data storage unit. Links are created in Oracle to apply common policies and to create associations between databases.

digital certificate A password-protected and encrypted file that holds the identity of a user or object.

inference A way that unauthorized users can obtain sensitive information by making assumptions based on the database's reactions or query responses to nonsensitive queries.

Kerberos An authentication protocol that was built by MIT to provide secure means for authentication using symmetric-key cryptology to verify the identity of a client to a server and a server to a client.

login An object that is mapped to a user account within each database and is associated to users by the security identifier or SID.

Mixed Mode Authentication A form of authentication that allows both Windows authentication and SQL Server authentication to be used. The database will accept both Windows and server logins.

principle of least privilege A security standard by which each user added to a system is given the minimum set of privileges that he or she requires to conduct legitimate business within that system.

privilege The ability to access a specific database resource or to perform a specific action within a database.

polyinstantiation A strategy that allows the database to contain multiple instances of a record, all pointing to the same primary key, but contain and display different values to users of different security classifications.

role A set of related privileges that are combined to provide a centralized unit from which to manage similar users or objects of a database.

service ticket A unique key that is used to validate a person's identification (similar to a driver's license), for the purpose of gaining access into a secured environment.

user profile A set of rules that limits a user's access to database resources, and can be used to set password restrictions as well.

Windows Authentication mode A form of authentication that allows only Windows authentication to be used for accessing the database; those users logging in to the database must have a Windows login to access it.

Review Questions

1. Explain the difference between *authentication* and *authorization*.

2. Explain the difference between a login and a user account. Which is used for authentication?

3. List and explain the two authentication methods.

4. Define and explain the process of Kerberos.

5. Define and explain the difference between the authentication modes of at least two of the three database vendors mentioned in the chapter (SQL Server, MySQL, Oracle).

6. Explain at least two server-enforced password policies.

7. Identify two written password policies that you find to be the most important. Explain why you chose those two.

8. Identify and explain the default logins or user accounts for at least two of the database vendors discussed in the chapter.

9. Identify at least five best practices when adding and removing users.

10. Explain the principle of least privilege and how it should be applied within a database environment.

11. Identify three actions that can be applied to a database environment to manage user access.

12. Explain the circumstances in which roles should be used and identify the reasons for using roles.

Case Projects

Case Project 6-1: Database Password Policies

Create and document a written password policy to be given out to database users in an organization.

Case Project 6-2: User Management Policies

Define a set of standards and policies for adding, modifying, and removing users from a database.

Case Project 6-3: MySQL User Accounts

Using MySQL's Web site (*http://mysql.com*), identify how to create a user in MySQL. Write the steps for creating a user in MySQL.

Case Project 6-4: Oracle, User Management, and PL/SQL

Using Oracle's Web site (*http://Oracle.com*), identify how to create a user in Oracle. Write the steps for creating a user in Oracle PLSQL.

Case Project 6-5: SQL, Users, Server Management Studio, and Transact-SQL

Using SQL Server's Web site (*www.microsoft.com/sqlserver/2008/en/us/*), identify how to create a Windows authenticated login using SQL Server's Server Management Studio and Transact-SQL.

Case Project 6-6: Roles

Provide a scenario in which a role is assigned to another role to fulfill a specific need.

Hands-On Projects

Hands-On Project 6-1: Securing the Oracle Environment

You have been hired as the DBA for Haphazard, Inc. You are asked to fulfill the following needs of the Oracle Database environment.

1. Users, roles, and privileges need to be added to the database. Identify the statements that would be used for creating the following users, roles, and privileges that match the following requirements:

   a. Create a user account NLitzinger identified by the password Dubrucr90.

   b. Grant NLitzinger the SELECT and UPDATE permissions on the table called *clients*.

   c. Create a user account HMimnaugh identified by the password EvCsvds01.

   d. Grant HMimnaugh the select and delete permissions on the table called *clients*.

      e. Create a user account TylerM identified by the password Fwdtwet12.

      f. Grant TylerM the select and insert permissions on the table called *clients*.

      g. Create a role named Most_Privileged without a password.

      h. Grant the Most_Privileged role the Update and Delete permissions on the *clients* table.

      i. Add all users to the Most_Privileged role.

2. Identify the most privileged users. (Which user has the most permissions?) Discuss the way in which the preceding steps could have been made more efficient.

3. A password policy needs to be enforced at Haphazard. Identify the statements required to create a server-enforced password policy with the following requirements:

      a. Complexity is a necessity.

      b. The password should be a minimum of seven characters.

      c. Allow the user to reuse the password after a minimum of 10 password changes.

      d. Lock accounts that have had more than three failed attempts.

      e. Expire the password every 60 days.

4. What security suggestions would you provide to Haphazard in terms of authentication and authorization? Explain what policies you would develop as well.

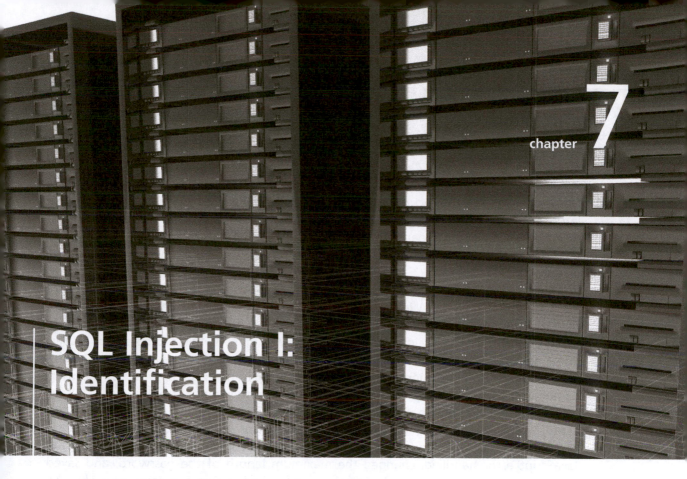

chapter 7

SQL Injection I: Identification

After reading this chapter and completing the exercises, you will be able to:

- Describe a SQL injection and identify how injections are executed
- Identify how a Web application works and its role in SQL injections
- Define how to locate SQL vulnerabilities using error messages
- Apply inferential testing
- Review source code manually to locate injection vulnerabilities
- Describe methods for automatic traversing of source code to locate injection vulnerability

Mazlo, an experienced security professional, was hired as a consultant by TJRigging, a large warehouse and storage facility in the Pittsburgh area. Clients of TJRigging have direct access to the company database through TJRigging's Web site. The Web site provides a convenient way for customers to check on their own stored product inventory.

Mazlo was told that his first task on the job was to conduct a Web server security audit for the TJRigging's Web site. From his home, and without any prior knowledge of the database, Mazlo attempted to obtain access to the company's database. He typed the company's URL into his browser and was immediately prompted for a user-name and password. Unaware of the authorized credentials, he decided to use a com-mon SQL injection statement —`'or '1'='1--"`— placing this statement in the user-name and password fields. The site returned the following error message: "Your password can only contain numbers, letters, or the underscore." Based on this message alone, Mazlo was able to tell that the database was vulnerable. Next, he used his browser to view and modify the source code for the company's site. He removed the JavaScript error handling, changed the maximum length of the password, and saved the file on his local hard drive. This time, instead of typing the company's URL, he used the path to the file of his newly modified version kept on his local hard drive.

Voilà! He obtained access and with administrative privileges to the database as well!

This scenario is not an exaggeration. SQL injections are not that difficult to execute and they accounted for about 30 percent of the over 500,000 Web site intrusions last year. With the right amount of knowledge, or access to the Internet, any vulnerable site can be attacked within a matter of minutes. Protection and awareness is becoming more important each day!

Understanding SQL Injections

It only takes one brief Internet search to understand the ease with which SQL injections can be used for unauthorized access to company databases and Web sites. In fact, on popular vlogging sites, such as YouTube and Metacafe, you can find several tutorials less than two minutes long on using SQL injections to break into organizations. The information is extremely accessible to anyone who wants it, and if not appropriately prepared, an organization can be devastated by the results. **SQL injections** are the methods by which intruders use bits of SQL code and SQL queries to gain database access. SQL injections are extremely dangerous, as they create vulner-abilities and provide the means by which an intruder can obtain full administrator privileges to sensitive data such as usernames, passwords, Social Security numbers, credit card numbers, and general account information. Having access to execute all queries within a database gives an intruder the power to also manipulate anything that is available to the database, including the operating system.

There are three common strategies for execution of SQL injections: single channel, multichannel, and observational. In a single-channel attack, an intruder uses only one channel for which to execute SQL injections and obtain the returned results. For example, using a Web application to input SQL injections in place of text to obtain immediate use of unauthorized data would be considered a single-channel attack. A multichannel attack involves the intruder using one avenue, such as with Web applications, to initiate the injection and a different one to obtain the results. In this scenario, an intruder could use a Web application to exploit a system and then change the Web script so that the results from a Web application query are sent to another account, such as the intruder's personal e-mail account. Intruders can also send SQL injections with no intention of receiving data from the database; these are known as inferential injections and they are used only to observe and learn from the returned behavior of the server for later attacks.

Injections and the Network Environment

Most SQL injections are performed through a Web application that acts as an interface to a back-end database. **Web applications** are programs that are available on a network and provide a way for users to interact with remote systems or databases. With the popularity of the Internet and the prominence of networks in today's society, the use of Web applications to access a database has been widely adapted within the database industry. In fact, most of the Web pages that exist on today's Internet can be considered a Web application of some type; in addition, well over half of the time that the average Internet browser spends online involves using these applications to access some type of sensitive data (e.g., e-mail messages, bank account information, credit card information). This is the reason that Web applications are the primary target for today's intruders. Common uses for Web applications online include e-mail access (e.g., Gmail, OWA), auctions (e.g., eBay, ubid), shopping (e.g., Amazon, Overstock), banking, bill paying, vlogging, blogging, and online gaming.

Let's take a look at the method for which data is retrieved and manipulated using Web applications beginning at the Web browser. The process is pretty straightforward and involves the following general steps:

1. A user accesses the specific Web site where the Web application resides by opening up a Web browser on their local machine and typing in the desired Web address (*www.amazon.com*). The Web site displays forms with fields and buttons that the user can use to input requests. The form resides on the Web server and is built using a combination of Hypertext Markup Language (HTML) and some type of scripting language (e.g., PHP, JSP, NET). HTML organizes and formats the form, while the scripting language makes it interactive by correlating some type of action with its components (buttons and fields).

2. A scripting language (PHP) residing on the Web server (*amazon.com*) reacts to the user's submission and passes the SQL statements to the company's application, or middleware server.

3. The middleware server contains applications that enforce business and database rules. These servers act as the interfaces to the database by managing the number of concurrent connections to the database as well as the Web content that is returned. The two primary responsibilities for middleware in a Web-based data retrieval environment are to initiate the database connection and to pass along the query.

4. Once received, the database executes the query and returns the results to the application server.

5. The application server returns the results to the scripting language on the Web server.

6. The scripting language, along with HTML, displays the results on the screen.

SQL injections are deployed in the very beginning of this process. There are two ways that SQL injections can cause destruction and create vulnerabilities. Lethal SQL code can be directly placed into user input fields and executed at the database, or ill-written code can be sent to be stored in the database. Either way, if Web applications are not prepared to detect and filter SQL injections, our most sensitive databases are at risk. The most common way to prepare an application to detect injections is to ensure that the application validates the data being received by the user before sending it to the database. SQL is used to communicate to Microsoft SQL Server, MySQL, and Oracle, so all three databases are at risk if applications are not properly secured.

It is important to note that SQL injections can exploit any client/server system that uses SQL Server and that relies on remote authentication. Although Web applications account for the majority of SQL injection intrusions, vulnerabilities also exist elsewhere.

In an environment where SQL statements are sent remotely through a Web application or client/server architecture, static, hard-coded SQL statements are not the optimal choice because query statements in this type of environment are reliant on users' input into the Web application form. A **dynamic SQL statement** is a SQL statement that is generated on the fly by an application (such as a Web application), using a string of characters derived from a user's input parameters into a form within the application itself. A **static SQL statement** is a statement that is built by the user and the full text of the statement is known at compilation. With dynamic SQL statements, developers build applications that handle most of the SQL code in real time, building the full query before being executed within the database because the full query is not known until the user inputs the information.

To illustrate the difference between a dynamic and static SQL statement, suppose that Smith is working on a Web application that displays input fields to users, who fill in certain criteria that the application uses to search the database. Let's say there are three fields, name (ClieNm), title (ClieTitl), and department (Depart). If Smith were to create this code using a static SQL statement, he would have to take into account all combinations of the various possible user inquiries because the statement depends on user input. This can be very cumbersome as possible parameters increase. For instance, imagine the number of potential combinations of possible inquiries search parameters are enabled on: client's name, address, phone number, department, title, age, starting date, status, sex, and race—and the use of AND or OR is allowed.

Dynamic SQL statements are best for Web database access, yet, as mentioned previously, if the input is not validated before being sent to the database, an attacker could input SQL statements, rather than search criteria into the input fields of the form. These statements will be interpreted as code and results will be generated based on the attacker's SQL syntax. Consider this scenario: A user types a URL into the browser to obtain access to a company's Web application and is prompted to provide a username and password. Rather than supplying a real username and password, the attacker can place SQL syntax into the fields to pull data from the database itself to be used for authentication. For example, the syntax `'or '1'='1--` often returns the first entry in a given table. So if the attacker places `'or '1'='1--` into the username and `'or '1'='1--` into the password fields of a vulnerable Web application, the Web application will create a SQL statement that essentially checks the table that holds the username and password information and uses the first username and password from this table as credentials for the attacker. There is always certainly at least one user in the database, so authentication is inevitable, and the attacker gains access with the privileges of the first user listed in the database. Furthermore, because usernames are often listed in this table in alphabetical order, the user account the attacker could potentially log in as is the *administrator* account.

TIP

Developers often write script within Web applications to handle a user error, such as if a user is missing data required for a field, an error message might state "Missing or invalid information." These error messages can also give clues as to how an error is handled within a system. These messages, if descriptive enough, provide the attacker with just enough information to change the error-handling code to meet his or her needs. For example, some sites have restrictions as to what symbols can be used for a person's username or password. Given the previous scenario, let's assume that the attacker attempts to use the code `'or '1'='1--` to obtain access into a database in which equal signs are not valid username characters. If the developer has written a script that informs users of this error by displaying the message "Invalid password characters," the attacker has just learned the error of her ways. Armed with this information, the attacker can review the scripting language by choosing to "view source" of the HTML page, and change the script by allowing the use of equal signs or removing error handling altogether. Therefore, developers should take caution when using error-handling messages.

7

Identifying Vulnerabilities

As an administrator, the primary step toward securing data is identifying vulnerabilities with the system. Without knowledge of the system weaknesses, security actions would be fruitless. One of the most effective ways to find vulnerabilities within an environment is to play the role of an intruder. Just as with any other area of security, having an understanding of the possible attacks that an environment might face is vital to the protection against SQL injections. Determining possible SQL injection attacks is not a simple task. There are several different types of attacks, different areas of the network can be attacked, and different methods can be used to deploy injections. Understanding these things from both a user and administrator perspective is very important to the protection of any database environment. This section explores these topics and explores ways to observe the behavior and code of the applications and systems to find SQL vulnerabilities. Much of the focus is placed on Web applications. As mentioned previously, Web applications are prominent in today's networks and they currently provide the primary means for SQL injection intrusions.

Inferential Testing for Locating SQL Injections

This section looks for clues of SQL injections using behaviors that are returned from the database in response to a controlled attack.

To find the SQL injection vulnerabilities through server behavior responses, an administrator must approach testing from the database user perspective, inputting parameters from the client side of the database environment. Once inputs have been made, the database server behaviors can then be analyzed and abnormal responses documented as potential vulnerabilities. For this type of testing, the administrator must be able to recognize abnormal server response and be capable of distinguishing these responses from the more typical or expected ones. The first step to acquiring this skill is becoming very familiar with the way the application and Web browser behave during normal data retrieval. This includes a basic understanding of the applications, the scripting language, the way the browser typically sends statements to the application server, and normal database returns given a specific return. Basically, an administrator must first familiarize herself with the environment in its normal state.

Using HTTP

All network communication is based on the same basic principles. A request to obtain a resource is sent from a source machine or application (client) to a destination machine or application (server). The request is received and processed and the client's privilege is checked to determine allowable permissions for the requested resource. Once approved, the requested resource is packaged and sent from the server to the client. Each step is handled using a set of standards or protocols that determine the who, what, when, where, and how of the communication process. For example, Transmission Control Protocol or TCP defines a set of rules that ensures a reliable virtual connection for delivery of data from one machine to another, and Hypertext Transfer Protocol (HTTP) is a set of rules that defines the method by which hypertext requests and responses (Web requests and responses) are formatted and packaged.

HTTP plays an important role when using Web applications for access into a database. When a request is made from a Web application to a database server, HTTP submits these requests by first initiating a TCP connection as the transfer agent. HTTP includes eight predefined actions that can be performed on a resource during the request or a response from a server: HEAD, GET, POST, PUT, DELETE, TRACE, OPTIONS, and CONNECT. Each of these define some way a request or response of a client or server should be handled. Although administrators should become familiar with all of these actions, only two are relevant to this discussion of SQL injections, as they deal primarily with network forms. These are GET and POST.

GET requests are encoded by the browser into a URL and the server will execute whatever parameters are appended to the URL itself. In other words, once a user fills out a form and clicks the submit button, the information that the user inputted into the fields of the form, which in this case is a query, is attached to the URL and sent to the server. The Web server will look for queries found within the URL and send them on to the database.

If using GET for Web forms, the information that the user has inputted into the fields of the form is included within the body of the request, rather than the URL. In this case, the application server recognizes the POST action and searches within the body of the request for particular statements to send on to the database to execute.

So, let's review this process. A Web application is presented to a database user through their local Web browser. This application includes some type of form, which the user must fill out to initiate a query and which sends a request to the Web server. The information that is provided within the form (user input) is sent either by HTTP GET or by HTTP POST to the Web server, where the scripting language retrieves the information and dynamically builds the SQL statement to be forwarded to the application server or middleware. The middleware applies business logic (depending on the type of middleware) and based on restrictions within the application server, it forwards the SQL statement to the database to be executed. The database server executes the query and returns the results to the application server, which in turn sends it back to the Web server. The Web server displays the results using HTML to format the view for the users.

This is an important concept to understand because user requests can be intercepted during transit from Web application to the Web server and user data can be switched with SQL injections. The user (if unauthorized) can also place SQL statements into the fields of the form instead of normal text. In both of these cases, the user input is switched or inaccurate prior to reaching the scripting language, so without filters and protection, the scripting language dynamically creates corrupt SQL statements to send on to the application server. An administrator searching for these vulnerabilities requires a close analysis of the data throughout the process, from the user browser to the database. Intercepting the data as an intruder would help provide a clear view as to what is being sent and received at the Web server.

Intruders can intercept and even modify GET and POST parameters in a few different ways. Administrators should use the following techniques to test their own environment and observe what is found when data is intercepted:

- *Third-party applications*—Several applications are accessible for free download on the Internet to intercept and manipulate HTTP data. Some of these applications are specific for either GET or POST, but most can parse both GET and POST information from a data transfer session.

- *Browser add-ons and plug-ins*—Because the data is sent directly from the Web browser, intercepting and modifying GET and POST requires browser-specific applications. Easier than third-party applications, add-ons have been created to provide browser-specific interception. These add-ons are also available online and can often be found on the individual browser support page. For example, a well-known add-on named TamperData is available for Mozilla Firefox and can be downloaded from Mozilla's browser add-on page.

- *Proxy servers*—Proxy servers are computers or applications that are used to monitor and mediate internal and external communication. Proxy servers are the "gatekeepers" of the network; they monitor all incoming and outgoing requests and use an administrator-defined set of criteria to filter traffic that is coming into and leaving a specific network or area of a network. As part of this process, proxy servers intercept client requests and analyze these requests based on a given set of rules. Therefore, a proxy server enables the interceptions and modification of HTTP requests, including GET and POST parameters.

- *Using one of the preceding tools*—An administrator can intercept and observe a network's GET and POST parameters prior to the SQL statement build to identify any abnormal requests.

Determining Vulnerability Through Errors

As mentioned a few times throughout this chapter, finding data vulnerabilities requires administrators to gain a strong understanding of the overall database request and response process. Although malicious SQL code can be injected at several points of this process, it is not executed until it reaches the database. The Web server does not test the data for errors or inappropriate database responses. Middleware could be designed to apply some logic to the statement, but in general, once injections are executed by the database, nothing gets in the way of returning the unauthorized results to users. With this said, administrators testing an environment for potential vulnerabilities may be presented with a few errors along the way. Although the errors come directly from the database, the scripting language determines how to present the errors and what to state within an error, and errors will not always occur because of SQL injection. It takes a strong familiarity with the errors that a system returns as well as knowledge of how these errors are presented to users to find vulnerabilities. If not filtered correctly, an error can give potential intruders information to help in the attack. In addition, as an administrator is testing the environment, the error messages will give clues as to what input has caused the issue, providing more information about potential SQL injection vulnerabilities.

Errors can be handled by application developers in different ways. The application's scripting language can be coded to display specific error messages in response to a user error. These messages, such as "usernames and password cannot include numbers," can give intruders information about the system that they can use to find a way to break in to the system. For example, the message "usernames and password cannot include numbers" tells an intruder that usernames and passwords do not include numbers and saves an intruder a great deal of time in his efforts to obtain authorized credentials for a particular system. Web applications can also be configured to respond to user error with generic messages. This approach would include errors such as "Please check your username/password," and is the best way to minimize the opportunity for intruder inference because these types of error messages do not typically give the user any information about the system. Administrators can also choose not to handle errors at the Web application, allowing HTTP to handle the errors instead (generating "Server Error" messages). This can help to minimize intrusions as well, yet, as we discussed previously, this technique is not without faults. Inferential testing conducted on error messages offers administrators and security professionals great insight into their own systems. Using inferential techniques, professionals can take note of the location in which error messages are being handled as well as the content of the messages that are being displayed and use this information to minimize potential vulnerabilities.

This section explores the different types of errors that can occur and should be monitored as events within a system. It is intended to help administrators and security professionals learn ways to distinguish between general errors and those that indicate vulnerability.

When testing for SQL injection vulnerability by observing error messages, you can organize information in four categories. These categories are typical conditions with no error, typical conditions with typical error, injection conditions with no error, and injection conditions with injection-caused error.

Typical Conditions with No Error

To determine vulnerability of a system using error messages received, you must first understand the typical error-free condition. This section displays a typical or baseline condition in which data is processed successfully and no error messages are present.

Imagine a scenario in which a local online specialty grocer allows customers to search and purchase their products on their Web site *www.yum.com*. This site allows patrons to choose from different types of foods, such as dairy, produce, and meat. Each category has its own respective button on a Web form; when visitors click a button, a new page appears displaying a list of available products for that food category. Dairy's button may link to the following URL:

http://www.yum.com/index.asp?category=dairy

For example, imagine that the Web site contains a button titled "Click here to view all dairy products." This button, when pressed by users, will result in the preceding URL. The scripting language will receive the output URL from the button and send a statement to the database requesting for all items whose category=dairy. In this case, the scripting language is ASP and so the request sent to the database will look something like this:

```
food_cat = request("category")
sqlstr= "SELECT * FROM products WHERE Food_Category = '"&food_cat&"'"
set rs-conn.execute(sqlstr)
```

In this case, the ASP would create the following SQL statement to be executed by the database:

```
SELECT * FROM products WHERE Food_Category = 'Dairy'
```

In this case, the database would return one or more rows that match the WHERE clause, which in this case is Dairy. No errors are generated for this scenario. Keep in mind that when using SQL, alphanumeric values must be enclosed using single quotes (e.g., `'Dairy'`).

Typical Conditions with Typical Error

Even under the most typical data-processing conditions, errors can occur. Administrators and security professionals should be very familiar with the error messages that are produced primarily as a result of a common user error. These types of errors are often not viewed as potential threats or vulnerabilities to a system, so they are often overlooked, but unfortunately, any error that is produced within a database environment can be an indication of system vulnerability. Therefore, these messages should be carefully monitored and considered over time.

Let's assume that through inferential testing, an administrator changes the URL manually to state:

http://www.yum.com/index.asp?category=Hungry

In this case, the ASP would create the following SQL statement to be executed by the database:

```
SELECT * FROM products WHERE Food_Category = 'Hungry'
```

Knowing that the value of *Food_Category* determines what should be displayed to the user, errors will be generated with this scenario if *Hungry* is not a category of food within the system. These errors might or might not indicate vulnerability, as mentioned previously, as it could be returned due to user error or due to an intruder's attempt to obtain information from the database. For this scenario, the database would return an error informing the user that the column does not exist in the products table. Although this is not necessarily an indication of injection vulnerability, it displays that URLs can be changed manually if database information is not hidden.

Injection Conditions with No Error

SQL injections executed without an error returned from the database are known as a successful injection. These are often caused by unprepared Web applications that do not filter user input and URLs that do not hide database information. When testing inferentially for vulnerabilities, injections that are successful need immediate attention.

Below is a common SQL injection technique, which when not filtered correctly, does not generate an error. The statement, `'or '1'='1` is used often in SQL injections. It always returns *true*, which can prove to be very useful when attempting to gain information about an environment. This statement's counterpart is `'or '1'='2`, which always returns *false* and can be very useful in injections and testing as well.

Several variations of this statement accommodate the different types of databases and code structures that exist in the networking environment. For example, an equivalent true statement for Microsoft SQL Server is `'or 'ab'='a'+'b`, for MySQL it is `'or 'ab'='a' 'b`, and in Oracle the statement is `'or 'ab'='a'\\'b`. Attacks using statements similar to these examples are most often used in *blind injections*. Blind injections are attacks made with little to no knowledge of the system. Similar to throwing a dart at a dartboard while blindfolded, sometimes blind injections will be successful and other times they will miss the target altogether. A series of true and false SQL statements is used to attempt to discover information from a system. Blind attacks can be very difficult to detect due to their subtle nature.

Assume that the Yum URL can be manually changed to state:

http://www.yum.com/index.asp?category=dairy `'or '1'='1--`

This would result in the SQL statement:

`SELECT * FROM products WHERE Food_Category = 'Dairy' 'or '1'='1 --`

In this case, the database (if not filtered) returns everything from the products table even if Food_Category is not equal to *Dairy*. This is because, as mentioned previously, the statement 1=1 is always true. The statement `'or '1'='1--` can be quite dangerous and can be used to provide access to an unauthorized user (by placing it in a password field) and help an intruder retrieve all of the data from a database (by being injected into a statement while it is dynamically created). This statement works effectively, causing no errors in return. The single quote in the beginning of the statement is the correct syntax to complete a statement, avoiding the return of errors, and adding double dashes at the end starts a comment in SQL, so all values after the injection are ignored by the system.

Single quote characters can be extremely helpful during inferential testing. They can provide a great resource for detecting injections and exploitations. When testing a database response, single quote characters are inserted in different places to determine vulnerability. If a database reacts the same way with single quotes added to the SQL statement through manual manipulation, as it reacted without changes being made to the statement, this is a great indication that vulnerability exists. To test this, the specific database SQL language needs to be considered, as syntax rules will be different. For example, in Microsoft SQL Server and MySQL, a manual change of the variable value using single quotes, such as in changing *category=dairy* to category=da' 'iry, should result in an error. Because Oracle uses PL/SQL, the manual change required to test this would be similar to changing *category=dairy* to category=da'+' iry,. If the type of language is not considered, the error generated would be caused from true syntax errors and a false sense of security would exist.

Injection Conditions with Injection-Caused Error

Depending on the database being used, some error messages will provide clear indications that a vulnerability has occurred. To effectively secure an environment, administrators need to rigorously test their environments to become aware of those error messages that indicate that a vulnerability does exist. These messages will differ from one type of database to another and will depend on how the environment's application is built to handle errors, so there is no definitive list that can be provided. Obtaining a strong understanding of one's own environment's behavior will help an administrator and security professional develop a list of their own. This scenario provides one example of how an injection can cause an error. The difference between this and the examples previously given is that the syntax being used is not appropriate for the database being queried and Web applications will not typically and dynamically create statements that are using incorrect syntax. This scenario uses `'or '1'='1`, which is a variation of the statement in the previous example.

Assume that the Yum URL can be manually changed to state:

http://www.yum.com/index.asp?category=dairy "or "1"="1 --

```
SELECT * FROM products WHERE Food_Category = 'Dairy' "or "1"="1 --
```

Here an error would be returned. The database would claim a syntax error because of the double quotes that have been appended to the SQL statement from the SQL injection. This error is also often a result of blind injections, as the attacker is attempting to determine the dialect of SQL (e.g., PL/SQL versus T-SQL), the type of database (e.g., MySQL versus Oracle), and the error handling of the Web application. With blind injections, the attacker does not have knowledge of the system, and because SQL comes in a number of different varieties, the database or SQL dialect must be determined before an injection can take place. An attacker will often use trial and error to determine these things.

Generic Error Messages

As mentioned previously, error messages can be displayed in many different ways and by many different means. Application developers typically make the determination as to how, and what, an error message will display by creating code within the Web application itself. In some cases, applications will show generic errors messages with no reference to the type of event that returned the error, and on some occasions, no message will be presented at all. This poses a challenge for intruders and database administrators alike because it is difficult to determine whether the error has occurred within the database or exists within the application itself. It is possible that the application is not built to handle errors, that there isn't code created to display a message or redirect a user to a page developed for error handling. A number of generic errors returned by a Web application during testing can mislead administrators by giving the perception that the system is extremely secure, while in reality the Web application could be causing the error. To rule out an error within the application error-handling system, an administrator must use a SQL statement that does not initiate an application error, but tests the database error returns instead. This can be done by inserting controlled successful SQL statements into parameters, such as the appropriate true statement for that particular database. For example, using `'or '1'='1--` as input parameters into a field would not cause an application error but would test the database for SQL injection vulnerability.

Direct Testing

Using inferential testing, you can uncover a great deal of information from the behavior of the database. Potential weaknesses are identified through system behavior observation and at this point, theories about vulnerabilities have been made based on abnormal behavior that was identified. Before the exploitation or removal of the injections can take place, further investigation is necessary. The next goal is to actively execute potential SQL injections, testing theories that were made during inferential testing. Doing this requires an understanding of the whole process as it is translated into programming language. Thinking like a program developer, you need to obtain a clear vision of the transfer of data from the Web application to the scripting language, to the middleware, and on to the database. In the mind-set of an intruder, SQL statements are built to actively test the environment. Determine just how far an outsider is able to reach into the system, bypassing authentication, and actively manipulating the data. Find out to what extent unauthorized access can be obtained and how much data is available for view. Active testing prepares an administrator for the removal of the injection, narrowing down the vulnerabilities and adding a focus to the exploitation efforts.

Using the Code for Locating SQL Injections

Inferential testing is a great way to find SQL injection vulnerabilities, much like security penetration testing. It allows administrators to view the system security from an attacker's point of reference. The second most common approach to locating SQL injection is through source code analysis. This strategy requires less time and resources, but it might require the database administrator to work with the application developer. Much information can be gained from reviewing the source code. Administrators can ensure that dynamic statements are being created and filtered without SQL vulnerability as well as determine how and where user input is being accepted—both of which are important aspects of maintaining a safe environment. This section discusses these topics as well as provides tips on how to identify vulnerable code.

Source Code Analysis

Analyzing source code can be quite a tedious and painstaking task. Depending on the approach, reviewing the source code of a piece of software one line at a time can take months, yet identifying problems at the source code level is one of the most effective ways to manage SQL injection vulnerabilities. Several tools are available to help automate the process, but many of these focus primarily on security and lack strength in locating errors that SQL injections can exploit. Source code can be analyzed in different views—while the code is running and while it is not. Analyzing the code while it is running is known as conducting a *dynamic analysis*. **Dynamic analysis** is an attempt to find errors or vulnerabilities in the source code of a program dynamically while it is being executed, whereas **static analysis** is an effort to find problems while the program is inactive. Static code analysis requires less resources and expense and is much more effective at identifying vulnerabilities within the code.

To effectively sanitize source code and rid it of its SQL vulnerabilities, you must first be able to identify potential problem areas. Problem areas can be poorly written functions or user input that is not verified. As shown earlier in the chapter, SQL injections can be input as parameters within fields on a form. Vulnerable sites are often those that do not validate a user's input by ensuring that it meets a certain predefined criteria prior to being included within the dynamic build of the SQL statement. For example, as shown in the scenarios presented earlier in the chapter, many of the successful SQL injections used a single quote as the starting character as a way to append to the existing statement. For the malicious input to be included within the dynamic statement, it has to be added without any type of filtering process. Including filtering processes between the user input and the dynamically created statement that define certain limitations for a user's input can easily reduce the number of SQL injection attacks.

Identifying these issues can be quite a large task, one for which the time requirements depend on the size of the program and the code's overall logic structure. You must first identify where in the code each SQL statement is built. It is here that the name of the variables that hold user input can be identified. Working backward in the code, the goal is to follow the path of the variable back to its origin: the place where the user input enters the code. Traversing through the code, an administrator must identify if restrictions have been placed on the user input anywhere in the code. Consider the following scenario.

The user inputs some type of information into a text field of a Web application online. The text field has a name assigned to it, such as *TFName*. A variable in the scripting language of the Web application is defined, named, and assigned to *TFName* (e.g., *UserInput*= "TFName"). The variable *UserInput* transfers the content of the text field (*TFName*) to a function (predefined and based on the language being used) that dynamically creates the SQL statement. If at no time the variable (*UserInput*) is verified to have an appropriate set or type of characters, anything can be inserted into the text field and transferred directly into the SQL statement. This is the reason that it is important to trace the path of all variables that contain user input, looking to find any verification that the user's input fits a certain set of defined criteria for that text field.

Keep in mind that this example is only considering the transfer of the data within the scripting language of the Web application. It is equally as important to consider how the data is being transferred from the form into the scripting language. As mentioned earlier in the chapter, this transfer involves the HTTP actions GET and POST. The actions of HTTP are identified in the HTML code, so the HTML code should also be reviewed to ensure the desired settings. How SQL statements are constructed is specific to the scripting language being used, as the functions are predefined. Prior to using functions to construct SQL statements, research the function thoroughly to ensure that validation is being applied.

Tools for Searching Source Code

Throughout this chapter, different strategies for identifying and testing SQL injections have been explored. Many of these strategies are time consuming and resource intensive, yet none are as time consuming as traversing line by line through hundreds of pages of source code. Several tools are available to help facilitate this process, yet none are as reliable as manual searching. There are essentially three methods for analyzing static source code: string-based pattern matching, lexical token matching, and data flow analysis. This section explores these techniques in terms of their reliability and methodology.

String-Based Matching

String-based matching is a simple detection tool that searches for, and locates, user-defined strings and patterns found within source code. It is the most basic of the three strategies and produces the highest number of false results. Signatures are created for typical SQL injection variables, and other types of dangerous source code and string-based matching systems attempt to find strings or patterns that match these signatures.

Data Flow Analysis

Data flow analysis is a method for obtaining information about the way variables are used and defined in a program. It determines the dynamic behavior of a program by examining its static code. Source code is divided into blocks of data for which data flow analysis tries to collect information at each point in a procedure. Data flow analysis uses control flow graphs to display how events in a program are sequenced during execution. Data flow analyzers help database administrators obtain a map of each variable as well as the assigned value each step through the program.

Lexical Analysis

Lexical scanning is the process by which the source code is read from left to right and then grouped into tokens, based on some type of similar criteria. A lexical analyzer can identify common symbols that the initiating programming language defines. Some tools implement an approach known as lexical analysis.

If used correctly, tools that utilize one of these methods to parse source code can provide a great deal of help for detecting dangerous code and potentially risky variables. Yet, this is not an exact science and no one automatic source code parsing tool should be relied on solely to provide protection against inaccurate code. Developers and database administrators ideally would pair up and choose a tool with the method that they desire the most. The tool in combination with an expert can provide an effective and reliable tool for analyzing source code.

Chapter Summary

- SQL injections can create vulnerability and provide the means by which intruders can obtain full administration of a database.

- SQL injections can exploit any client/server environment that uses an application to obtain remote connection of a database.

- There are two types of SQL statements, static and dynamic. Dynamic SQL statements are created by applications in an online environment, whereas static SQL statements are used when accessing the database directly.

- Administrators can test for SQL injections either by sending a series of requests while observing the reaction of the server or by reviewing the source code.

- HTTP and TCP are two of the several protocols used for sending information over the network. When a request is made from a Web application to the database, HTTP submits these requests by first initiating a TCP connection as the transfer agent.

- HTTP data can be intercepted and manipulated using third-party applications, local proxy servers, and browser add-ons and plug-ins.

- Becoming familiar with typical database errors is important for identifying the anomalies and vulnerabilities within a system and its environment.

- It is important to keep in mind that applications and databases handle errors differently. An error that may be returned on one database might not be returned on another under the same circumstances.

- Testing for SQL injections should be included within an environment's security penetration testing process.

- Source code can be analyzed while the program is static, or dynamically as the program is being executed.

- Single quotes are an important aspect to error testing; they can be used to identify vulnerabilities.

- Several tools can automatically analyze source code, yet they are not as accurate as a manual user analysis.

- String-based matching tools review source code looking for patterns and strings of data that match vulnerable and dangerous code. This is the most basic form of automatic source analysis tools.

- Data flow analysis tools use control flow graphs to display the sequencing of procedures and variables found within source code. This helps administrators find and verify the safety of the input of variables.

- Lexical analysis scanning tools group code into tokens based on similar criteria, allowing administrators to find dangerous code through tokens.

- Automatic source code analysis should be used by security professionals and in conjunction with manual source reviews.

Key Terms

dynamic analysis An attempt to find errors or vulnerabilities in the source code of a program dynamically while it is being executed.

dynamic SQL statement A SQL statement that is generated on the fly by an application (such as a Web application), using a string of characters derived from a user's input parameters into a form within the application itself.

SQL injections Methods by which intruders use bits of SQL code and SQL queries to gain database access.

static analysis An effort to find problems while the program is inactive.

static SQL statement A statement that is built by the user; the full text of the statement is known at compilation.

Web applications Programs that are available on a network and provide a way for users to interact with remote systems or databases.

Review Questions

1. Discuss the three common strategies for execution of SQL injections.

2. Discuss the relationship between a Web application and a scripting language.

3. Describe the steps involved in the user input reaching the database.

4. Discuss the challenges of typical conditions that create typical errors.

5. Describe the difference between dynamic and static SQL statements. Provide an example to support your discussion.

6. Explain inferential testing.

7. Explain the difference between the HTTP actions GET and POST. Which is more vulnerable to SQL injections? Provide an example to support your statement.

8. Identify and explain at least one way that HTTP data can be intercepted and changed.

9. Explain how studying error messages can help identify SQL injection vulnerability.

10. Explain why active testing is just as important as inferential testing when searching for SQL injection vulnerability.

11. Identify at least one method that source code analysis tools use to locate dangerous source code.

12. Identify how the common injection `'or '1'='1` can be used to test for SQL vulnerability.

Case Projects

CASE PROJECTS

Case Project 7-1: Web Applications

Search the Internet and find three Web applications. Write a paper that discusses the purpose of a Web application; include the three that you found as support for your discussion.

Case Project 7-2: Source Code Analysis Tools

Search the Internet for at least two static source code analysis tools. Identify which method described in the chapter these tools use for source analysis.

Case Project 7-3: The Data Retrieval Process

Describe the steps involved from the user input to the database results displayed on the screen. Identify the different points of the process described in Review Question 3 in which SQL injections can occur.

Case Project 7-4: SQL Server SQL Injections

Identify at least two T-SQL injection warnings or tips found on the Microsoft Web site or elsewhere online that are specific to Microsoft SQL Server.

Case Project 7-5: Oracle SQL Injections

Identify at least two PL/SQL injection warnings or tips found on the Oracle Web site or elsewhere online that are specific to Oracle Database.

Case Project 7-6: MySQL SQL Injections

Identify at least two SQL injection warnings or tips found on the MySQL Web site or elsewhere online that are specific to MySQL.

Hands-On Projects

Hands-On Project 7-1: Securing the Oracle Environment

You have been hired as the security consultant for TJRiggings. As your first task, you have been asked to complete a security audit of their Web applications. Answer the following questions:

1. What are the first steps that you would take to test the sites for SQL injection vulnerability?

2. How might you apply the concept of inferential testing?

3. What is your strategy for identifying dangerous source code now and far into the future?

4. What suggestions would you offer TJRiggings in reference to their Web clients?

7

SQL Injection Exploitation and Defense

After reading this chapter and completing the exercises, you will be able to:

- Define SQL injection exploitation
- Identify ways intruders gather information from a network infrastructure
- Describe common strategies for exploiting database infrastructures
- Identify common SQL statements and SQL constructs used to exploit weaknesses
- Apply exploitation for the purpose of identifying infrastructure weaknesses
- Identify defense strategies against SQL injection exploits

MerryH@K is a self-proclaimed hacking genius of the underground. Notorious for her successful intrusions into the world's most secure systems, she takes great pride in her ability to identify and exploit infrastructure weaknesses. Armed with close to 15 years of experience breaking into private networks, she has obtained a strong understanding of the inner workings of both network architectures and network administrators. Through practice, she has matured her skill for reading basic machine responses and has developed an accurate understanding of the behavior of a typical administrator. In general, MerryH@K's success stems from her refined ability to blindly gather information from foreign systems. Given the extraordinary value of data stored within today's databases, SQL injections and the database infrastructure have become her areas of focus for the last five years. Her latest triumph involved a high-profile company from which she extracted sensitive data, gave herself administrative rights, and ultimately took control of the entire system, which surprisingly began with a single SQL statement created to initiate a delay in the system response. When asked by her peers to describe the most effective technique for extracting data from a secured database, she responds, "Observation."

Achieving success in database intrusion today requires keen observation skills above all other things. Although some database knowledge is necessary, most of what an intruder needs can be found through basic Internet searches and database vendors' Web sites. Intrusion requires the know-how to take a very little bit of information and use it to piece together a larger picture of the target system's construction.

All great security defense strategists attempt to master both the psyche and the behavior of their potential enemies. This is also important for those attempting to defend their infrastructures from SQL exploitation. It can be viewed as a chess match of great proportions. As the intruder is attempting to predict the behavior and strategy of the administrator, the administrator is attempting to predict the behavior and strategy of the attacker. Unfortunately for administrators, the attacker's odds of winning this battle are much greater because security strategies are never foolproof. Whereas security professionals have several reliable applications to help them detect and protect an infrastructure from viruses and intrusion detections, locating and fixing SQL injection vulnerabilities require a great deal of manual configuration, diligent exploration, and constant observation.

Obtaining hands-on knowledge of the various means by which an infrastructure can be exploited is vital to the success of a SQL exploitation defense strategy. This chapter offers insight into the many common and successful techniques intruders similar to

(continued)

MerryH@K use to exploit a system. This chapter, like the previous one, requires the reader to explore and take on the role of a potential attacker who might be working to obtain control over a foreign system.

Please use caution when using the techniques and tools introduced in this chapter. These techniques can cause changes to the database that might interfere with the integrity of the storage system and its interconnected applications. When possible, practice these techniques and tools within a test environment.

Exploitation and Information Gathering

Exploitation is the act of using system vulnerabilities and carefully crafted SQL queries to gather information and subsequently peel away at the infrastructure's security defense for the purpose of gaining access or control of a system. Exploitation does not always result in the control of a system; it depends on the effectiveness of the SQL query injection techniques and the usefulness of the output generated from the system as a result of the SQL query injection techniques. Essentially, the success of exploitation is dependent on the amount of information derived from that system during the exploitation; the more information an attacker can find out about the system, the more freedom they will have within that system. To defend a system from successful exploitation, a security professional must be aware of the means by which information can be derived as well as which information to protect. This section displays the common techniques and exploits used to find different types of information from a system and identify information that those who are exploiting are attempting to obtain.

Information That Aids in Exploitation

As discussed in the previous chapter, inferential exploration is a valuable strategy that can be used by both system administrators and potential intruders for gathering information about a system and its infrastructure vulnerabilities. Locating a weakness is only the first step in the process of intrusion. These weaknesses provide an open door through which intruders can obtain further information about a system and its applications in order to take control. For example, an attacker may obtain access to a particular database, but is not aware of the structure or type of information contained with the tables and records within it. Therefore, the goal is to construct a theoretical picture of the infrastructure, identifying all of the layers and their associated parts. A variety of details, such as the type of Web application, scripting language, Web server, and middleware, combined with the knowledge of the number and type of databases that exist, aid in the goal of obtaining access to the system. Every piece of information helps by providing clues that eventually lead to an intruder developing an understanding of the database schema. The database schema is the overall logical structure of the objects within the database. The schema includes the default stored procedures, tables, views, and users. Obtaining a map or schema of the database subsequently leads to the intruder finding the path to the desired access. This map must be obtained before specific targets can be identified and significant power can be obtained. The end goal of an intruder is often to obtain information residing within the database. Each piece of information that can be gathered about the functionality of the system strengthens the intruder's power over the system, bringing the intruder closer to his or her goal. Therefore, identifying and securing valuable information can be a strong step toward intrusion prevention. This section reviews a few of the most important pieces of information necessary to begin an exploit.

Information About the Database   To successfully exploit a given system, an intruder must first obtain information about the database system itself. Without an understanding of the vendor or version of the database, an exploit is nearly impossible to pull off. The vendor and version of the database provide an intruder a great deal of information, allowing more of an opportunity for attack. Furnished with this information, the intruder can infer such things as the SQL language syntax to use to construct injections, the available default procedures that can be called to obtain more information, the way the database processes queries, and the storage mechanisms utilized. A great portion of the schema can be determined as well because each database vendor (e.g., Oracle, Microsoft) contains default tables and objects, so that identifying the vendor and version number can provide an intruder with important information as to the name of the tables in which sensitive information might reside. If an intruder is able to use the information gathered to construct an accurate map of the database scheme, the entire database is in great jeopardy. The vendor provides a jump-start to understanding the database schema of a target database. For example, finding out that the database is Oracle informs the intruder that the SYS user is installed by default and contains the critical system tables and privileges, whereas in Microsoft SQL Server, the database administrator (DBA) can access and control all database items. This is a simple example, but the important thing to understand is that there are variances between database vendors, as well as different versions under the same vendor, that enable intrusion. Finding this information is the first step toward exploitation.

Identifying the Vendor   The database vendor can be identified in several different ways. Locating this information is quite easy for the knowledgeable intruder, as many clues are available to help. The following list of clues aid intruders in identifying the database vendor. Keep in mind while reviewing these items that they are only clues; by themselves, none of these clues is reliable enough to draw a conclusion. An intruder often needs to identify more than one of the following clues to conclude with a sufficient level of certainty the vendor and type of database being used:

- *The scripting language*—There are standards and commonalities between the scripting languages being used within Web applications and the underlying database vendor. These standards came to fruition as database vendors began to build relationships with specific languages by including additional support for improved compatibility. Database vendors often lean toward one or two languages, building additional support for these languages to increase the transparency and interoperability. For example, PHP is often used to communicate with MySQL as it offers native PHP drivers allowing for alternative connections to the database through PHP scripting. On the other hand, .NET was developed by Microsoft and from the introduction of SQL Server 2005 until today, a great amount of support for integration with the .NET Framework is included with SQL Server. This relationship offers the highest compatibility and transparency, which has been extended to include ADO.NET. Oracle has offered support for Java since its introduction into the coding world. More recently, Java's acquisition of Sun Oracle has made this relationship even stronger. Therefore, the presence of PHP can indicate that MySQL exists, whereas .NET implies that SQL Server is the underlying database and Java Script used within a Web application can almost provide certainty that the database being used is Oracle.

- *The platform*—The operating system on which the database resides provides clues as to the version of database in place. As discussed in earlier chapters, Microsoft SQL Server is based on the foundation of Microsoft Windows Server 2008, so any indication that the underlying operating system is Microsoft Windows can also be a clue that points toward a SQL Server database. One the other hand, open source operating systems such as Linux and UNIX are often used to support MySQL and Oracle. The platform provides only one small clue as to the underlying database. Many factors unrelated to the database can play a role in choosing an operating system. These factors include cost, complexity, and support, so be aware that the operating system alone is not a reliable indication of the database in use. Every configuration is different and every network, as well as the applications that reside on it, has its own unique and individual needs. Therefore, the platform being used within an infrastructure can only provide supporting evidence when combined with other information. For example, the discovery of Microsoft Windows is hardly an argument for an underlying SQL Server database. Windows is an extremely popular operating system onto which both Oracle and MySQL can be installed, so to make this assumption would be a grave mistake. On the other hand, combining the discovery of a Windows platform with the identification of the usage of .NET within the Web application can make for a much stronger argument that SQL Server is in use.

- *The database response*—Database responses, if present, can provide the most reliable means by which to identify the database. This is true for almost any piece of technology that exists today. It only takes one informative error message to give away the identity of the database being used. This is due to the differences in syntax and error format from one database to another. One apparent way to identify the database from an error message is by using the error code provided. A database error will often include a number or code in hopes of offering the user or administrator with some means by which to obtain further information about the cause of the error; each database vendor has its own convention for numbering errors. Therefore, becoming familiar with the naming convention of the different database vendors provides intruders a way to immediately identify the database. To make matters worse, vendors maintain an area on their Web sites where administrators can search for an error number and find the meaning of the code itself. This is intended to aid in the troubleshooting process, yet if an intruder is unfamiliar with the error code naming convention of each database vendor, he or she can simply search for the corresponding error number on each vendor's site until the correct vendor is found. Table 8-1 provides a list of the vendor Web sites where error code searches can be found. In some cases, error messages include the name of the database, the version number, and the last patch applied to the system. Obviously, generating an error with this information included within the message would be the easiest way to obtain the information, yet these messages are not as prevalent in today's security-conscious society. The amount of information included within a database error is dependent on both the vendor and the type of error. Databases can also be configured to eliminate the return of error messages or to return a generic message for all errors despite the type of error encountered. These circumstances are intended to avoid passing along unwanted information to intruders.

It is important to point out that not all databases will return error messages as described in this section. A database can be configured to allow the Web application to handle errors or to provide a generic message to a user despite the error the database encountered. Ideally, a database is configured to eliminate external error messaging altogether, having no response to an erroneous query, and in turn offering no information to an external user.

When combined, the clues identified in this section can provide an intruder with information about the type or vendor of the database. Having this knowledge, an intruder gains an understanding of how to speak with and manipulate the database to ensure further exploitation and ultimately aids in helping the intruder achieve his or her desired goal.

Vendor	Error code search Web site	Sample
Microsoft SQL Server	www.microsoft.com/technet/ support/ee/ee_advanced.aspx	Login failed for user *'DOMAINNAME\ACCOUNTNAME'* (Error code: 18456)
MySQL	http://dev.mysql.com/doc/ refman/5.1/en/error-messages-server.html	error 2003: access denied for user @ localhost (100061)
Oracle	www.ora-code.com/	ERROR: ORA-01017 invalid username/password; login denied

Table 8-1 **Error code identification**

Identifying the Version Identifying the version can be equally as important to an intruder as identifying the vendor. Finding out which version of the database is in use provides an intruder with better insight into the capabilities of the system. Each version of a database management system is different. They can include new features, missing features, or have subtle changes in syntax that could deter the attack, and many new versions are created as a way to patch known security vulnerabilities from previous versions. Therefore, armed with the knowledge of the version of the database system, an intruder will be certain to ensure the correct approach for injection and can potentially identify and take advantages of known vulnerabilities for that version and use these as an advantage toward obtaining control.

With the database vendor identified, locating the version number can be an easy task. Each database management system has standard queries meant for returning the version number of that system. For example, executing the command *SELECT @@VERSION* will return the version of the underlying Microsoft SQL Server as well as the processor, operating system, service pack, and build, which is quite a lot of information for such a small statement! For MySQL, the equivalent statement is *SELECT VERSION()*, and for Oracle, *select * from v$version where banner like 'Oracle%';* will return the version and build number. Using the injection techniques discussed in the previous chapter, dynamic SQL can be used to send these queries to be processed by the database by injecting the statements as a string parameter within the Web application or from the URL. One of three things will occur:

- *Results returned*—In cases where the application input or output has not been filtered and the application or parameter is expecting a string (the ideal scenario for an intruder), the database will return the results of the injected statement and provide the version number.

- *Error returned*—If a number is expected within the application or as a parameter, as opposed to the string that was input, or the statement is constructed incorrectly, an error will be generated. Surprisingly, depending on the vendor, this error message may also provide the necessary information.

- *Nothing returned*—For scenarios in which the application does filter the input or output or is configured to handle error messages in such a way that messages either do not return anything or return a generic response, nothing will be returned. Under these circumstances, finding the version will be more difficult. Each version of the database will have subtle changes in the way that some statements are constructed. To identify the correct version, the intruder will have to take a trial-and-error approach by choosing the statements that have been subtly changed with each version of that particular database management system. These statements will then need to be injected one by one into the application or URL until the correct syntax returns a result. The correct syntax will then identify the correct version of the database.

Standard statements for identifying the version of a database management system are helpful, yet they are not the only standard statements that exist. Several other standard statements are also available with every database management system. These statements can be used to gather useful information, such as the name, the location, and the language being used on the database. Administrators should familiarize themselves with these statements so as to understand the amount of information that can be gathered during an initial trial at exploitation.

Extracting the Real Data

The information gathered using the techniques discussed in the previous section acts as a building block for an intruder, opening the door of possibilities tremendously. Based on the knowledge obtained about the database, the intruder can make inferences (e.g., SQL syntax, data structure) that will enable the construction of meaningful queries that will provide data to assist in the further development of the intruder's understanding of the database schema. In other words, the exploitation attack is equipped to delve deeper into the system, adding more of an understanding of the data stored within it. Targets can be located and data can be extracted as each layer of integrity is taken apart piece by piece, or bit by bit.

Statement Exploits

Once vulnerability has been exploited and the appropriate syntax has been identified, an endless number of SQL statements can be injected into the database. The intruder has the capability to access the database as a typical user. Restricted only by the privileges of the user for which the queries are being processed, which can be liberal depending on the configuration, thoughtful statements can be constructed for further exploration. This section explores the most common statements constructed for SQL injection attacks as well as the inventive ways they are used to uncover more information about the internal workings of the database. Later sections explore ways privileges can be manipulated and granted to extend the intruder's capabilities, but for this section, it is assumed that the intruder is working under restricted conditions.

Using UNION

UNION statements are very powerful tools of SQL injection attacks. They provide an opportunity for an intruder to attach his or her own queries onto already existing legitimate statements. UNION statements are SQL statements that include the UNION operator, which combines two or more SQL statements from which the output is combined. If a UNION operator is placed at the end of one SQL statement and a SELECT query is added after the UNION statement, then both queries will produce output. For example, imagine a scenario in which a local online specialty grocer allows customers to search and purchase products on its Web site, *www.yum.com*. This site allows patrons to choose from different types of foods, such as dairy, produce, and meat. Each category has its own respective button; when visitors click this button, a new page appears displaying a list of available products for that food category. For example, Dairy's button may link to the following URL:

http://www.yum.com/index.asp?category=dairy

This URL shows the variable as *category* and the value *dairy*. The scripting language will take the output from the button (the preceding URL) and send it as a request to the database. Again, we are using ASP, and so the code to request this information may be similar to this:

```
food_cat = request("category")
sqlstr= "SELECT * FROM products WHERE Food_Category = '"&food_cat&"'"
set rs-conn.execute(sqlstr)
```

In this case, the ASP would create the following SQL statement to be executed by the database:

```
SELECT * FROM products WHERE Food_Category = 'Dairy'
```

In this case, the database would return one or more rows that match the WHERE clause, which in this case is Dairy. No errors are generated for this scenario. Keep in mind that when using SQL, alphanumeric values must be enclosed using single quotes (e.g., 'Dairy').

If a UNION statement is injected after 'Dairy' and a new statement is created as such:

http://www.yum.com/index.asp?category=dairy **union select Table_Name from Information_ Schema.Tables- -**

both results will be combined and returned, given the syntax is correct. In this case, if the syntax is correct, the table name from within the Information_Schema.Tables will be returned. The statement Information_Schema.Tables is the location from which a user can view all of the tables from within the SQL Server database. The Table_Name call is essentially asking the database to provide all of the names of the tables in the Information_Schema area. Initiating this procedure will return all tables for a specific database. The double dashes (--) comment the rest of the statement.

The difficulty involved with using the correct syntax for UNION statements is that the data type must be the same for each column that the original statement is returning and the number of columns being requested in the new statement must be the same as the results of the original statement. Therefore, using the previous example, if the original statement has more than one table and it is of a different data type than that of "Table_Name," this statement will fail. Without complete knowledge of what is being returned from the original request, it can take a bit of trial and error to successfully pull this off.

The first step is to try to figure out how many columns are being used in the original query. If error messages are being returned, there is a technique that will help identify this number. The trick is to keep adding null expressions in place of the SELECT statement in the URL until the error messages disappear, such as:

http://www.yum.com/index.asp?category=dairy **union select null from Information_Schema .Tables- -**

http://www.yum.com/index.asp?category=dairy **union select null null from Information_Schema .Tables- -**

http://www.yum.com/index.asp?category=dairy **union select null null null from Information_ Schema.Tables- -**

http://www.yum.com/index.asp?category=dairy **union select null null null null from Information_ Schema.Tables- -**

Depending on the number of columns being requested in the original statement, this can be quite a long process. Yet, if null is accepted (which it is in most modern databases), it is an effective technique. Because null is being used, the data type is irrelevant, ensuring that the focus is on finding the number of columns avoiding data type errors.

Once the number of columns being called from the original request has been determined, the data type necessary for each column can also be determined. Again, this involves trial and error, but can be determined by replacing each column one at a time with a specific data type. For example, assuming that it was discovered that the original statement contained only three columns, the following strategy would determine the correct column from which to extract table names from the Information_Schema.Tables view:

http://www.yum.com/index.asp?category=dairy **union select Table_Name, null, null from Information_Schema.Tables- -**

http://www.yum.com/index.asp?category=dairy **union select null, Table_Name, null from Information_Schema.Tables- -**

http://www.yum.com/index.asp?category=dairy **union select null, null, Table_Name from Information_Schema.Tables- -**

For those data statements in which an error is returned, the incorrect data type exists, so the choice is to either attempt a different data type for that column, or leave it as null and out of the statement altogether, such as:

http://www.yum.com/index.asp?category=dairy **union select Table_Name, null, Table_Name, from Information_Schema.Tables- -**

Automated tools have been developed by both administrators and intruders to assist with this effort. They can be found by searching online. These tools can be used in cases where *null* is not able to be used or when the columns are much too large and the task becomes much too time consuming. As you can see, table names can be extracted using these techniques: *Table_Name* can be replaced with *Column_Name*, whereas *Information_Schema.Tables* can be replaced with *Information_Schema.Columns* to identify and view all of the columns in the database using the same strategy!

Using Conditions

Conditional statements can also be quite handy in providing the intruder with clues adding to the theoretical database schema mapping. Essentially, conditional statements assert that if a certain condition shows true, then a specified action should be taken and if a certain condition shows false, then an alternative action should be taken. This section shows how conditional statements can be used iteratively to expand the intruder's view of the database and allow further collection of information. Conditional statements are greatly advantageous in situations where UNION statements are not allowed.

Using conditional statements as injections is like playing a game of *Twenty Questions* with the database. For example, an intruder can ask the database *Am I the Administrator?* by constructing a statement that asserts if the username for which my queries are being processed is equal to the administrator account for the database, then return a 1 otherwise error. This is the constructed statement for SQL Server:

```
IF ((select user) = 'sa' OR (select user) = 'dbo') select 1 ELSE
select 1/0
```

Because the expression 1/0 cannot be calculated, the statement will generate an error, if the "if" condition is not true. Otherwise, it will return a 1. In cases where applications are configured to never display error messages, the intruder's question, *Am I the Administrator?* can still be answered because a 1 will not be returned to the user. Generating error messages is often not the best approach for an intruder who wants to ensure that his or her actions are transparent to the system and the system administrator. Conditional statements similar to the previous one do not return a great deal of information and it is likely that several statements will be required to gather the desired amount of information about the database scheme. With each statement, an error message is generated and recorded within the error logs of the database. Network and database monitoring systems provide an administrator with the capability to set up alerts under certain conditions. For example, an administrator can create a rule within a system that states *If the number of error messages that the database experiences exceeds the baseline or number of error messages that are typically experienced, alert staff.* If this rule is created within an environment, then an intruder who is generating excessive numbers of error messages to obtain information will be identified through alerts. It is important to point out that the absence of an error message does not indicate the absence of an error; only a returned result indicates error-free processing. Cases where errors are not sent to external users (blind environments) typically indicate that errors are being handled and deterred by the Web application as a safety measure to minimize the impact of a SQL injection, yet these messages are still being logged by the database. Therefore, although conditional messages are effective in nonblind circumstances, they should not be used in situations where a great number of iterative conditional statements are necessary. There are several alternative and less-alarming ways to obtain an answer from a conditional statement.

Initiated delays or time-based responses are alternative means that have been proven to be an effective means to finding an answer to a constructed conditional statement, in both blind and nonblind environments. Time-based response strategies involve the intruder creating statements that either keep the servers busy or delayed for a certain amount of time to indicate the yes-or-no answer to the constructed statement. For example, if a conditional statement asks the server to respond displaying a 1 for both true and false conditions, yet adds a delay of the response (let's say five seconds) on the false condition, then the presence or absence of a pause is what will provide the intruder with the correct answer.

```
IF((select user) = 'sa' OR (select user) = 'dbo') select 1 AND WAIT
FOR DELAY '0:0:5' ELSE select 1
```

Table 8-2 provides the statements used to pause a system for different database vendors.

Platform	Procedure	Comments
Microsoft SQL Server	WAIT FOR DELAY '0:0:5'	Delays a system for five seconds
MySQL	BENCHMARK(100000, encode('Hello'))	Causes the system to encode the word *hello* one million times, resulting in a delay; the exact time of the delay can be determined by practicing the commands prior to using them
Oracle	Pg sleep(5)	Delays a system for five seconds

Table 8-2 Initiating server time delays

The disadvantage of using time delays is the delay itself. Keep in mind that the goal is to gather enough information to better understand the database schema. This will require quite a bit of information and can require a number of conditional statements or yes-and-no responses. This alone takes a lot of time. If each conditional statement includes a time delay of five seconds (which might not be enough time to distinguish between normal system delays and the statement-forced delay), the process takes five times as long as without the delays. Therefore, although this is an effective injection alternative for blind scenarios, it adds a lot of time to the overall process.

Another option for using conditional statements to gather information is designing statements to return different results for true statements as for false statements. For example, constructing a statement that returns a 1 if the condition is true and 2 if the condition is false will provide a clear indication of the correct response.

```
IF ((select user) = 'sa' OR (select user) = 'dbo') select 1 ELSE
select 2
```

Although this might seem to be the simplest and most effective choice for gathering information using conditional statements, because there are no error messages or time delays, it is important to be aware of all the strategies that exist to effectively defend against conditional statement injections. This point will become clearer as the chapter continues. Despite the type of conditional statement chosen, the process of gathering information using only yes-or-no responses is quite a laborious and time-consuming task. However, depending on the defense strategies of the database administrator, conditional statements might be the only means by which information can be gathered. Depending on the value of the data stored within the target database, using conditional statements might just be well worth the trouble!

Large-Scale Extraction

As this chapter has stressed thus far, each bit of information gathered from a system provides a building block to obtaining information and the deeper the discoveries, the more capabilities that will result. Therefore, although the strategies discussed in previous sections might seem tedious and time consuming, they are effective at providing intruders with the necessary data to extend their search. As the data scheme becomes more understood and a partial database scheme is created, the strategies presented thus far can be combined to extract data on a much grander scale. Equipped with the basic information collected thus far, the intruder can now delve much deeper into the infrastructure by identifying the number of accessible databases and by extracting the tables and columns from within them. This section explores the strategies used to locate and extract large scales of information from target databases.

Obtaining Database Names The first step to obtaining large amounts of information is identifying a list of accessible databases that reside within the infrastructure. Once these have been discovered, one or several can be targeted and tables and columns can then be extracted. Here, the intruder will need to use the information that has been gathered thus far, as the exact statements injected to find this information will be dependent on the vendor for correct syntax. Table 8-3 displays a list of potential statements that can be used to extract the names of the surrounding accessible database for the current users. These statements can be injected into an application field or added to an application URL as previously described.

Platform	Statement	Comments
Microsoft SQL Server	SELECT name FROM sysdatabases	Returns a list of databases; the *sysdatabases* is installed with SQL Server and contains entries for each major database, which includes the *master*, *model*, *msdb*, and *tempdb*
MySQL	SELECT schema_Name FROM information_schema.schemata	Returns a list of databases; *Information_schema* allows access to the metadata of the databases and *.schemata* is a table that holds information about the databases
Oracle	SELECT global_name FROM global_name	Within Oracle, a user can only maintain one connection to one database, so the only list that can be retrieved is that of the name of the current database

Table 8-3   **Database discovery**

Obtaining Table Names Once a list of accessible databases is discovered, the next step is to extract the tables within the target database. This is done by finding the table that holds the number and names of all of the tables in that particular database. Each database vendor has a table called sysobjects that will provide this information. Table 8-4 displays the statements that can be constructed and injected into Web applications or URLs to extract the list of database tables.

Obtaining Columns At this point, the intruder has the names of all of the accessible databases, has targeted a database, and has identified the names of the tables within that database. Having these names, the intruder can construct statements to extract the columns

Platform	Statement	Comments
Microsoft SQL Server	SELECT name FROM systables	Returns a list of tables found in the *sys.tables* view of the target database
MySQL	SELECT Column_Name FROM information_schema .tables	Returns a list of databases; *Information_schema* allows access to the metadata of the databases and *.tables* is a table that holds information about the tables
Oracle	Select Table_Name from all_tables;	Returns all of the tables in the database

Table 8-4 **Table identification**

from the data and, subsequently, the data from within these columns. Table 8-5 displays a few statements that can be constructed and injected into Web applications or URLs to extract this data.

Platform	Statement	Comments
Microsoft SQL Server	SELECT name FROM syscolumns	Returns a list of tables found in the *sys.columns* view of the target database
MySQL	SELECT Column_Name FROM information_schema.columns	Returns a list of databases; *Information_schema* allows access to the metadata of the databases and *.columns* is a table that holds information about the columns
Oracle	Select column_name from all_tab_columns;	Returns all of the columns in the database

Table 8-5 **Identifying columns**

If successful, the intruder now has a pretty clear picture of the database schema and the partial mapping can be completed.

Advanced Techniques

Often, filters are used within Web applications as a way to identify and defer an injection. These filters will often use string comparisons to identify dangerous code being input or displayed as output. These filters will search for and block certain known SQL injection characters or statements. Unfortunately, intruders have found several ways to evade and trick these filters. Often, these filters are configured to compare strings or characters that may be found in the application URL or input fields with those common characters and well-known SQL injection keywords. Even the most basic detection systems filter strings such as SELECT and UNION. So, as a way to push injections through filters undetected, intruders use variations of these strings and keywords. The following list describes ways attackers can trick the system or hide from filters:

- *Encoding*—Changing characters from the expected standard (e.g., ASCII) to a different unexpected one (e.g., URL, Hex, Binary) that direct string comparisons will not detect and that can evade basic filters. For example, instead of using a single quote (') within an injection because it is often filtered, the URL encoding standard of a single quote, %27, is used instead.

- *Case sensitivity*—If the Web application that is filtering common strings such as SELECT or UNION is case sensitive, variances in case can be used to avoid detection. For example, the word UNION might be found through a basic string comparison, whereas uNiON will not.

- *Breaking it down*—Another way to avoid basic string comparisons from filters is to break the common word up using URL code so that the word is pieced back together once processed. For example, SELECT could be expressed in an injection statement as 'S'+'ELE'+'CT.

- *Using alternatives*—There are several different ways to express statements, so if one injection technique fails and filtering is suspected, alternative words can be used to express the same statement and avoid filters. For example, when using conditional statements, *Case* statements can be used instead of *If .. Then* statements. In case of numbers, 2+2 can be used in place of 4.

These techniques, when used together, can be very powerful. Considering the amount of possible combinations of variations that are possible, they can make detection almost impossible.

Exploitation of Privileges and Passwords

The success of all of the statements described in the previous sections is dependent on the permissions of the user for which the injection statements are being processed within the database. Therefore, if the users for which the injection statements are being executed only have the right to view one database, a query injected with the intention of gaining access to view all of the remote databases will only display the one for which the privileges exist. This can be quite limiting, especially with newer versions of a database management system. As was discussed earlier in the book, a great deal of granularity is offered to administrators when setting up privileges for the database users. Therefore, to apply the techniques in this chapter and gain an understanding of the target database's schema, privileges must be identified and, if possible, increased. This section explores a few of the most common techniques for identifying and obtaining administrator privileges.

Identifying Privileges

Using techniques that were already discussed in this chapter, an intruder is able to locate and read tables and columns within the database. Assuming that the goal is to locate and potentially escalate user privileges, the intruder must first know which privileges are grantable on the system. Therefore, user privilege tables must be located and viewed. Table 8-6 displays the SQL statements that can be constructed and injected into vulnerable Web applications and URLs to identify the available grantable privileges on the database.

Platform	Statement	Comments
Microsoft SQL Server	EXEC sp_helprotect NULL, 'myusername'	Returns a list of all permissions for the username provided in single quotes, for that particular database. It is necessary to change *myusername* to the name of the current user; therefore, the current username must be found first for this statement to be effective
MySQL	SELECT Grantee, privilege_type, is_grantable FROM information_schema .user_priviliges	Returns a list of grantable privileges on the current database; *Information_schema* allows access to the metadata of the databases and *.user_privileges* is a table that holds the grantable privileges
Oracle	Select * from user_sys_privs Select * from user_role_privs Select * from user_tab_privs Select * from user_col_privs	There are four different types of privileges within Oracle: System, Role, Table, and Column. *Sys_privs* holds all current user-grantable system privileges; *Role_privs* holds all current user-grantable roles; *Tab_privs* holds all current user-grantable table privileges; *Col_privs* holds all current user-grantable column privileges

Table 8-6 Identifying grantable privileges

8

Obtaining Passwords

On all database management systems, user passwords are stored using a nonreversible hash within a table for which privileges are needed to access. A **password hash** is a cryptology-encoded string version of a user or system password. Passwords are often stored within a database as a hash to increase security of the password, yet not all passwords are saved as a hash. Some are saved as text strings and pose a great risk to the data integrity. This section focuses on the injection methods by which the text and hash version of stored passwords can be extracted and decrypted for the purpose of escalating one's privileges within a system.

If an intruder uses the techniques discussed throughout this chapter to obtain the names and fields of the tables for which passwords are stored within a database, the intruder can then extract passwords and use them to log in to the system, elevating his or her rights on that system. Whether the password is stored as a hash or a simple text string will determine the ease with which the intruder can put the passwords to use. For example, if a database is stored as a text string in the user table of the database, and an intruder locates the field in which these passwords are stored, a simple SQL statement can be constructed to extract the string value of the field and with very little effort obtain the actual characters of the password. Although password hashes are much more secure, these too can be extracted using injected SQL statements. You can find programs online that are built to automate the processes of decoding hashed passwords, so even the strongest hash does not guarantee safety when stored in a database. Table 8-7 provides examples of SQL statements that can be constructed to retrieve text passwords stored within a system.

Platform	Statement	Comments
Microsoft SQL Server	2000- SELECT name.password FROM master.dbo.sysxlogins 2005- SELECT password_hash FROM sql_logins	In SQL Server 2000, login information is stored in the *sysxlogins* table of the master database; this table was discontinued in later versions and the login information was moved to the *sql_logins* table
MySQL	SELECT user, password FROM mysql.user	Passwords are located in the *mysql.user* table in MySQL
Oracle	SELECT name, password FROM sys.user$ where type#=1	Text passwords can be found in *sys users* in the *system.mgmt_credentials2.table* by default

Table 8-7 **Extracting passwords**

Obtaining Privileges

Obtaining user passwords is one sure way of obtaining higher privileges within a system, yet very often the tables that hold this information require high privileges themselves. More often than not, intruders must find a back-door strategy for viewing the tables that can cause the greatest harm. Unfortunately for database administrators, but fortunately for attackers, these back-door strategies do exist. Unlike many of the strategies that were discussed thus far, obtaining administrator privileges from a system is vendor and version specific, so these strategies vary greatly from one system to the next. This section identifies and explores the vulnerabilities that offer an intruder the potential for escalating privileges.

Brute Force Attacks Brute force essentially means to use every possible combination. Brute force attacks often involve the act of obtaining passwords or specific pieces of information through iterative trial and error. For example, a brute force attack on a lock combination would involve several attempts of each number of the lock in each order possible until the safe is cracked, so to say. Brute force attack complexity depends on the information that the intruder is attempting to obtain. For example, if the combination of a lock is only three numbers in length and only the numbers 1, 2, and 3 can be used, then the attack will be quick and successful. With this said, brute force attacks are often more successful if a great deal of background knowledge is obtained prior to the attack. For example, information such as the length of a desired administrative password as well as the available characters allowed within the password both can support a brute force attack. It often also involves stages. A brute force attack on an administrative password might begin with a brute force attack on a user password, so as to gain access to database tables from which it is necessary to gather information. Brute force attacks are not uncommon approaches to successfully elevating privileges.

Automated Tools Several tools can be found online that are created for gathering information about a database to assist in taking control through privilege elevation. As was mentioned earlier in the chapter, blind attacks can be very time consuming and laborious, and much like brute force attacks, they involve iterative tasks for obtaining information from a system that provides little to no response. In addition, several tools are available online that are created to automate the process of SQL injection. Some are intended to speed up or decrease the complexity of brute force attacks and others are created specifically for attacks on certain platforms. Either way, these tools can be very dangerous and offer an intruder a way to attack several system vulnerabilities at once.

OPENROWSET Any of the SQL statement strategies provided earlier in this chapter can be used to escalate privileges because they can be used to gather information from a database. The possibilities for injecting conditional statements are endless and certainly not limited to the examples provided in the chapter. With a little ingenuity, anything is possible. One specific procedure worth noting is OPENROWSET. OPENROWSET is a common procedure available in SQL Server and can be used for escalating privileges within SQL Server. OPENROW-SET allows a user the ability to remotely connect to the database to retrieve information as a user different from that defined by the Web technology. OPENROWSET was developed to provide administrators an alternative way to access tables in a remote server one time, using their database credentials. The requirement of OPENROWSET is that the credentials provided to log in remotely must match those on the database for which the connection resides. Therefore, a username and password must be obtained to use OPENROWSET, as mentioned previously, but OPENROWSET does not have a time-out for failed attempts at logging in. Therefore, an intruder can use brute force strategies and tools to obtain the necessary credentials. Once the credentials are achieved, OPENROWSET offers a remote connection to the database in a way that data can be manipulated and changed in bulk, providing the necessary door for an intruder to achieve full control of the system.

E-Mail Most modern database systems provide an e-mail function that automatically sends messages via e-mail to administrators or users. These messages can be alerts or general responses from the server. For example, in large environments to better support database users, the database will automatically generate an e-mail that includes a user's password if the password was lost or forgotten. An attacker can take advantage of this system by creating malicious code to redirect or copy the information being sent. Although the information that the intruder will receive is unpredictable, it does provide a channel for escalating database privileges and obtaining sensitive information.

Defending Against Exploitation

Now that vulnerabilities have been identified through the diligent attempts of exploit against one's own infrastructure, vital information has been obtained. For administrators, the only question that remains is *How do we defend our systems?* By now, it is clear that the answer involves much more than code and user restriction alone. Becoming aware of the weaknesses of an infrastructure is the first line of defense, as awareness alone arms administrators by providing them with areas on which to focus their defense. A strong defense includes meticulous system monitoring and thoughtful action. There isn't a simple and quick answer to what is necessary, and SQL injection defense isn't an exact science. As this section explores the strategies for limiting the potential of a SQL injection attack, it is important to understand that this is an ongoing effort and that not one strategy identified here will work alone. The most effective approach is to combine all of these strategies, creating a very strong force to be reckoned with.

Using Bond Parameters

Although this chapter has identified several alternative methods to accomplish a SQL injection attack, the most common intrusions involve malicious SQL statements that are inputted as parameters. **Bond parameters** are placeholders for which to bind user input. Once bonded, the input is placed into an already constructed SQL statement and sent to the database to be processed. Statements are predefined, so dynamic SQL is not necessary, and because of the way that the statements are constructed, the user input has nothing to do with the SQL statement parsing. The user data is treated as data alone and cannot affect the SQL statement, so if the data is an injection, it isn't processed by the database in a malicious way. This is a very effective defense, yet bond parameters cannot be used for every user variable, only data values.

Sanitizing Data

By this point, it should be clear that some type of input filter needs to be applied. Although this chapter identified ways input and output filtering can be defeated, security requires multiple layers of defense. Each layer adds complexity for the intruder, and blocking well-known characters and keywords plays an essential role in limiting the intruder early on. It is important to note that *word filtering* is not synonymous with *word blocking*. **Word blocking** refers to the act of blocking keywords that are not allowed to be used as input within a Web application or a Web URL. **Word filtering** is a balance of blocking those known keywords that are not allowed to be used as input within a Web application or Web URL, and identifying those keywords that are allowed to be used as input within a Web application or Web URL. It is much better to place the majority of one's effort into defining only those words or characters that can be inputted in a specific field, than to spend hours fruitlessly attempting to identify every single variation and combination of potentially dangerous items that could come across the network. Therefore, when possible, limit and mask data fields. This is not to say that blocking is not necessary; common keywords should still be blocked, just to a reasonable extent.

Restricting and Segregating Databases

As was discussed several times throughout this book, granularity is the key to setting permissions. At this point, it should be clear that privileges on the database should be assigned with the greatest granularity available, yet what is often overlooked are the permissions of the users on the Web server. Because the injections will be processed with the privileges of the Web application, the Web server should have the most restricted privileges possible. The ideal strategy is to provide the Web application with rights only to access limited tables on an isolated server until the appropriate credentials are supplied. At that point, some of the restrictions would be lifted, corresponding with the user's rights for whom credentials were provided. Related to this, the administrator should design the infrastructure so that the Web server and database server are segregated. Therefore, if users are not configured properly on the Web server, it will not affect their capabilities on the database management system.

Security-Conscious Database Design

One goal of this chapter was to provide administrators with an outsider's view of their infrastructure. Great insight can be gained from this, so use what you learned. When designing the data infrastructure, consider where things are stored and how this is viewed by an outsider. Does the organization give away too many clues? Consider how objects are named; what information does the name give to an external visitor? Try changing default names on sensitive data whenever possible and do not use object views for critical database objects. It can also be beneficial, if the resources are available, to create a honeypot environment. A **honeypot** is a fake environment that includes false data to mislead intruders who are attempting to gather information about the database.

Diligent Monitoring

Monitoring is equally as important as all of the other security techniques available. Through logs and monitors, an experienced security professional can identify a potential attack. For example, conditional statements that rely on errors will generate a great number of database connection pool errors, so tracking this will show indications of real-time attacks. Automated tools used in brute force attacks increase resource usage, so recording database queries per minute and database requests per minute can also be an accurate alert of potential attack. Use information gathered through inferential observation to create baselines. Use the baselines to create thresholds that sound an alarm in situations where resources are exceeded. If configured correctly, the network management logs and tools can be a significantly valuable security defense tool.

Chapter Summary

- SQL injections are used to identify and exploit weaknesses within a database management system.

- Through inferential explorations and vulnerability exploitation, intruders are able to obtain enough information to obtain a picture of the infrastructure as well as the database schema itself.

- An intruder who has obtained an accurate database schema of a particular database is aware of how the data is structured and is able to find any information that is desired.

- The more information a potential intruder can gain from a system or infrastructure, the better equipped he or she is to obtain control. Valuable information about a database includes its vendor, operating system, supporting applications, and version.

- Standards exist for how systems are configured. For example, certain Web applications are better supported when combined with certain scripting languages or database applications. These standards help intruders make assumptions and gather information to aid in their attack.

- Database errors often include the vendor's name. Therefore, databases that return errors provide intruders with a clear view as to what system they are trying to attack.

- Union statements are powerful components for an attack. They provide intruders with the capability to append malicious code onto legitimate SQL statements.

- Conditional statements can be used in several ways to help intruders obtain access and subsequently gain control over a system. Using conditional statements is the way unauthorized individuals ask the database yes-or-no type questions.

- Union and conditional statements combined offer a powerful strategy to obtaining control of a system using SQL injection. With these statements, privileges can be identified, data can be retrieved, and a theoretical database schema can be created.

- Intruders can evade Web application filters by using alternative encoding, case, and words that are unexpected.

- Privileges can be escalated by obtaining passwords through brute force attacks, automated tools, e-mail redirection, and OPENROWSET.

- Bond parameters defend against exploitation by ensuring that malicious SQL statements are not processed.

- Sanitizing data is an important component to keeping Web application data legitimate and the database secure. Sanitizing data can be done by applying filters and blocking words.

- Segregation of the database servers will ensure that they can be closely monitored and secured.

- When designing a database infrastructure, you should be considerate of what can be seen from outside the network. For example, tables and critical database items should be named so as to not identify their contents to outsiders.

Key Terms

bond parameters Placeholders to bind user input.

exploitation The act of using system vulnerabilities and carefully crafted SQL queries to gather information and subsequently peel away at the infrastructure's security defense for the purpose of gaining access or control of a system.

honeypot A fake environment that includes false data to mislead intruders who are attempting to gather information about the database.

password hash A cryptology-encoded string version of a user or system password.

word blocking The act of blocking keywords that are not allowed to be used as input within a Web application or a Web URL.

word filtering A balance of blocking those known keywords that are not allowed to be used as input within a Web application or Web URL, and identifying those keywords that are allowed to be used as input within a Web application or Web URL.

Review Questions

1. List and explain at least two ways that an intruder can identify the vendor of a database.

2. Identify the SQL statement for identifying the version of an Oracle, MySQL, and Microsoft SQL Server database management system.

3. Define a UNION statement and explain how it can be used to exploit a system.

4. Explain the constraints of the UNION statement. Provide an example to support your answer.

5. Provide an example of a UNION statement used in conjunction with a SQL injection.

6. Define a conditional statement and explain how it can help an intruder gather information from a system.

7. List the SQL statement to obtain the list of all database names within a Microsoft SQL Server envrionment.

8. List and explain at least two ways that intruders can defeat Web application filters.

9. Identify at least two ways that privileges can be escalated or obtained by an intruder from within the system.

10. Explain how the use of bond parameters can help defend against Web application exploitation.

Case Projects

Case Project 8-1: Defending Against Web Application Exploitation

Create a plan detailing steps that should be taken to defend against SQL injection exploitation within Web applications.

Case Project 8-2: Time Delays

Provide a scenario where time delays can be used to gain information from a system and provide an example to support your statement.

Case Project 8-3: Oracle Vulnerability

Using Oracle's Web site *www.Oracle.com* and the Internet, locate at least one security vulnerability in a current version of an Oracle application.

Case Project 8-4: Microsoft SQL Server Vulnerability

Using the SQL Server Web site *www.microsoft.com/sqlserver/2008/en/us/* and the Internet, identify at least one vulnerability in a current version of a Microsoft SQL Server application.

Case Project 8-5: MySQL Vulnerability

Using My Server's Web site *www.mysql.com/* and the Internet, identify at least one vulnerability in a current version of a MySQL application.

Hands-On Projects

Hands-On Project 8-1: Exploitation Awareness

Nathan is a security consultant for Tyler & Haley financial, a large mortgage lending company in New York City. He has been hired to raise the company DBA's awareness about SQL injections.

1. Nathan is giving a speech on the four steps of exploitation. What four steps do you anticipate him including within his speech?

8

2. Nathan is planning to describe at least three ways a database management system can be identified. What three ways for identifying a DBMS should Nathan cover?

3. Nathan plans to provide a few examples of SQL statements that can be used to gather information externally. Provide two examples of SQL statements that Nathan can provide.

4. What suggestions do you expect Nathan to provide for securing the company databases against SQL injections?

chapter 9

Security Auditing

After reading this chapter and completing the exercises, you will be able to:

- Provide an overview of security auditing fundamentals
- Describe the different phases of auditing and identify activities within each phase
- List the goals and objectives of a security audit
- Provide an overview of database auditing fundamentals
- Identify the auditing activities that are specific to database security auditing
- Identify the auditing tasks that are specific to supporting database tools

Security In Your World

Rae Ann has been running the IT department for a small financial accounting firm in Arizona for a little over a year now. She was hired into the position after the previous administrator, Gary, retired. Gary had worked for the company for over 15 years and built the network from the ground up. Luckily for Rae Ann, Gary was meticulous in his documentation and left several instructional papers that Rae was able to follow throughout the year. One of these documents was a set of strict instructions for how to maintain the company's database storage backup. According to the instructions, full backups are to be run once a day, at the end of the day, while inferential backups are to be completed every hour. An external hard disk is used to store the data at the end of the day. Rae Ann is to walk the hard disk to the local bank and place it in a safety deposit box from which she retrieves it the next morning. This was a solid routine to maintain the integrity of the organization's data, or so it seemed.

Friday was the start of a typical day at the office; the backups were in place and everything was running smoothly. Rae Ann was working on her daily administration tasks when she received a call from the owner of the company explaining that he was unable to access his files from his computer. When she arrived at his desk, she realized that the files were no longer accessible from the file server. After a bit of troubleshooting, she discovered that the file server was out of service. Unable to get the server back up and running, Rae Ann had to find a way to retrieve the owner's files and return them to him, so she decided to use the previous day's backup. As Murphy's Law would have it, the backup server was not reading the files from the backup and she was unable to restore them. She checked Gary's documentation for some type of resolution, but there was nothing in terms of troubleshooting instructions. It seems that Gary never tested the backups or attempted to restore the files once they were saved—so no controls were built into the system to handle a situation like this. As a result, Rae Ann found herself in quite a difficult situation—one that could ultimately have a big impact on her job security.

All of the security measures in the world are insignificant without internal controls and plans to support them. If managers create policies that forbid users to open suspicious e-mails, but do not have a control in place to deal with those who defy the policies, then, in reality, how effective is the policy? It is not easy to identify missing internal controls or poorly written backup plans within an organization's architecture, so often no one is aware that a step is missing until disaster has struck. This is where auditing comes into play. Auditing helps to prevent disasters and improve an

(continued)

environment by locating risks within that environment that exist due to a lack of secondary internal controls.

This chapter explores the security and database auditing processes. It defines the different types of security audits, explores the phases of an audit, and provides tips for locating vulnerabilities within a database environment. Auditing in itself is a strong security practice, and is vital to maintaining the confidentiality, integrity, and reliability of database environments.

Security Auditing

To thoroughly explore the process of database auditing, we must first identify the purpose of a security audit in its most general form. This can be achieved by formulating a basic appreciation of the auditing process and identifying an audit's goal within an environment. This section defines the term *audit*, identifies the purpose of a security audit, and explores common characteristics of the auditing process.

The term **security audit** refers to the procedures by which all of an environment's security controls and systems are thoroughly reviewed to identify and report weaknesses within an organization. Security audits are meant to provide an accurate view of the organization's internal security controls and to initiate positive changes for identified weak areas. Security audits focus specifically on the security of an environment, testing and exploring each layer of security to identify potential existing risks or weaknesses within security controls. They offer great insight into the effectiveness of an organization's security practices.

Security audits are often the means by which companies begin to realize the sheer vulnerability of their security efforts and are important security measures in themselves.

Audit Classification

Security audits can be conducted for many reasons, and the frequency with which they take place is dependent on the nature of the business. Audits should be conducted informally as part of an organization's yearly self-assessment, as a result of a recent security intrusion, or in reaction to an identified elevated risk. They can also be conducted formally, as a way to satisfy a group of industry standards or a set of industry-specific laws (e.g., the Health Insurance Portability and Accountability Act, the Sarbanes-Oxley Act, the Gramm-Leach-Blilely Act).

The reasoning for which an audit is conducted will dictate the individuals chosen to conduct it. For example, audits intended to satisfy legal obligations will be conducted externally or by a third-party group, whereas those that are conducted for the purpose of self-assessment will likely be conducted by an internal committee developed within the organization. The following list identifies different auditing classifications and their typical usage:

- *Informal audits*—Conducted as a way to provide organizations evidence that their security policies and practices are effective and working properly. Although informal audits are most often conducted internally using a committee of the organization's own employees, some organizations hire third-party security consultants to audit the network to obtain the most objective review.

- *Formal audits*—Most often conducted to satisfy specific industry standards that are required by law for certain types of organizations. Formal audits utilize an external group of individuals who are hired or employed by the government or other standard-setting groups for the purpose of conducting an audit. A hospital is an example of an organization that would commonly conduct a formal audit. In a hospital, security is bound by HIPAA, a privacy act that dictates which network security standards must be in place and effectively practiced in network environments that maintain and share sensitive medical records, so informal audits are conducted regularly to ensure compliance with these standards.

- *Internal audits*—Conducted using a committee of individuals who are employees of the company itself. The committees are often composed of individuals from an organization's senior management team and advisory board. Often informal, internal audits that are initiated from within the organization are most likely done as a way to self-assess an organization, to ensure that the company is meeting its auditing standards and complying with its own policies. They can also be conducted in reaction to a certain incident or intrusion, and are used as a way to determine the cause of the negative event.

- *External audits*—Conducted using a third-party group or a number of individuals from a source outside the organization itself. Often formal, these audits are usually conducted to satisfy a requirement or certify that a company is complying with a certain group of standards or laws established by governing bodies or financial institutions. These audits can also be requested by governing bodies or financial institutions out of concern for noncompliance or corrupt undertakings.

- *Automated audits*—Conducted using tools that are either installed onto a machine or embedded within an application for the purpose of recording the typical behavior of a system. The recorded behavior is stored within some type of system or application log. These logs are used to create administrative reports that are analyzed to troubleshoot or validate the system's behavior.

The Goal of an Audit

As mentioned previously, security audits are meant to provide an accurate view of the organization's internal security controls. What are internal security controls and why are they important? **Internal security controls** are the systematic measures and checks put into place to ensure that networks remain sound and secure. This section provides a real-world example of a security control and identifies its important role in the security auditing process.

A common misconception about security audits is that they are used to remove and eliminate a company's security vulnerabilities. As was explained in Chapter 1, there is no such thing as a foolproof security implementation; no security can be guaranteed with 100 percent certainty. This is true even after a security audit. In fact, a security audit does not remove vulnerabilities at all; it only tests to ensure that the proper policies and procedures are in place to handle a potential vulnerability and that these policies and procedures are followed as needed. The goals of an auditor are as follows:

1. Identify the purpose of a security measure implemented within systems or areas of an organization.

2. Locate any risk on the network that might prevent security measures from achieving this purpose.

3. Search for some type of process or practice already in place to lessen the harm that these identified risks can cause.

4. Report any areas in which risks are identified *and* no process or policy is in place to lessen the harm that these risks can have on the main purpose of a given security measure.

For example, let's say that an auditor learns of a policy that forbids users from leaving their desktops unattended and unlocked. The policy is put into place to lower the potential for unauthorized access to the network. (1. Identify the purpose of a security measure implemented within systems or areas of an organization.) The auditor finds that some employees leave their desk without locking their PCs, disregarding the policy altogether. (2. Locate any risk on the network that might prevent security measures from achieving this purpose.) The auditor waits to see if the desktop automatically locks after a certain period of inactivity. (3. Search for some type of process or practice already in place to lessen the harm that these identified risks can cause.) The PC does not lock automatically after 10 minutes of inactivity, so the auditor writes the incident down for reporting. (4. Report any areas in which risks are identified *and* no process or policy is in place to lessen the harm that these risks can have on the main purpose of a given security measure.)

As this example shows, the goal of auditing is not to fix issues on the network or to identify security holes, but to ensure that processes are in place to deal with potential risks that may exist and that the controls comply with these processes and policies.

The Auditing Process

Although many different types of security audits can be conducted within an organization, the characteristics of the overall process remain consistent for all. The auditing process generally includes three steps: prepare, audit, and report. This section explores these three steps and provides a clear picture of what each entails.

Planning and Preparation Phase The first step in preparation for an audit is the planning and preparation stage. At this time, the auditor is to determine exactly what systems, department, or component of the organization will be included within the security audit. In planning for an audit, the organization will conduct a number of preliminary interviews to ensure that an auditor is thoroughly informed about the network and business structure itself. The tasks included in this phase are defining the audit scope, becoming familiar with the organization or department for which the audit will take place, listing and prioritizing assets, and identifying potential threats. Preparation for an audit will vary greatly from one organization to another, but, for the most part, preparation is highly dependent on the reason for which the audit is taking place (e.g., formal or informal).

The **audit scope** is the area or system on which the security audit will focus. Defining the scope of the audit is one of the most important steps of the auditing process. During this phase, the priority assets are identified and a conceptual perimeter of the security audit is determined. Related and central assets are studied and classified as being either in or out of the perimeter of the security audit.

This phase requires the auditor to develop a strong understanding of the network and organizational structure. Knowledge of the people, policies, systems, and controls is a necessity that should include an understanding of the relationships and correlations that exist among them. A list of assets must be made by reviewing inventories, table schemas, network design plans, and organizational hierarchies. Both tangible (e.g., computers, servers, printers, individuals) and intangible (e.g., data, e-mails, Web applications, passwords) items should be included. Threats to these assets must be identified and considered, while prioritization is handled using the results of a risk analysis combined with the objectives of the management personnel. It is good practice to check previous security audit results for clues as to where priorities have been placed in the past.

Once the perimeter has been created and the assets prioritized within it, the objectives of the audit can be clearly defined and a solid plan can be created. The plans will likely include the logistical details as well as the information already gathered. Information such as the date and time of the audit, the backup strategy, and the effect the audit will have on daily operations should all be included.

Because of the many layers (e.g., files, servers, applications, data) and techniques (e.g., policies, firewalls, biometrics, encryption) involved in security, it is nearly impossible to conduct a security audit on all areas of the network at the same time. Therefore, to ensure that enough resources are available for the entire network, several small security audits are scheduled for an organization at different times of the year, each focusing on only one area of the environment. A common breakdown of areas of a security audit includes physical security, operating systems, Web applications, Web server security, database server, policies and procedures, central help desk, and network equipment security.

Often, rotating schedules are used in an attempt to ensure that all areas of the organization are audited over a certain period of time. Rotating schedules appear to work well at first glance, but should be used with caution. As was mentioned in the earlier sections, an audit can be initiated (or take priority) as a result of an elevated risk or recent network intrusion. In these cases, it is almost certain that the existing condition will take precedence over the current rotating schedule, and adjustments will need to be made to the existing table to accommodate the new priority. Whether the items that are listed toward the end of the rotating schedule are reached in a reasonable amount of time is dependent on the number of incidents that may occur in a given period of time.

For example, Table 9-1 displays a potential security auditing rotating schedule for an organization. The first column of the table displays the original rotating security audit schedule for a given organization and the second column displays the same schedule after adjustments were made due to a detected SQL injection intrusion on day one. As shown, the schedule was affected greatly as the priorities shifted and urgent security audits potentially related to the intrusion were pushed to the top of the list, while less urgent tasks, like the physical security audit, were bumped quite a few weeks.

Although this might not seem urgent now, continued future priority shifts can cause certain areas to be left unchecked for an extended period of time. In the example provided in the table, there is a potential that the environment would become a reactive one where only those items that were compromised would obtain highest priority, defeating the security audit's purpose of creating an effective proactive security strategy.

Until now, there has been no mention of the ways an organization prepares for an audit. This section has solely focused on ways an auditor becomes prepared. This is because besides gathering requested information for the auditor, very little preparation should be done on the organizational end. The goal of a security audit is to report an accurate view

Priority listing for normal rotating schedule security audit	Priority listing after Web application intrusion occurs	Schedule
Domain controller management	Web applications	Week 1
Web server management	Web server management	Week 2
E-mail server management	Database server management	Week 3
File server administration	Server security	Week 4
Network wireless access	Network wireless access	Week 5
Remote access	Remote access	Week 6
Web applications	Domain controller management	Week 7
Network equipment	E-mail server management	Week 1
Physical security	File server administration	Week 2
Security policy	Network equipment	Week 3

Table 9-1   Sample security auditing schedule

of the organizational control weaknesses, so the desire is to audit the organization while conducting daily activities in its most typical and raw form. Unfortunately, audits are often not welcomed with great anticipation, particularly in situations of formal external audits.

Many insecure organizations fear that the outcome of an audit—if too many weaknesses are found—will result in negative consequences or severe penalties (which may certainly be true in cases where privacy laws are broken) for the organization. These are often organizations that are insecure about the way they create, maintain, and enforce effective internal controls. They tend to overprepare by spending weeks prior to the audit conducting quick but vast cleanup efforts across the company in an attempt to hide or minimize weaknesses that may be found. Some companies even go as far as forging documents and bribing employees to get rid of any evidence of inconsistency. It is an unfortunate reality, but one that is important to be aware of. This type of behavior will skew the audit results by providing an inaccurate view of the typical environment, leaving no room for real growth.

Audits are meant to provide an accurate view of the organization's internal controls and to initiate positive changes of identified weaknesses. To achieve the highest accuracy through an audit, the auditing process itself must be standardized and little to no preemptive preparation should be made within the environment. Figure 9-1 represents all that is involved in the planning and preparation stage of an audit.

The Audit   At this point, perimeters have been identified and objectives are well understood, so the detailed security audit plan is put into action. This phase involves activities that help the auditor analyze the environment for potential vulnerabilities. As risks or concerns are identified, they are validated using the business policies and specifications gathered in the planning stage, and are also verified by asking customers to explain issues as they are found. This phase takes the most time in an auditing process. The activities involved in the actual audit depend on a great number of factors, including the type of audit, the audit scope, and the organization. Obviously, an audit that is meant to review the internal

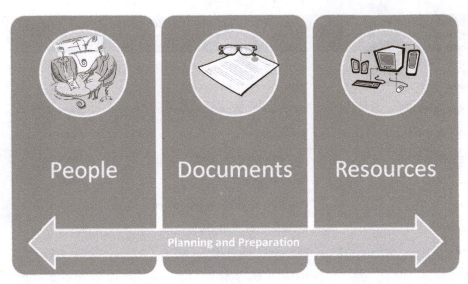

Figure 9-1 Planning and preparation
© Cengage Learning 2012

controls of physical security will involve much different activities than one that is intended to audit internal administration of a database management system (DBMS). Table 9-2 displays a list of common activities that are conducted during the security auditing process for different system type audits.

Security audits of:	Common activity
Web server management	Ensure that only authorized services and protocols are accessing the server
E-mail server management	Verify that spam filters are in place and active
File server administration	Validate that the appropriate permissions exist for files and directories
Network wireless access	Ensure that rogue access points are not being used
Remote access	Verify that remote access is being logged
Web applications	Verify that input filters are appropriate and in place
Physical security	Ensure the use of proper physical access control systems
Security policy	Validate that company security policies are disseminated appropriately
Database security	Review database permissions to ensure accuracy and granularity

Table 9-2 Common security auditing activities

Reporting a Security Audit The final step of the security auditing process is a debriefing meeting in which the auditor or committee of auditors communicate verbally and in writing the results of the audit. This communication usually involves the company's owners, senior managers, and other major stakeholders. It provides a detailed view of the organization's internal security controls, including vulnerabilities and risks and, in some cases, the strengths are defined as well. The format of the written report is dependent on the classification of the audit (e.g., informal, formal, internal, external, automated) as well as the individual auditors or auditing committee.

Although the format and content will vary, some important commonalities are found within all audit reports. These common components include the background information, the defined perimeter and scope, the objective of the audit, the key findings, the methodology used to identify the risks, and the remediation recommendations. The auditor or auditing committee's recommendations are typically followed by a specific set of remediation actions. If the review was that of a formal audit or external audit, all remediation actions are defined by a set of expected deliverables. The time frame for the submission of these deliverables is set forth and is required for the organization to become compliant. If the review was that of an informal audit or internal audit, all remediation actions need to be tracked internally and the deadlines for deliverables must be met for the audit process to be completed and senior management to be informed of compliancy. In some cases, reports provide recommendations with no remediation actions or requirements.

Database Auditing

With a general understanding of the security auditing process, we can now explore the security auditing process for a database. This section focuses primarily on the audit phase itself. It revisits the planning and preparation phase to discuss those planning needs that are specific to database management systems, but the primary focus here is the auditing phase itself. Different areas of the database environment are identified and explored and the tasks that correspond with these areas are discussed. This section provides the reader with the tools to perform a security audit on a database management system. Again, it must be reiterated that this process is a cumbersome and laborious one that does not ensure the security of a network. In reality, database auditing takes a great deal of time, effort, and resources, and is not conducted as often as is necessary. Database audits must be conducted frequently and thoroughly to contribute to an environment's security measures. Intruders are sophisticated and their knowledge grows each day; so even under the best of circumstances with best practices put into place, there is no guarantee that an audit will keep a database environment secure.

Preparation and Planning for a Database Security Audit

As mentioned in the previous sections, the preparing and planning stage is the time the auditor takes to get to know the system and the environment. It is at this stage that the audit scope and work perimeter are identified for the area in which the audit will take place. Along with the suggestions provided in the previous section, a few considerations specific to database environments must be addressed during this stage. This section discusses these database-specific planning topics to help an auditor complete a DBMS security audit.

Preparing for a database security audit requires the auditor to gather as much information about the database environment as possible to define the specific perimeter. A perimeter should address all layers of a database environment. It should include detailed information about the people, data, technology, and documents that will play a role within a particular audit. Figure 9-2 provides examples of each of these layers of the environment.

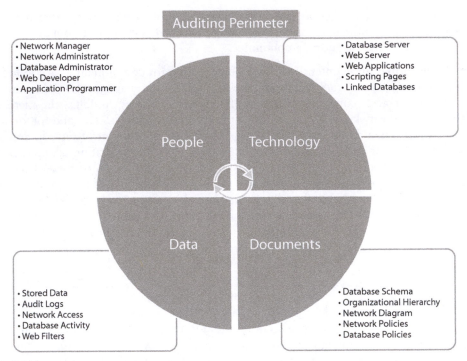

Figure 9-2 Database audit perimeter
© Cengage Learning 2012

Gathering information involves interviews with the database administrator (DBA) and the database system team as well as an examination of the database schemas, network diagrams, and database-related policies and procedures. Organizations often contain several database management systems, so a decision as to how many systems will be audited must be made with purposeful intent.

An understanding of the functionality, purpose, and structure of all database management systems must also be obtained in this stage to conduct an effective and comprehensive audit. Information such as the vendor of the database or the operating system on which the data-base resides is important, as well as knowledge of the backup strategy that is being imple-mented. An analysis of the data and how it is stored within the database must be examined and coupled with the organizational hierarchy so as to build an understanding of the rela-tionship between the individuals within the organization and their data storage and manipu-lation needs.

Risk and threat analysis is another important aspect of planning for a database audit, as it helps to define a prioritized checklist of activities that can be developed as a starting point for the DBMS audit. As was shown in previous chapters, many components of a network interact and communicate with a database. This is especially the case within an environment where the database is accessed remotely or from the Web because many more components are involved in the data-retrieval process. Therefore, to ensure that all measures have been taken to secure the database and that all risks are considered, the entire database infrastruc-ture should be considered any time a security audit is conducted within a database environment.

A thorough audit can be conducted on a database, ensuring that proper security controls are in place for that management system, yet if a Web application that communicates with this database has not been audited, a potential SQL injection risk remains. Database audits can be done in one of two ways. An auditor can choose to focus initially on the database-supporting components (e.g., Web applications, Web servers, middleware, scripting pages) before moving on to the database itself, or the audit can begin at the database and work through the other components thereafter.

Although the rest of this chapter focuses more on the database and less on the database infrastructure's supporting components, a comprehensive and complete audit should include activities that involve the exploration of both.

The Database Audit

Due to the sheer size of a database environment and resources that are required to complete a database audit, they are often conducted in small pieces, focusing on specific functionality or areas of concentration. These different areas of concentration can include server maintenance, account administration, access control, data privileges, passwords, encryption, and activity. This section reviews each of these areas and discusses the activities involved in the auditing process of each.

Server Maintenance Measures should be taken to ensure that servers are being maintained appropriately and policies exist that standardize the maintenance of the database server. Auditing server maintenance includes the review of software updates, backup strategies, application version control, resource management, and hardware updates. Following is a list of audit check examples:

- The latest security patches are applied.
- The latest DBMS critical updates have been applied.
- The current version of the DBMS is supported.
- A procedure exists for maintaining patches and software versions.
- An appropriate backup policy exists that includes disaster recovery.
- A feasible and appropriate backup schedule exists.
- A procedure exists to test the integrity of backups.

Account Administration Account administration is a vital component to database security. The way user accounts are handled is important to access and privilege controls. Auditing account administration includes a review of how the administrator is defining and creating user accounts; removing user accounts; applying security policies; and assigning groups, roles, and privileges. Some sample audit checks include the following:

- Roles for administrators are clearly defined.
- Administrative accounts are distributed appropriately.
- Inactive or unneeded user accounts are removed.
- Generic accounts are not utilized.

- Default accounts are disabled or removed.
- Application object owner accounts are disabled.
- The backup's integrity is tested.

Access Control Access control is the act of minimizing, handling, and detecting user access to the database and its resources. Appropriate access control is essential to ensure the confidentiality, integrity, and availability of the DBMS. Auditing access control is very time consuming and can require the logging of access to the database over a period of time. Some sample audit checks include the following:

- Only trusted IP addresses can access the database.
- Sensitive data is accessed only by those who require it.
- Database links are appropriate.
- Linked databases have applied the appropriate access controls.
- Administrators are not able to make changes to the database remotely without special authentication.
- Access to backups and disaster recovery are restricted to administrators only.

Data Privileges Monitoring privileges very closely to ensure security and granularity is a must. Ensuring the appropriateness of privileges during an audit is the most time-consuming task that often requires quite a bit of collaboration with the network administrator. Some sample audit checks include the following:

- PUBLIC is revoked from the system.
- Implicit granting of privileges is carefully considered.
- The principle of least privilege is utilized.
- Account privileges within the underlying operating system are restricted.
- Privileges are granted using groups rather than individuals.
- Privileges to stored procedures are restricted.

Passwords Strong passwords are critical in a secure environment, as they are the first line of defense that intruders will encounter. Most database management systems can be configured to ensure that passwords meet a specific policy automatically to ensure the strength of the password. Auditing password management involves the review of a written policy, the server configuration, and default user accounts. Some sample audit checks include the following:

- Password management capabilities are enabled within the DBMS.
- The password policy includes specifications for failed logins, aging, complexity, history, expiration, and content.
- Default passwords have been changed.
- Passwords are not stored within the database if possible.
- Passwords are encrypted using strong encryption if stored in the database.

Encryption Without effective and strong encryptions, data might as well be stored as text. Encryption utilization and sensitive data storage are two considerations that must be included in any database security audit. Encryption should be checked for both stored and moving data throughout the database. Some audit checks include the following:

- Stored data is encrypted using strong encryption techniques.
- Moving data is encrypted using strong encryption techniques.
- Encryption is configured accurately.
- Symmetric keys are used for data encryption.
- Sensitive data is documented and labeled as such.
- Passwords are encrypted while remotely logging in to the database.

Activity Auditing activity automatically and between larger security audits is a best-practice technique to keeping the database secure. Much information can be discovered using embedded monitoring tools and even logs. In fact, auditing the activity of the database is the means by which much of the information in this section can be identified by an auditor during the database security audit itself. Sample audit checks include the following:

- Auditing has been configured on the server in a way that coincides with the security policy.
- Failed logins are being monitored.
- Failed queries are being monitored.
- Changes to the metadata are being monitored.
- The dynamic SQL that is being executed within a stored procedure is being validated.
- Resource consumption baselines have been set and alerts are being monitored.

Reporting a Database Security Audit

The final step of the security auditing process is a debriefing meeting in which the auditor or committee of auditors communicates verbally and in writing the results of the audit. This communication usually involves the company's owners, senior managers, and other major stakeholders. It provides a detailed view of the organization's internal security controls, including vulnerabilities and risks and, in some cases, the strengths are defined as well. The format of the written report is dependent on the classification of the audit (e.g., informal, formal, internal, external, automated) as well as the individual auditors or auditing committee. Although the format and content will vary, some important commonalities are found within all audit reports. The common components include the background information, the defined perimeter and scope, the objective of the audit, the key findings, the methodology used to identify the risks, and the remediation recommendations. The auditor or auditing committee's recommendations are typically followed by a specific set of remediation actions.

If the review was that of a formal audit or external audit, all remediation actions are defined by a set of expected deliverables. The time frame for the submission of these deliverables is set forth and is required for the organization to become compliant. If the review was that of an informal audit or internal audit, all remediation actions need to be tracked internally and the deadlines for deliverables must be met for the audit process to be completed and senior management to be informed of compliancy. In some cases, reports provide recommendations with no remediation actions or requirements.

Vendor-Specific Auditing Information

Most types of databases contain their own unique automatic functions or tools for aiding in the process of auditing database and user activity. These tools often require some type of configuration, but once set up, they can offer great value to the auditing process, saving both time and effort. While reading through this section, keep in mind that many of these tools create logs that contain the information gathered and that the logs are often saved within the database itself. Depending on which actions are selected, these logs can become quite large and resource intensive. It is important to choose your audited activities carefully and to purge your logs as often as needed. This section describes the unique auditing tools found within Microsoft SQL Server, Oracle, and MySQL.

Microsoft SQL Server Microsoft SQL Server enables the tracking and logging of activities throughout all levels of the database. Several features are available that allow administrators to create an auditing trail that best fits their needs. Auditing can be created at the server level or the database level. The recorded activity can be sent to a target file, or to event logs within Windows that the creator of the audit can specify. Audits can be enabled, reviewed, and created using the Object explorer in the SQL Server Management Studio. On this page, the administrator can choose one of two paths, depending on which audit records are desired. These are Security/Audit/Server Audit Specification and Database/Database Name/ Security/Database Audit Specification.

To create audits in Microsoft SQL Server, an administrator must first create a server audit object to record the server or database level actions (or groups of actions) that are desired. These are created at the instance level and more than one audit can be created for each instance. The next step is to create a specification object that will belong to either the server audit object or the database audit object previously created. Database-level auditing provides an administrator with the ability to create custom audits to be defined for any given action (e.g., SELECT, UPDATE, INSERT, DELETE, EXECUTE) on the database or a database object (e.g., tables, views, functions, procedures). Server-level auditing can be defined to record actions performed on the server itself and includes login information, password changes, backups, server role changes, maintenance procedures, schema changes, and permission adjustments.

Oracle Oracle provides several ways to audit the database both manually and automatically, yet the configuration for these embedded tools can be quite complex in their setup. Three basic levels of auditing are available: database, application, and external. Ideally, auditing would be configured at each level to ensure the most comprehensive audit trail, yet resources are not always available. To achieve the best auditing results, both application- and database-level auditing should be configured. Application-level auditing provides information about changes made by a specific user session; therefore, application-level auditing monitors sessions. Database-level auditing provides information about changes made to a specific database object; therefore, database-level auditing monitors databases. Together, they essentially inform auditors what is changed and by whom it has been changed. Therefore, both must be applied for a comprehensive picture of the activities on a database.

The most basic step in beginning the auditing process within anOracle Database is enabling the default security settings. This can be done within the Security Settings window found in the Database Configuration Assistant (DBCA). Enabling this setting will begin the default auditing procedures that include the following:

- Statements that use the ALTER function on procedures, tables, databases, profiles, systems, and users
- Statements that use the CREATE function on libraries, procedures, tables, jobs, database links, public database links, sessions, and users
- Statements that use the DROP function on procedures, tables, profiles, and users
- Statements that use the GRANT function on privileges, roles, and object privileges
- AUDIT SYSTEM statements
- EXEMPT ACCESS POLICY statements

The default security settings will also enable the audit_trail function, which allows granular administration of systemwide auditing at both application and database layers. There are essentially four options for setting the parameter for the audit_trail function. These options determine whether database auditing is enabled and identify where the audit records will reside. Here is a list of the options for the audit_trail function:

- None—Disables auditing altogether.
- DB—Enables auditing and sends the log to the database SYS.AUD$ table. This is the default setting chosen when Security Settings is enabled.
- OS—Enables auditing and sends the log to the operating system.
- XML—Enables auditing and sends the log to an XML operating system file.

Table 9-3 provides a list of these options as well as a description of what these options determine. When the security settings are enabled, audit_trail is set to DB, but can be changed by locating the parameter found in int.ora.

Once audit_trail has been enabled, the administrator can begin to audit activities and system characteristics at the application and database levels. As part of the auditing process, an auditor can take note, or log, user login information, unsuccessful password attempts, processes that are executed, processes that are concurrently running, row and table changes, and tables that are accessed frequently. Table 9-3 displays a few common SQL statements used to audit information in Oracle.

Statement	Comments
Audit user	Audits statements that create, alter, and drop users
Audit session	Audits connections to the database
Audit statement	Audits statements that create, alter, or drop objects
Audit object	Audits objects that are created, altered, or dropped
Audit database	Audits statements that create or drop database links

Table 9-3 Sample Oracle auditing

MySQL At the time of this writing, MySQL has no built-in tools available to aid in the auditing process. The auditing process within MySQL involves the manual exploration of logs and objects, following the general database security auditing guidelines provided earlier in the chapter. Third-party automated tools can be found online to aid in the process of auditing a MySQL database.

Chapter Summary

- Security audits are implemented as a way for companies to identify the vulnerabilities of their security efforts and internal controls.

- Security audits can be formally conducted to ensure compliance with industry standards and privacy laws.

- Informal security audits can be conducted as a way to provide organizations with a clear picture of their internal security controls, or in reaction to an intrusion as a way to identify the vulnerability related to the intrusion.

- External security audits are usually conducted by third-party companies and are most often formally done; the results are reported to government or financially supportive organizations.

- Internal audits are most often conducted informally by an internal auditing team; the results are reported to senior management and CEOs.

- In general, an auditor first identifies a security measure and determines its purposes. Next, the auditor locates any risks associated with the identified measure, and then searches for a company policy or process that exists for handling that risk. So, the primary goal of an audit is to ensure that controls are in place for handling security vulnerabilities and risks.

- Gaining familiarity with typical database errors is important in identifying the anomalies in the system.

- In preparing for an audit, the auditor must first gather as much information as possible from an organization, including network diagrams and employee hierarchical structures.

- An audit scope is created as a way to specify the area of the infrastructure and identify those tasks that will be included and excluded from the security audit.

- An audit perimeter is a specific area of the infrastructure's network diagram that is identified to define those components and areas of the network that will be included and excluded from the security audit.

- Informal security audits are often too resource intensive to be conducted in all areas of an organization at the same time. Therefore, informal security audits are often conducted by breaking the organization into smaller parts for which a rotating schedule is developed to ensure regular maintenance.

- The security audit report will include the background information, the scope, the defined perimeter, the goal, the methodology, and the key findings.

- Remediation actions are defined by a set of deliverables and should include a schedule for completion.

- Database audit planning and preparation include a review of the database schema, the network diagrams specific to the database management systems, and data usage policies.

- Database auditing can be divided into different areas of concentration, such as server maintenance, account administration, access control, database privileges, passwords, sensitive data storage and encryption, and auditing activity.

- Oracle provides several ways to audit the database, including both manual and automatic methodologies. To achieve the best audit results in Oracle, both application- and database-level auditing should be configured.

- The audit_trail function allows granular administration of systemwide auditing and is a requirement before any type of automatic auditing can take place within an Oracle database.

- Microsoft SQL Server allows auditing at both the application and database level and the reports can be sent to the operating systems to lessen the database resources used by the report logs.

- Microsoft SQL Server enables administrators to create custom audits for all SELECT, UPDATE, DELETE, and EXECUTE actions on a database or database object.

- MySQL requires manual auditing, which involves the review of logs and database objects in hopes of identifying anomalies.

9

Key Terms

automated audit An audit conducted using tools that are either installed onto a machine or embedded within an application for the purpose of recording the typical behavior of a system.

audit scope The area or system on which the security audit will focus. Defining the scope of the audit is one of the most important steps of the auditing process.

external audit An audit conducted using a third-party group or a number of individuals from a source outside the organization itself.

formal audit An audit most often conducted to satisfy specific industry standards that are required by law for certain types of organizations.

informal audit An audit conducted as a way to provide organizations evidence that their security policies and practices are effective and working properly.

internal audit An audit conducted using a committee of individuals who are employees of the company itself.

internal security controls The systematic measures and checks put into place to ensure that networks remain sound and secure.

security audit The procedures by which all of an environment's security controls and systems are thoroughly reviewed to identify and report weaknesses within an organization.

Review Questions

1. Identify the purpose of an internal audit and an external audit.

2. Identify those persons who might be included within an auditing team for both formal and informal audits.

3. Explain the goal of an auditor. Provide an example to support your response.

4. List the documents that would likely be reviewed in the planning and preparation phase of a formal external audit.

5. What is the difference between a scope and a perimeter?

6. List the typical sections of information included within an audit report.

7. Identify documents that would likely be reviewed in the planning and preparation phase of a database-specific informal audit.

8. List database-supporting components that would require an audit to ensure reliability of the database.

9. Identify and explain the different areas of concentration for database security audits.

10. Explain the purpose of audit_trail found within Oracle.

11. Describe the difference between a database-level audit and an application-level audit.

Case Projects

CASE PROJECTS

Case Project 9-1: Auditing Organizations

Use the Internet. Find and describe at least one company for which security audits would be required to be compliant with a standardization organization.

Case Project 9-2: Internal Controls

Provide a list of internal security controls that your current school or company has implemented.

Case Project 9-3: Database Auditing

Use the Internet. Find and describe one automated tool that aids in database security auditing. (It is not recommended to install the tool.)

Case Project 9-4: Auditing Oracle

Use the Internet. Identify the steps for creating a custom audit within Oracle.

Case Project 9-5: Auditing MySQL

Use the Internet. Identify a third-party application that can aid in the auditing of MySQL databases.

Case Project 9-6: Auditing Microsoft SQL Server

Use the SQL Server Web site *www.microsoft.com/sqlserver/2008/en/us/*. Identify the steps for creating a custom audit for Microsoft SQL Server.

Hands-On Projects

Hands-On Project 9-1: Creating and Implementing an Audit

You have been hired as the lead auditor within your own company. You are to create and implement an internal, informal database auditing schedule for the organization. Create a paper that responds to the following:

1. Create a table that includes a rotating schedule for the 12 months of auditing. Include columns that identify time estimates for each audit listed.

2. Create a planning and preparation checklist common to all audits as a whole.

3. Identify any special planning and preparation needed for each individual audit.

4. Identify the scope for each audit and identify any special considerations that need to be addressed.

5. Create a list of at least five audit activities for each audit.

6. Describe any special considerations unique to Oracle that must be addressed.

7. Describe any special considerations unique to MySQL that must be addressed.

8. Describe any special considerations unique to SQL Server that must be addressed.

9

chapter 10

Security Testing

After reading this chapter and completing the exercises, you will be able to:

- Provide an overview of security testing fundamentals
- Identify the difference between security testing and security auditing
- Describe the methodology used to perform a security test
- Define common techniques that intruders use to gather information
- Describe common methods used to gain unauthorized access into a system
- Identify common strategies used to escalate one's privileges in a system

Security In Your World

Erin and Jeff have been dating for several years. Erin is a network engineer who runs her own consulting firm out of the home, while Jeff is a business entrepreneur who develops custom database applications on the side to make ends meet. They both had their own separate clientele, but they occasionally referred clients to one another to increase their businesses and better support their customers' needs. Living together side by side, they worked for several years without combining the two businesses for fear of the personal conflict that might result from sharing a business.

Over time, Jeff and Erin's personal relationship deteriorated and they agreed on a trial separation. Jeff moved into a leased space temporarily, hoping for some type of near-future reconciliation, while Erin remained at their previously shared home. After a few months apart, Jeff received a call from one of his customers inquiring about a message that Erin had left with their answering service. It seems that Erin had been in contact with many of Jeff's clients in hopes of promoting an expansion of her business that included custom application development. Furious and taken aback, Jeff realizes that he must immediately take steps to protect his company and the data within it. Not only does Erin have the passwords to his main business accounts, but she was also an integral player in the initial construction of his company's security architecture.

Aware of Erin's level of expertise, Jeff calls a security professional for support in the rebuilding of his company's security architecture. Sparing no cost, the two of them completely replace the existing architecture, changing both the physical and logical environment in hopes of thwarting any attempts that Erin may make at obtaining more information. Excessive measures were taken to secure the network. Confident in his efforts as well as in the security professional whom he hired, Jeff was excited about the end results.

A few weeks had passed when Jeff's security alerts suggested that an unauthorized intruder had obtained remote access to the environment. To his dismay, and despite all of his efforts, it appeared that Erin had found her way back into his network. Further exploration discovered that documents had been destroyed and customers had been removed from the database. Forced to inform his customers of the recent intrusion, many began to search elsewhere for application development needs. Jeff's future was jeopardized due to this incident.

So where did Jeff go wrong? Regardless of the level of security that Jeff had put into place, he did not schedule resources for security penetration testing. Confident that his excessive measures of security would prevent any intrusions (a common

(continued)

misconception), and being aware of the enormous time and cost associated with the security testing process, he did not find it necessary.

The amount and level of security put into place is irrelevant if penetration testing is not conducted at the end of implementation. In the end, penetration testing should be the final confirmation that an environment is reasonably secure. The strength of security offered to a network can be measured by its weakest component, so identification of a weakness is vital within all architectures. This chapter explores the process of security and penetration testing and provides models from which security testing plans can be developed. Time and resources will be considered as well.

Security Testing

There is much confusion and conflicting data regarding the distinction between security auditing and security testing. **Security testing** refers to the process of identifying the feasibility and impact of an attack or intrusion of a system by simulating active exploitation and executing potential attacks within that environment. It offers a way to actively evaluate the security measures implemented within an environment in terms of strength and loss potential by focusing primarily on the actual security measures implemented (e.g., hardware, software). It is conducted from an attacker's perspective and is typically outsourced to a third-party organization or application developed specifically for testing weaknesses of a system.

Security audits, on the other hand, are conducted to locate potential weaknesses found within the company's internal controls. Security audits are different from security testing in that they include areas such as security policies, human resource information, and legal or standards compliance, areas security testing does not cover. Auditing compares the documentation with the architecture to ensure accuracy and reliability of an environment, whereas security testing measures the strength and effectiveness of the environment. Auditing also requires a great deal of knowledge about the infrastructure to be completed, whereas security testing can be conducted with no prior knowledge at all.

Although both security auditing and security testing are laborious and resource intensive, penetration testing is more costly and time consuming. Therefore, security tests are better suited for evaluating the security on a small group of assets, such as when broken down departmentally. They become too impractical if the goal is to test an entire architecture complete with hundreds of systems; when compared with audits, given this scenario, they provide less information at a much higher cost. Security testing provides a more accurate picture of the strength of architecture, but because of lack of resources, testing is often conducted with a very narrow scope defined.

Characteristics required for a security tester are very similar to those needed for a security auditor. The main difference is that a security tester must have the ability to think and act like a potential intruder. Often, security testing focuses on a specific well-known attack (e.g., spoofing an account) and lacks a strong understanding of the steps that an attacker might take to achieve a goal, which makes effective testing virtually impossible. Effective

10

security testers understand how attackers think and behave. They are armed with a tool-box full of ideas for ways to break a system, and they are creative in their attack attempts.

 It is important to point out that auditing is no more effective than security testing, just as security testing is no more effective than audit-ing. An effective security strategy includes both auditing and testing, but these are only two of the several components that should exist in the process of securing an environment.

Security Testing Classification

As mentioned earlier, you must understand the behavior and mind-set of a potential attacker to effectively test the security of a network. Therefore, successful security testing in a database environment is conducted from the attacker's perspective and is categorized in terms of the viewpoint from which it is conducted. We most often think of an attacker as an external force whose primary goal is to break into a network or a database envi-ronment, but, as mentioned earlier in the book, intruders can exist internally as well. Internal users are just as dangerous, if not more dangerous, than those unauthorized external ones. Therefore, to be successful, testing that is conducted from the attacker's perspective must include both internal and external vantage points. The following list identifies the different perspectives from which security testing within a database environ-ment can be conducted:

- *Internal testing*—**Internal testing** is conducted within the organization's security bor-der. This type of testing will display vulnerabilities that exist among internal users such as employees and contractors. Testing will identify attacks and the damage that can be caused within the database environment itself. A task conducted during an internal security assessment might include an evaluator who logs in to a user's com-puter in an attempt to extend his or her privileges on a particular database system.

- *External testing*—**External testing** is conducted outside the organization's network security border. This type of testing will display attacks and liabilities that can be exploited externally from competitors, remote users, and hackers. Initial tasks most commonly completed during external testing outside a database environment primarily involve information gathering—because an intruder must gain information about an infrastructure to break into it. A security consultant who attempts to use SQL injec-tions to gather information about an environment using external Web forms and Web applications is an example of someone conducting external security tests within a database environment.

- *Black box testing*—**Black box testing** is conducted with no prior knowledge of the system or infrastructure that is being tested. This testing is most often conducted externally because external intruders do not typically have prior knowledge of the existing infrastructure. Black box testing can also be seen as a type of exploratory testing. There is not one specific focus and not all systems will be tested. A black box test often weighs heavily on gathering information because the ability to gather information is what provides external intruders a way into the system. Because of this, the test identifies the most fundamental weaknesses of an infrastructure. Overall, this test will determine just how far external users can get into the system without prior knowledge. SQL injections, more specifically, blind loop statements used in SQL injections, are most often used to obtain information through black box testing.

- *White box testing*—**White box testing** (**target testing**) is conducted by an intruder who already has existing information about the system or the infrastructure. It is also known as *targeted testing* because prior knowledge exists and known weaknesses within the infrastructure allow intruders to focus on specific areas of the infrastructure. The goal is to assess the damage that can be done by those users who understand the infrastructure they are attempting to intrude; the results will provide a more comprehensive, thorough picture of specific system weakness than that found in black box testing. White box testing is most often associated with internal testing. The assumption is that internal users will most likely have some knowledge of the infrastructure, yet white box testing can be conducted internally or externally. Consider the external intruder who obtains information by using blind SQL injections. This intruder has obtained information about the system and can now target an individual database, or table within a database, based on the information he or she has obtained. Another example of someone who might have information about a database system and might attempt to intrude is a disgruntled former employee. These individuals have information about the environment from their work history and can use this information to aid their efforts to access a system.

One last note to consider about the different categories of testing is the skill sets required to conduct each type of test. External and black box testing require assessors who hold a more broad and diverse range of skills. The tester must have a great amount of knowledge of the different network and security technologies to defeat them and gain access. The tester also needs to be flexible and creative in his or her attempts because the possibilities and potential for different types and combinations of security measures are endless. Although a tester should be experienced and flexible, internal or white box testing can be conducted by someone with less expertise because these testers have more knowledge and awareness of the environment that they are trying to intrude.

The Goal of Security Testing

The general goal of a security assessment within any environment is to test the strength of security measures put into place. A security assessment can be conducted to test database security measures both broad and narrow. It can be used to test an intruder's potential for breaking into the environment or to test the appropriateness of the privilege assignment within a particular database. Therefore, the goals of a security test vary and depend on both the type of test conducted (e.g., black box, external, white box, internal) as well as the scale for which the testing takes place. For example, external black box tests are often not focused on one particular area of the network because little is known about the environment, so the goal of these tests is typically to determine how deeply an intruder can obtain access. In contrast, internal or white box testing involves a specific target within the database environment, so the goals are likely to be further defined. A security tester may assess the security measure's ability to block intruders from obtaining administrative rights to a mission-critical database.

Other common testing goals within a database environment include the ability to block access to the physical location of the database; retrieve stored, confidential information; use SQL injection to exploit; escalate privileges within the database; deny users access to their tables and records; destroy applications or files; and evade an intrusion-detection system.

Testing Methodology

The security testing process, even in its narrowest form, can be a painstakingly time- and resource-intensive process. An unstructured approach to security testing is very ineffective and can result in wasted resources. Knowing this, even attackers do not conduct their attacks in a haphazard fashion. Having a clearly defined, well-thought-out standardized testing methodology allows an assessor to do the following:

- Address resource constraints through prioritization.
- Decrease the time required for an assessment by avoiding redundancy.
- Create an improved picture of security strength using enforced consistent testing.
- Communicate recommendations more efficiently by utilizing standardized reports.

Therefore, a structured and methodical approach is greatly beneficial to any organization. This section identifies a methodical strategy to security assessment and penetration testing using a phased approach.

Planning and Preparation Phase

In this phase of the security assessment methodology, the assessor defines a scope, gathers information about potential weak areas of the network, identifies potential attacks, classifies and prioritizes assets, specifies objectives and goals, and lists resources required.

Defining the Scope
The **security scope** defines the perimeter of the overall security assessment, the physical and logical area included within the assessment. Areas for security testing can be defined as a group of systems or applications (e.g., database servers), a department within the organization (e.g., Finance), an attack strategy (e.g., injections), and, in some cases such as those scenarios that include white box testing, the level of access achieved (e.g., privileges escalated). This section identifies the process for developing a scope, a scope perimeter, and white box and black box scenarios.

As mentioned in the previous sections, due to the resource-intensive nature of security testing, the scope of a security assessment is often narrow in size. Therefore, in scenarios that include white-box-type assessments, defining the perimeter of the scope is a pretty straightforward process. The goal of a particular security test is the primary factor used for defining the area and tasks included within the assessment. The white-box-type assessments provide the assessor with information about the infrastructure prior to testing, so the infrastructure can be used to determine those things that should be included within the scope. For example, if the goal is to ensure that privileges cannot be escalated by unauthorized users on the database servers, then the infrastructure can be analyzed and all hardware, software, and related tasks that the assessor needs to utilize in testing would be included within the scope. All other hardware, software, and unrelated tasks would be considered out of scope.

Defining the scope in a black-box-type assessment scenario is much more difficult. Because little to no information is given to the assessor prior to the test, the perimeter cannot be defined in terms of the locations of the systems within the infrastructure unless the target system is completely isolated from the rest of the network. In these situations, scopes are often defined by analyzing the level of access achieved by the attacker necessary to achieve the goal of the assessment. Potential intrusions are analyzed prior to testing and a determination is made as to how much information would need to be obtained to access differ-ent levels of the infrastructure and subsequently achieve the assessment goal. The scope bound-ary is then defined in terms of the assessor's ability to reach this specific depth within the envi-ronment. For example, consider a scenario in which an exploratory black box test is planned within an environment where the goal is to ensure that database privileges cannot be obtained by unauthorized external users. Prior to the test, no information is given, so the scope perimeter is much broader and is defined as the point at which the assessor either cannot access any more information or has obtained the escalated privileges. Having information about the infrastruc-ture prior to testing poses a great advantage to defining the scope perimeter.

Other tasks involved in developing a scope for a security assessment include defining a contract or service-level agreement, conducting a threat assessment, scheduling an assess-ment, and listing the resources needed to complete the assessment.

Gathering Information There are two types of information gathering: that which is done prior to the assessment as a way to prioritize and identify goals and that which is done during the assessment as a way to identify information leaks within the infrastructure. Infor-mation gathering that occurs during assessment is also known as information reconnaissance and will be discussed in later sections. This section explores the information that is often acquired prior to testing. Information that should be obtained prior to the database security assessment includes the following:

- Infrastructure information found in network diagrams and database schematics
- A prioritized set of data storage server and information assets
- Weak areas of the database infrastructure, those areas lacking sufficient defense
- Areas that have the highest potential for an attack (sensitive data)
- Areas that can offer entry points for intruders
- Potential attack strategies based on infrastructure or recent and past trends of intruders

This information can have a big impact on the assessment. Depending on what information is obtained, this gathering process can change the original course of direction for the assess-ment, help to prioritize assessments, and dictate the goals of the security assessment. The list just provided is not exhaustive and the more information that you can obtain about the net-work and security trends, the better the results of the security assessment. Also, keep in mind that this information is only provided in a white box scenario; black box scenarios do not offer any information prior to testing.

Much of the preassessment information gathering can be done with the help of network tools available throughout the industry. For example, port and vulnerability scanning tools can be utilized to identify open areas of the network, patch configuration levels, and patch known bugs for system versions. Surveillance cameras can also be used to identify weak-nesses in the physical security of the network.

Execution Phase

In this phase, the actual database security assessment is conducted. The tasks completed here are dependent on a great number of factors, including the area tested. the type of test being conducted, the scope of the test, and the priority of a particular test. For instance, an external test that is conducted on the mission-critical database is going to be quite different from an internal test that is conducted on the privileges of users. This section covers the techniques of a black box security assessment execution, from the perspective of an intruder. This is to ensure that the most comprehensive approach is covered. Keep in mind that not all actions listed within this section are necessary for white-box-type assessments.

Information Reconnaissance The complex nature of today's network structures works as an advantage toward the efforts of keeping our environments secure. Intrusion would require much less time and energy were the environments less varied and multifaceted. The first step in obtaining access from any infrastructure is information gathering. Unfortunately for administrators, finding information is much easier than hiding it. With remote access becoming more necessary, and intrusion aid tools increasing by the minute, no system infrastructures are completely hidden from the outside world. Given enough time and resources, some information can be discovered either directly or indirectly from any existing system or infrastructure. The greatest security defense is time. Security measures that are built strongly enough to keep intruders busy for long periods of time are more likely to thwart those who are looking for a quick avenue, and the longer an intruder attempts to access the system, the better chance there is that security logs will capture their presence. This section discusses information reconnaissance and explores techniques that intruders use in an attempt to gather information from a system infrastructure.

Information reconnaissance is the process of gathering information either directly (e.g., actively) or indirectly (e.g., passively) from a system or the system's environment. There are two types of information reconnaissance, passive and active.

- *Passive reconnaissance*—**Passive reconnaissance** involves the use of passive investigation methods to gather information about a system or an infrastructure indirectly. An example of a passive reconnaissance attack is a user who utilizes tools such as a network sniffer to obtain information about a system or network infrastructure. A **network sniffer** is a utility that monitors and captures network activity, enabling the owner of the utility to gain an understanding of the amount, frequency, and type of communication occurring on a network. A network sniffer combined with a bit of expertise provides a great tool for gathering information about a network environment, including things like the type of applications that are running and a general idea of the number of users within a network. Database and SQL sniffers exist that are intended to help database administrators and developers monitor their own database systems. These tools can provide unauthorized individuals the means by which to obtain information from the database without ever having to directly communicate with it. Information gathered through passive reconnaissance is not necessarily directly applicable, but it provides information that will eventually lead toward more active information-gathering methodology.

- *Active reconnaissance*—**Active reconnaissance** involves the use of active investigation methods to gather information about a system or an infrastructure directly. An example of an active reconnaissance attack is a user who sends SQL injections to a system in hopes of generating some type of error or system response to use to make inferences about the system or environment. Automated tools are also available that will send pings and packets to systems to initiate a response. Many of these tools will also make determinations based on system responses they receive, providing data to the user, such as the current operating system, the services running, the firewall, the applications, or the topology of an infrastructure.

Active and passive reconnaissance are two very useful methods for gathering information. Passive reconnaissance requires much more time than active reconnaissance, but it is very difficult to detect. For both active and passive reconnaissance, several freely downloadable tools are available to aid in the information-gathering process. Although it offers more information, active reconnaissance can lead to detection of an intruder on a system. Because it involves active communication with the system, logs and activity reports can potentially show the identity of an attacker; therefore, the less time spent actively gathering information, the better.

It is important to point out that information reconnaissance does not always involve technology. Social engineering can be used as a form of active reconnaissance. A person sitting outside a company warehouse taking notes of incoming and outgoing packages is an example of a nontechnical application of passive reconnaissance.

To better understand the concept of passive and active reconnaissance, consider this scenario. A man decides that he is going to rob the local convenience store. He begins by using passive reconnaissance methods to gather information about the store security. He sits in his car across the street day after day taking notes of shift changes, looking for security guards and outdoor cameras. He watches the counter clerks as they interact with customers, gaining a basic understanding of their personalities, enabling him to form assumptions as to which clerks are most likely to fight rather than flee. He pays attention to their routines, finding out when they stock shelves, change the register drawers, and open the safe. After obtaining enough information about the store security and management from the outside, active reconnaissance can commence. At this point, he begins to actively shop at the store, taking note of the position of the internal cameras and talking to the clerks to obtain a better understanding of their psyche. He takes a closer look at the positioning of the safe, and looks for phones, alert buttons, or any way that the clerk could call for help. With all of the information gathered, the robber can plan his attack, and, having built a relationship of trust with each of the clerks, they won't know what hit them!

Obtaining Access A common initial milestone in the security assessment process is obtaining access into a system infrastructure. The way this milestone is achieved will depend on system responses as well as the goals of the security assessment. Several different entrance doors provide access into a network; from the physical server to the wireless network, an opportunity for penetration exists within each. This section explores the most common doors through which intruders obtain access into a foreign environment externally and blindly.

The Use of Automated Tools Several automated tools have been developed to defeat network security measures. These tools contain features that enable their owners to capture data transmitted during transit, to crack passwords, and to find vulnerabilities within an infrastructure. Many of these tools also have the capability to identify software, hardware, and network devices found within the infrastructure and some go as far as providing a map of the overall topology of a network. All of the tools listed in this section are downloadable free from the Internet and offer significant means by which to gain access to a system infrastructure and network environment:

- *Network port scanners*—Network ports are the most common way to access resources available throughout the environment. **Network port scanners** are automated tools that are designed to traverse the network in an attempt to locate available vulnerable ports and identify the services that they use. Why is this important? A network port is a number-addressed channel created for communication to and from services and processes. Ports are assigned addresses ranging from 0 to 65,535, and most port numbers are designed to indicate a specific type of service request that is associated with that port. The term associated is used lightly here, because port numbers can be changed and services can be forced to communicate on different ports than those for which they were originally intended. For example, port 21 is reserved for FTP communication; this means that, in theory, this port should only accept FTP-type service requests, but services and ports can be manipulated. Although some ports have been deemed more dangerous than others, they all offer a way to access a system and intruders can abuse ports by passing Trojans and other types of malware through them. Therefore, if an open port is available on a router or within an operating system, an intruder can hijack the port and send malicious code by way of it. Code such as a key logger can be inserted into the port to further obtain information. A **key logger** is a piece of malware constructed to log every stroke a user types on the keyboard. Key loggers record the keystrokes of a user into a text file that is sent back to the attacker for a specific period of time and frequency. Not only do ports offer access into an infrastructure, but key loggers provide a grand opportunity for attackers to retrieve passwords and sensitive data from a machine. Imagine the amount of information that can be gathered from a key logger that remains on a database server for over a month, logging every action the database administrator takes. The amount of sensitive information that would be compromised is immeasurable. Refer to Table 10-1 for a list of common port addresses and their associated services.

- *Password scanners*—Essentially, **password scanners** traverse the network searching for passwords from remote authentication systems. Password scanners capture, record, and return passwords as they are sent across the network. The risk that a password scanner poses is obvious and is the primary reason passwords should never be sent to a remote machine without some type of encryption. Some password scanners include the capability of cracking the passwords as well. This adds significant complexity for those attempting to protect transmitted passwords, but as a rule of thumb, the greater the complexity of the encryption, the more difficult and time consuming it is to decode.

- *Network sniffers*—Essentially, network sniffers traverse the network searching for packets of data from which information can be extracted. Network sniffers can identify missing software patches, application types, application version numbers, open ports, operating systems, and firewalls, to name a few. Sniffers offer a quick way for an intruder to search for all vulnerabilities within an infrastructure. Like all of the other scanners, network sniffers can be found and downloaded free online.

- *Wireless scanners*—With wireless network popularity, wireless scanning applications are at an all-time high. **Wireless scanners** identify vulnerabilities within a wireless network, which includes missing encryption keys and poor security measures. Some wireless scanners can also locate vulnerability and risks within Bluetooth environments. Wireless networks can be scanned both actively and passively. Passive wireless

Port address	Service	Comments
21	File Transfer Protocol (FTP)	Used for FTP file transfers, uploading and downloading files from a server
23	Telnet	Used for all Telnet sessions, connecting to a remote machine
25	Simple Mail Transfer Protocol	Used for sending outgoing mail
53	Domain Name Service (DNS)	Used to transfer domain name information
67	Dynamic Host Configuration Protocol (DHCP)	Used for allocating new leases and IP addressing information
80	Hypertext Transfer Protocol (HTTP)	Used for Internet traffic and requests
110	Post Office Protocol 3 (POP3)	Used to support incoming e-mail messages
161	Simple Network Management Protocol	Used to gather information about network device status
1433	SQL Server and SQL Server Replication	Used as the default connection to a Microsoft SQL Server database and for replication of Microsoft SQL servers
1434	SQL Server Monitoring	Used by Microsoft SQL Server for monitoring performance of the database servers
1521	Oracle	Used as the default connection to an Oracle database
3306	MySQL	Used as the default connection to a MySQL database

Table 10-1 Common port addresses

10

scanning captures information about wireless activity, device types, device addresses, and data transmitted, aiding the intruder looking to further explore unauthorized networks.

- *Wired Equivalent Privacy (WEP) crackers*—An encrypted-key password is often used to secure a wireless network environment. A wireless router creates an encrypted string of letters and numbers from an inputted user password; this is a WEP key and is used to log in to a wireless network environment. **Wired Equivalent Privacy,** or WEP crackers, are software applications that are used to decrypt WEP keys. They provide attackers with entry into a wireless environment by breaking its password-encrypted code.

Exploiting Network Hardware Network hardware can be used to access the network in several ways. Some of these techniques involve installing rogue devices, whereas others are exploited through identified vulnerabilities:

- *Rogue access points*—Wireless networks are expensive and difficult to secure. A wireless network can be compromised in several ways, but rogue access points are currently the most common and most difficult to identify. A **rogue access point** is a wireless access point (e.g., wireless router) that is installed within a company's wireless range without authorization, exposing the entire network, leaving it open for anyone and everyone to navigate. For example, let's say that an intruder purchases a wireless access point at the local computer store. Subsequently, this intruder installs his new access point, with an SSID of Finance, in the range of ABConsulting. The wireless devices within the existing ABConsulting (e.g, laptops, Blackberries) network will be redirected and begin to connect to Finance to access the network. The intruder is also able to connect to Finance, using his own wireless device to obtain access to ABConsulting, implement an attack, and obtain sensitive information. In fact, anyone within the wireless range of ABConsulting's new access point can connect as an unauthorized user as well.

* *Firewall penetration*—Firewalls are the largest contributors to the security of an infrastructure of all the security measures that can be placed within an environment. They work tirelessly to keep unauthorized users and traffic from entering a network. Although they are invaluable assets to an infrastructure, as with other security tools, they, too, can fall prey to intrusion attacks. The strength of a firewall, like many other technical devices, is dependent on the manufacturer, the hardware from which it is built, and the length of time that it has been in production. Firewalls tend to lose their effectiveness with time as new and improved attacks are discovered by intruders. Older firewalls contain services and default accounts with known security vulnerabilities. Network scans can provide intruders with information about a firewall's manufacturer and model number. Armed with this information, an attacker can conduct a simple Internet search to find out more information, and, in cases where the firewall is a bit aged, the attacker can exploit the services, accounts, and any other well-known vulnerability for the specific make and model.

Another well-known technique used to gain access to an unauthorized network via a firewall is by using port redirection and reverse Telnet. Port redirection works by redirecting packets into unauthorized territory, by taking advantage of an existing trust between the firewall and a system. Essentially, an attacker Telnets into a trusted system and through reverse Telnet redirects commands to another shell located within a firewalled perimeter.

Exploiting the Operating System An operating system manages every aspect of a computer, including resource allocation, data access, and user authentication. Without an operating system, our computers, servers, and networks would be useless. With this power comes great risk. The operating system was designed to make computers effortlessly interact with people, other hardware, other software, and all network environments, yet very little concentration has been placed on security. Operating systems are often placed on the market with a limited amount of debugging satisfied. Because it is virtually impossible for an operating system manufacturer to test the systems against every single component and custom-made application within our complex networks, many operating system vendors are left to rely on customers for reporting security vulnerabilities. Unfortunately, most security vulnerabilities that exist are not found until a breach occurs. Therefore, these vulnerabilities often go unnoticed for quite some time. To make matters worse, once patches are created to secure the identified risks, it is up to the administrators to apply these patches. This could result in even more time that the vulnerable operating system is in production and the network environment is virtually exposed. Outdated operating systems or those that have not had the most recent security patches applied are one of the most common vulnerabilities that are exploited through the network.

Exploiting Web Applications Web applications interact with servers, so they offer a legitimate way for intruders to gain access to the infrastructure. For example, network, database, and SQL sniffers can be used to obtain the identification of the database applications being used within the environment. A quick Internet search can identify vulnerabilities that exist within this application, and these vulnerabilities can be exploited as a way to gain access to the database itself. Once access has been achieved, SQL statements can be used to construct the database schema and escalate user privileges. Similar to operating systems, applications that have not been effectively debugged and patched provide a door into the network. Figure 10-1 displays this process of intrusion.

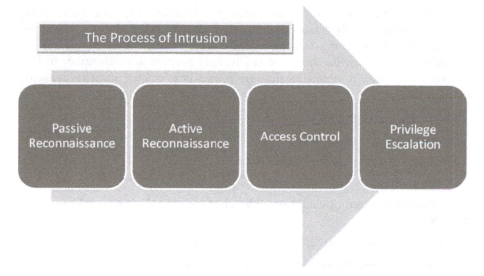

Figure 10-1 The process of intrusion
© Cengage Learning 2012

Escalating Privileges

Once access has been achieved, the next step for an assessor or an intruder is to escalate the privileges of the current user so that more rights are available. Once access has been obtained, privileges can be escalated by a few methods, but these methods depend on a number of factors, including the way the user is physically connecting to the database as well as the user account with which the attacker is currently logged in. The following list details the most common methods unauthorized users use to escalate their account privileges:

Note: SQL injection techniques described in Chapter 8 can be utilized in situations where the database is being accessed remotely.

- Guest accounts can be manipulated to provide improved account capabilities.
- Passwords can be obtained from the OS, from the network, or from within the database itself. If encrypted, using a password cracker can help to decrypt the passwords.

- Network sniffers can be installed locally to discover passwords traveling across the network.
- Windows services that are written to be executed as the local system account can be manipulated.
- Third-party tools that are designed to allow users to run code for escalating privileges can be used locally or remotely.
- Cross-site scripting techniques can be utilized to run malicious code on the local machine using the Web browser.
- Brute force strategies can be attempted as a way to increase user credentials and privileges.
- Passive information-gathering techniques can be conducted using the individual's current system privileges as an attempt to learn more about the system's security structure.

Reporting Phase

This is the final step of the security assessment. It is here that the results are analyzed and a report is drawn describing in detail the discovered security vulnerabilities as well as potential remediation. The format of the written report is dependent on the organization's standard, yet the writing should provide enough detail to fully prepare administrators to fix the problems at hand. Common components that are found in a written security assessment report include the following:

- The gathered background information
- The defined perimeter and scope
- The objective of the security assessment
- The key findings
- The remediation recommendations, including deliverables, required resources, and a time frame
- Information about the methodology that was used for penetration testing

Following up on the remediation recommendations is vital to the confidentiality, integrity, and availability of the network as a whole. Therefore, a process should also be identified within the report that clearly details the steps for remediation, including a schedule for a repeat security assessment for remediated areas.

Chapter Summary

- Security testing is the process of penetrating the security of an environment to measure its strength and determine the feasibility of an attack.

- Security auditing differs from security testing in that security auditing is used to determine vulnerabilities within internal controls and the reliability of the processes, whereas security testing measures the strength and effectiveness of an environment's security as well as the potential for an attack.

- Security tests are often too laborious and resource intensive to be conducted for all areas of an organization at the same time. Therefore, security tests are best suited for evaluating the security of small groups of assets within an organization.

- The security assessor should have a great amount of intrusion experience and must be able to think from the perspective of an attacker.

- Security testing and auditing are equally as effective, and an ideal security strategy includes both testing and auditing.

- Internal security tests are conducted within the organization's security perimeter and are most often conducted with information about the organization given to the assessor prior to the penetration.

- External security tests are conducted outside the organization's security perimeter and are often done blindly with little to no information given about the environment prior to the test.

- Black box testing is conducted under the assumption that the intruder has no prior knowledge of the organization's infrastructure. Black box testing is normally more broad and exploratory than white box testing.

- White box testing is conducted under the assumption that the potential intruder is internal or has some knowledge about the infrastructure. White box testing is typically focused on a specific target and is often done in reaction to a recent attack.

- An auditor requires much more expertise to conduct effective black box testing due to its ambiguous nature.

- To define an appropriate scope for security testing, both the physical and logical areas need to be included.

- Defining a scope for a black box test is much more difficult than for a white box test scenario. Because no prior information about the infrastructure exists, scopes for black box testing are defined by how successful an attack is in penetrating the system. The end of a security test is often identified by the intruder's ability to obtain a certain level of access into a system.

- Planning and preparation for a security test is dependent on the type of test being conducted. Planning for a white box test includes pretest information gathering, scope and perimeter definition, contract development, assessment scheduling, and threat prioritization. Planning for a black box test does not include threat prioritization and pretest information gathering.

- Information gathering for white box testing scenarios includes the review of network diagrams, database schematics, network assets, areas of weakness, areas with the highest potential of attacks, and historic attack strategies.

- Intruders attempt to gather information from a foreign environment in two ways, passive reconnaissance and active reconnaissance.

- Passive reconnaissance is a strategy for gathering information about an infrastructure indirectly—tools such as network sniffers and port scanners are included.

- Active reconnaissance involves direct system probing to obtain information. The strategy can be detected by logs and monitoring devices.

- Passive reconnaissance helps an intruder obtain enough information to conduct active reconnaissance, which in turn aids them in creating custom system attacks.

- Obtaining access is the initial goal of a potential attacker because it gives them the opportunity to escalate privileges and subsequently take over a system.

10

- Several automated tools are available from the Internet that help an intruder obtain access into a system. These include port scanners, network sniffers, password and wireless scanners, and WEP crackers.

- Rogue access points and firewall penetration techniques are two ways that network hardware can be used to obtain access into a system.

- Poorly written code and misconfigured applications are two ways that intruders can use software and operating systems to obtain access.

- Several techniques can be used to escalate privileges once access has been obtained, for example, automated tools and brute force attacks.

- The security test report will include the background information, the scope, the defined perimeter, the goal, the methodology, and the key findings.

- Remediation actions are defined by a set of deliverables and should include a schedule for completion.

Key Terms

active reconnaissance The use of active investigation methods for gathering information about a system or an infrastructure directly.

black box testing An assessment that is conducted with no prior knowledge of the system or infrastructure that is being tested.

external testing An assessment that is conducted outside the organization's security border; this type of testing will display attacks and liabilities that can be exploited externally from competitors, external users, and hackers. Initial tasks most commonly completed during external testing involve information gathering. An external intruder must gain information from a system or an infrastructure to break into it.

information reconnaissance The process of gathering information either directly (e.g., actively) or indirectly (e.g., passively) from a system or the system's environment.

internal testing An assessment that is conducted within the organization's security border that will display vulnerabilities that exist among internal users such as employees and contractors. It also identifies attacks and the damage that can be caused within the network itself. A task conducted during an internal security assessment might include an evaluator logging in to a user's computer in an attempt to raise the user's privileges on a particular system.

key logger Malware constructed to log every keyboard stroke that a user types on the keyboard.

network port scanner Automated tools that are designed to traverse the network in an attempt to locate available vulnerable ports and identify the services that they use.

network sniffers The utilities that monitor the network looking for a number of combined types of vulnerability. Network sniffers can identify missing software patches, application types, application version numbers, open ports, operating systems, and firewalls, to name a few.

passive reconnaissance The use of passive investigation methods to gather information about a system or an infrastructure indirectly.

password scanners Essentially, network sniffers that traverse the network searching for passwords from remote authentication systems. Password scanners capture passwords as they are sent remotely across the network and record them for the attacker to maintain.

rogue access point A wireless access point (e.g., wireless router) that is installed within a company's wireless range without authorization, exposing the entire network and leaving it open for anyone and everyone to navigate.

security scope This defines the perimeter of the overall security assessment, the physical and logical area included within the assessment.

security testing The process of identifying the feasibility and impact of an attack or intrusion of a system by simulating active exploitation and executing potential attacks within that environment.

white box testing (target testing) An assessment that is conducted by an intruder who already has information about the system or the infrastructure. It is also known as targeted testing because prior knowledge exists and known weaknesses within the infrastructure allow for intruders to focus on specific areas of the infrastructure. The goal is to assess the damage that can be done by users who understand the infrastructure that they are attempting to intrude; the results will provide a more comprehensive, thorough picture of specific system weakness than that found in black box testing.

Wired Equivalent Privacy (WEP) crackers Software applications that are used to decrypt WEP keys.

wireless scanners Utilities that identify vulnerabilities within a wireless network, including missing encryption keys and poor security measures.

10

Review Questions

1. Describe how a security test differs from a security audit.

2. List and compare the characteristics of internal and external security tests.

3. Explain how the planning stage for a black box test is different from a white box test.

4. Describe why a black box test requires more expertise than a white box test.

5. Explain why a scope is defined differently for a black box test than it is for a white box test.

6. For what scenario is a security test a better fit than a security audit?

7. List the typical sections of information included within a security test report.

8. Describe the benefits of a standardized security testing methodology.

9. What is the difference between information gathering for preparation of a security test and information gathering during a security test?

10. Explain the difference between passive reconnaissance and active reconnaissance.

11. List at least three ways an intruder can gain access to an infrastructure.

12. Identify at least two ways that an intruder can escalate privileges within a database.

Case Projects

Case Project 10-1: Database Security

Use the Internet. Find and describe one automated tool that aids in database security testing. (It is not recommended to install the tool.)

Case Project 10-2: Passive Reconnaissance Tools

Use the Internet. Find and describe at least two automated tools that can be used for passive reconnaissance. (It is not recommended to install the tools.)

Case Project 10-3: Active Reconnaissance Tools

Use the Internet. Find and describe at least two automated tools that can be used for active reconnaissance. (It is not recommended to install the tools.)

Case Project 10-4: Capturing Passwords

Use the Internet. Find and describe at least one automated tool for capturing and decrypting passwords within a database. (It is not recommended to install the tool.)

Case Project 10-5: SQL Server's Security Template

Using this chapter as well as the SQL Server Web site at *http://www.microsoft.com/sqlserver/2008/en/us/*, install the security template available within Server Management Studio. Describe the steps that were taken to do so.

Hands-On Projects

Hands-On Project 10-1: White Box Database Security Test

You have been hired as a security professional for your company. You are to create and implement a white box informal database security testing schedule for the organization. Create a paper that addresses the following:

- Create a table that includes a rotating schedule for the 12 months of security testing. Include columns that identify time estimations for each test listed.
- Create a planning and preparation checklist common to all security tests as a whole.
- Identify any special planning and preparation needed for each test.
- Identify the scope for each test and identify any special considerations that need to be addressed.
- Create a list of at least five testing activities for each audit.
- Provide recommendations for securing the database that are unique to Oracle.

- Provide recommendations for securing the database that are unique to MySQL.

- Provide recommendations for securing the database that are unique to SQL Server.

Hands-On Project 10-2: Black Box Database Security Test

You have been hired as a security consultant for XYZ Company. You are to create and implement a black box, external database security test. Write a paper that responds to the following:

- How will the scope be identified?

- What will indicate the end of a test?

- What special skills or characteristics will be required from the assessor that are not as necessary in white box testing scenarios?

- Identify and describe the first three main goals of the test.

- Explain at least three specific techniques that will be used to gather information.

- Explain at least three specific techniques that will be used as an attempt to obtain access to the system.

- Provide at least two special considerations unique to Oracle.

- Provide at least two special considerations unique to MySQL.

- Provide at least two special considerations unique to SQL Server.

10

Glossary

active reconnaissance The use of active investigation methods for gathering information about a system or an infrastructure directly.

adware A general term for software that uses typical malware intrusion techniques to obtain marketing data or advertise a product or service.

alternate key A field with values that are not chosen as a primary key, but can be used in cases where the primary key is not available.

attribute A characteristic or variable that describes or further identifies an entity.

audit scope The area or system on which the security audit will focus. Defining the scope of the audit is one of the most important steps of the auditing process.

authentication The process of confirming the identity of those individuals or applications that request access to a secure environment.

authorization The process of ensuring that those individuals or applications that request access to an environment or an object within that environment have the permission to do so.

automated audit An audit conducted using tools that are either installed onto a machine or embedded within an application for the purpose of recording the typical behavior of a system.

availability The efforts taken through policy, procedures, and design in order to create and maintain the accessibility of resources within a database environment.

back door A method created during the programming of a worm in which access is gained into a system by avoiding normal security, which gives the creator of the worm undetected access into the system.

backup An intentional copy of data, program files, and system configurations that is used to archive and store information in the event of network failure or malware attacks.

backup management plan A process developed to ensure the safety of the data on a network.

binary code installations Binary files that are packaged and ready to be installed without the need for compiling the code to enable it to be run as an executable file on a particular machine.

binary file A file that contains code that can be read by machines and run as an executable file.

black box testing An assessment that is conducted with no prior knowledge of the system or infrastructure that is being tested.

black hat Someone who breaks into computer networks without authorization and with malicious intent.

bond parameters Placeholders to bind user input.

boot sector An area of the hard disk that contains records necessary to the boot process of a computer.

boot sector virus Malware that infiltrates a system by loading itself onto the boot sector of a hard disk via an infected floppy disk left in a floppy disk drive.

bot (software robot) A form of malware that has the ability to perform a large array of automated tasks for an intruder at a remote location, ranging in severity from spamming a system to initiating DoS attacks on systems.

botmaster An individual who controls a network of bots and who accumulates a number of bots and then rents these botnets to other intruders and cybercriminals for the purpose of spamming, phishing, and other more serious types of cybercrime.

botnet A network of bots.

buffer manager A portion of the SQL Server responsible for accessing data pages and updating the database.

buffer pool (buffer cache) The area where data pages from a database are stored to minimize the need to read and write from the database file located on the hard disk.

caching The process of saving a duplicate of the requested data to another area of a system in hopes of saving resources and speeding up the future requests for that same data.

candidate key A field with values that meet the requirements for a primary key.

Client Access License (CAL) A unique license that allows users or devices access to gain a licensed Microsoft SQL Server 2008 server.

cold site A facility that provides the basic necessities for rebuilding a network. A contract that involves a cold site would promise the use of a facility that provides water, power, and air conditioning or heat.

column (field) The component of a table that maintains a general category of information with similar data types.

commit To make a change within a DBMS that is permanent and visible to other users.

compile The act of converting source code that is written in one language into a different programming language or machine language.

composite key A group of two or more fields where their values can be combined to be used as a primary key.

computer security A set of established procedures, standards, policies, and tools that is used to protect a computer from theft, misuse, and unwanted intrusions, activities, and attacks.

computer virus A form of malware intended to spread from one computer to another without detection.

concurrency The simultaneous access of resources and data.

confidentiality The efforts taken through policy, procedure, and design to create and maintain the privacy and discretion of information and systems.

control file A file within a database that contains the location and important credentialing information of other files.

cracker An individual who breaks into networks without authorization with hopes to destroy and/or steal information.

credential A piece of information that is used to verify identity, such as a person's username and password, an application's secure ID, or a host's network name and address.

database A collection of data stored on a computer using an application called a database management system.

database connection manager The component of the database architecture that manages connections to the MySQL server.

database link A link made between two databases that when created results in one logical data storage unit. Links are created in Oracle to apply common policies and to create associations between databases.

database management system (DBMS) An application that allows users to search stored data in order to locate specific information.

database model A representation of the way data is stored.

database security A set of established procedures, standards, policies, and tools that is used to protect data from theft, misuse, and unwanted intrusions, activities, and attacks.

datafile A file that contains the actual data for the database and holds the information for all logical structures (tables, records, and so forth) within the database.

data sending Trojan Malware that obtains sensitive data from your computer and transmits it back to a cracker.

deadlock A situation when two transactions cannot proceed because each user has data that the other needs.

denial of service (DoS) attack A concerted effort made by malware to keep system resources, such as Internet sites, from functioning correctly.

destructive Trojan Malware that is installed on a computer with the intent to destroy a system as a whole by randomly deleting files and folders and corrupting the registry.

differential backup An intentional copy of data, program files, and system configurations that only saves the data that has changed since the last backup was complete.

digital certificate A password-protected and encrypted file that holds the identity of a user or object.

digital signature Code that uses cryptography to verify the authenticity of a source of information.

disaster plan A plan developed to ensure the quick reinstatement of a network that has fallen victim to a human or naturally caused disaster.

DNS poisoning An intrusion where a cracker gains control over the DNS server and changes the domain name's respective IP address, redirecting requests to sites that the cracker has built and maintains.

dynamic analysis An attempt to find errors or vulnerabilities in the source code of a program dynamically while it is being executed.

dynamic SQL statement A SQL statement that is generated on the fly by an application (such as a Web application), using a string of characters derived from a user's input parameters into a form within the application itself.

encryption The transformation of data by using sophisticated algorithms in an attempt to make the data unrecognizable.

entity A person, place, or thing stored within the table of a database and for which attributes and relationships exist.

exploitation The act of using system vulnerabilities and carefully crafted SQL queries to gather information and subsequently peel away at the infrastructure's security defense for the purpose of gaining access or control of a system.

external audit An audit conducted using a third-party group or a number of individuals from a source outside the organization itself.

external testing An assessment that is conducted outside the organization's security border; this type of testing will display attacks and liabilities that can be exploited externally from competitors, external users, and hackers. Initial tasks most commonly completed during external testing involve information gathering. An external intruder must gain information from a system or an infrastructure to break into it.

fiber A subcomponent of a thread, which is handled by the server to accomplish a task.

filegroup A collection of one or more physical data files within a SQL Server database.

file-infected virus A form of malware that will attach itself to an executable file that requires a user to run before it can propagate and corrupt the system.

File Transfer Protocol (FTP) Trojan Malware that allows the attacker to use someone else's computer as an FTP server.

flat model A two-dimensional list of data entries, where all data within a field are understood to be similar, and all data within a record are understood to be related to one another.

foreign key A field within a table that contains a label used to build a relationship between two tables.

formal audit An audit most often conducted to satisfy specific industry standards that are required by law for certain types of organizations.

full backup An intentional copy of data, program files, and system configurations that stores all information, regardless of its critical nature, age, and prior backup activity.

grey hat An individual or groups of individuals who waver between the classification of a hacker and a cracker, and who either act in goodwill or in malice.

hacker Someone who has mastered the hardware and software of modern computer systems and enjoys the exploration and analysis of network security with no intent to intrude or cause harm.

hactivist Hackers and crackers who use their extensive experience and skill to use networks to share their ideologies regarding controversial social, political, and economic topics.

Health Insurance Portability and Accountability Act (HIPAA) Strict laws for health institutions throughout the United States that ensure the security and privacy of patient records by dictating the way in which files are accessed, stored, and transmitted on a network.

hierarchical database structure A treelike storage schema that represents records and relationships through the use of tiers and parent-child relationships.

hijacking A process in which Web sites are hacked into and rewritten to react differently to users than how the original Web site designer intended.

honeypot A fake environment that includes false data to mislead intruders who are attempting to gather information about the database.

hot site An exact replica of an organization's network, or a mirror site, that promises the vendor will assume all responsibility for ensuring that the network is readily available in the event of a disaster.

Hypertext Transfer Protocol (HTTP) The portion of an Internet address that informs the browser what protocol is used to send the request for a particular Web site.

incremental backup An intentional copy of data, program files, and system configurations that is conducted on only the data that has changed since the last full or incremental backup.

inference A way that unauthorized users can obtain sensitive information by making assumptions based on the database's reactions or query responses to nonsensitive queries.

informal audit An audit conducted as a way to provide organizations evidence that their security policies and practices are effective and working properly.

information reconnaissance The process of gathering information either directly (e.g., actively) or indirectly (e.g., passively) from a system or the system's environment.

instance A broad term that refers to the background processes and structured memory used during interaction with the database.

integrated services A valuable tool in data warehouses where different types of data need to be joined together for reporting and extrapolation.

integrity Efforts taken through policy, procedure, and design in order to create and maintain reliable, consistent, and complete information and systems.

internal audit An audit conducted using a committee of individuals who are employees of the company itself.

internal security controls The systematic measures and checks put into place to ensure that networks remain sound and secure.

internal testing An assessment that is conducted within the organization's security border that will display vulnerabilities that exist among internal users such as employees and contractors. It also identifies attacks and the damage that can be caused within the network itself. A task conducted during an internal security assessment might include an evaluator logging in to a user's computer in an attempt to raise the user's privileges on a particular system.

Kerberos An authentication protocol that was built by MIT to provide secure means for authentication using symmetric-key cryptology to verify the identity of a client to a server and a server to a client.

key A single field or group of fields used to identify an entry in a table.

key logger Malware constructed to log every keyboard stroke that a user types on the keyboard.

lock A mechanism within a DBMS that controls concurrency by preventing users from taking hold of data until changes being made are completed or committed.

log file A file that stores information about the transactions in the database to be used for recovery and backup.

logic bomb Malware that can lie dormant until a specific predetermined variable is met, whose variables typically depend on the environment in which it resides.

login An object that is mapped to a user account within each database and is associated to users by the security identifier or SID.

macro A small program that enables users to automate a large number of repeated processes within a document.

macro virus Malware that can either be attached to a macro, or can replace a macro within a document, and that runs automatically when the document containing the infected macro is opened or closed.

malicious software A programming code written and used by unauthorized intruders to perform a certain task on a computer.

malware An abbreviation for the term malicious software.

memory target The reserved space for the buffer cache.

misleading applications Applications that deceive users into believing that their computer's security has been breached, therefore tricking the user into downloading and purchasing rogue antivirus tools to remove the bogus breach.

Mixed Mode Authentication A form of authentication that allows both Windows authentication and SQL Server authentication to be used. The database will accept both Windows and server logins.

multipartite virus A form of malware that combines the characteristics of a boot sector virus with those of a file-infected virus.

network database model A treelike structure that stores information in the form of a hierarchy, using tiers and parent-child-like entities to represent relationships.

network port scanner Automated tools that are designed to traverse the network in an attempt to locate available vulnerable ports and identify the services that they use.

network security A set of established procedures, standards, policies, and tools that are used to protect data from theft, misuse, and unwanted intrusions, activities, and attacks.

network sniffers The utilities that monitor the network looking for a number of combined types of vulnerability. Network sniffers can identify missing software patches, application types, application version numbers, open ports, operating systems, and firewalls, to name a few.

nonresident virus The general term for malware that requires users to initiate it by downloading a program or opening up an e-mail attachment.

online analytical processing (OLAP), (decision support systems [DSS]) Databases that store large volumes of historical data for report generating and analyzing.

online transaction processing (OLTP) database A database that is created for real-time storage and manipulation of data within an organization.

open source A term that refers to software that has been written to be distributed for use and downloaded free of charge.

operational information security A term that refers to the secure operation of an organization through the development and reliability of an environment's policies and procedures that focus on security policies, change management, update management, and disaster recovery plans.

optimization The process of locating the quickest and most efficient way to retrieve the data being requested by a user.

OS upgrade The process of installing a new version of an operating system onto a host or a server.

page A fixed unit of storage that is transferred or swapped from one storage device to another.

pagefile The dedicated swap space for a page.

parallel processing When more than one server processes one query at the same time.

parsing The act of analyzing a construction of a query for correct syntax and semantics.

passive reconnaissance The use of passive investigation methods to gather information about a system or an infrastructure indirectly.

password hash A cryptology-encoded string version of a user or system password.

password scanners Essentially, network sniffers that traverse the network searching for passwords from remote authentication systems. Password scanners capture passwords as they are sent remotely across the network and record them for the attacker to maintain.

patch A small program that is used to fix or update software programs or hardware devices.

payload The component of a worm that holds all of the instructions on how to affect each computer that it encounters.

personal identifiable information (PII) Personal information that identifies a person.

phishing The attempt to obtain PII from people through the use of spoofed e-mail addresses and URLs.

point of sales (POS) system A system that is meant to handle cash register or sales transactions.

polyinstantiation A strategy that allows the database to contain multiple instances of a record, all pointing to the same primary key, but contain and display different values to users of different security classifications.

polymorphism The incidence of changing forms, or self-modification.

primary data file The main data file for a SQL Server database which is the file of origin for the entire database and references all other secondary data files.

primary filegroup The collection of files that contains all of the SQL Server system files, including the primary data files.

primary key A field that contains a unique label by which we can identify a record or row in a table.

principle of least privilege A security standard by which each user added to a system is given the minimum set of privileges that he or she requires to conduct legitimate business within that system.

privilege The ability to access a specific database resource or to perform a specific action within a database.

process A set of instructions that is executed by the operating system intended to complete a task.

Process Global Area (PGA) The central area where information is stored for background and server processes. It allocates space for each individual background process.

programming language A type of synthetic language developed with a specific syntax and semantic rules that allows individuals to create statements or functions to interface and control the behavior or functionality of a machine.

proxy Trojan Malware that enables a cracker to use someone else's computer to access the Internet in order to keep his or her identity hidden.

query A search initiated by a user in an attempt to retrieve certain information from a database.

query cache A memory component that plays a role in ensuring that query processing is successful.

query engine A component of the architecture that optimizes and manages queries and SQL statements.

query management The steps taken by a database management application to process a user query.

read consistency A term that refers to the accuracy and reliability of data within a database.

redo log A file within a database that contains information regarding all changes made to the data within the database.

relational database A storage model in which common entities are stored within separate tables that use unique key identifiers to build relationships between these entities.

relationship A term that defines the association between two entities and binds them.

remote access and administration Trojan (RAT) Malware that provides remote access capability to the cracker from whom the virus originated, who in turn is provided complete control of and access to someone else's computer from a remote location.

replication The act of sending copies of one database to another database within a network.

report A document that contains a formatted result of a user's query.

resident virus Malware that installs itself or takes residence directly in the main system memory of a computer.

response file A file that holds the specification of a typical Oracle installation for the purpose of creating silent installations.

rogue access point A wireless access point (e.g., wireless router) that is installed within a company's wireless range without authorization, exposing the entire network and leaving it open for anyone and everyone to navigate.

role A set of related privileges that are combined to provide a centralized unit from which to manage similar users or objects of a database.

row (record, tuple) The component of a table that holds distinct units of data identified using unique strings of numbers or characters.

script kiddie Amateur cracker who uses programs and scripts written by other people to infringe upon a computer network system's integrity.

secondary (alternative) key A field with values that contains nonunique data and that can refer to several records at one time.

secondary data file An optional data file found within a SQL Server database that is not a primary data file.

security audit The procedures by which all of an environment's security controls and systems are thoroughly reviewed to identify and report weaknesses within an organization.

security policy A document that defines the overall goal of security and identifies the scope of what to secure, as well as the roles and responsibilities of the people within the organization.

security scope This defines the perimeter of the overall security assessment, the physical and logical area included within the assessment.

security testing The process of identifying the feasibility and impact of an attack or intrusion of a system by simulating active exploitation and executing potential attacks within that environment.

service ticket A unique key that is used to validate a person's identification (similar to a driver's license), for the purpose of gaining access into a secured environment.

shared site agreement An arrangement between companies with similar, if not identical, data centers.

signature A pattern of characters that is identified for a specific family of viruses.

silent installation An installation of an application that completes without prompting a user for setting specifications.

social engineer An individual who uses human interaction to manipulate people into gaining access to systems, unauthorized areas, and confidential information.

software upgrade A combination of a number of software or hardware packages that creates a new version of software.

sort (control) key A field in which values are used to sequence data.

source code A group of statements or functions written using a specific programming language and that are combined to create a specific type of application or utility.

source code installation Allows a user to download the actual MySQL source code, change it, and compile it into a binary file for installation execution.

spoofing A process that involves hackers building Web sites to look identical to other popular sites in hopes of drawing in a user.

spyware A general term for any software that intentionally monitors and records a user's computer and/or Internet activities.

SQL injections Methods by which intruders use bits of SQL code and SQL queries to gain database access.

startup page The Web site that is displayed when the Web browser is started.

static analysis An effort to find problems while the program is inactive.

static SQL statement A statement that is built by the user; the full text of the statement is known at compilation.

storage engine A component of the MySQL database architecture that reads and writes data to and from the database and offers services to enable customization of an environment.

storage management A term that refers to the process of storing and retrieving data throughout the database.

System Global Area (SGA) The central area where all shared data and processes are stored, including information shared by users and database processes.

table One of the most basic units of storage within a database, typically representing unique and specific data objects.

Tabular Data Stream (TDS) A Microsoft-defined protocol that describes the specifications as to how the SQL Server and a client can communicate.

thread A process that runs independently from another process. It utilizes a portion of the CPU and contains tasks or executions that share the same resources, yet run independently from one another.

time bomb (time-delayed virus) Malware that can lie dormant until a specific variable is met, such as times, days, or specific days that are predetermined and written within its code.

transaction The group of statements or operations processed by a database to execute a user's request to update or change the database.

transaction manager A component of the MySQL database architecture that is responsible for avoiding and resolving deadlocks and corrupted data.

transmission packet Sensitive information about users or businesses compiled by spyware that is sent back to its original creators for use as they see fit.

Trojan (Trojan horse) Malware that disguises itself and its harmful code and often hides within enticing programs such as software updates, games, and movies.

update A change to a system that is added to software or firmware that is already installed on a network.

update management policy A document that includes procedures for patch updates, software upgrades, OS upgrades, and firmware changes.

upgrade Replacements for older versions of software or firmware.

user-defined filegroup A collection of files created by a user.

user profile A set of rules that limits a user's access to database resources, and can be used to set password restrictions as well.

virtual address space The complete virtual memory area allotted to a program.

virtual memory A technique for extending the availability of memory by which units of storage located on different memory devices are used to store data from one entity in such a way that it appears as though the data has been stored in one continuous block of the same memory.

warm site A facility that contains the basic environmental concerns, as well as computers, connection firmware, and software devices necessary to rebuild a network system.

Web applications Programs that are available on a network and provide a way for users to interact with remote systems or databases.

Web browser An application that acts as a user interface of the Internet, allowing users to interact and view Web pages on the World Wide Web.

Web page A document containing a specific programming language (e.g., HTML or JAVA) that is designed to be viewable on the World Wide Web.

white box testing (targeted testing) An assessment that is conducted by an intruder who already has information about the system or the infrastructure. It is also known as targeted testing because prior knowledge exists and known weaknesses within the infrastructure allow for intruders to focus on specific areas of the infrastructure. The goal is to assess the damage that can be done by users who understand the infrastructure that they are attempting to intrude; the results will provide a more comprehensive, thorough picture of specific system weakness than that found in black box testing.

white hat An ethical hacker; hackers who use their extensive experience and knowledge to test systems and provide security consultation to others.

Windows Authentication mode A form of authentication that allows only Windows authentication to be used for accessing the database; those users logging in to the database must have a Windows login to access it.

Wired Equivalent Privacy (WEP) crackers
Software applications that are used to decrypt
WEP keys.

wireless scanners Utilities that identify
vulnerabilities within a wireless network,
including missing encryption keys and poor
security measures.

word blocking The act of blocking keywords
that are not allowed to be used as input within
a Web application or a Web URL.

word filtering A balance of blocking those known
keywords that are not allowed to be used as input
within a Web application or Web URL, and
identifying those keywords that are allowed to be
used as input within a Web application or Web URL.

worker process A pool of either threads or fibers
that SQL Server keeps for all user connections.

worm Self-replicating malware that is able to
harness the power of networks and use this power
in its attacks against them.

Index